International Funds: A Practical Guide to Their Establishment and Operation

International Funds: A Practical Guide to Their Establishment and Operation

Catherine Turner

ELSEVIER

AMSTERDAM BOSTON HEIDELBERG LONDON NEW YORK OXFORD
PARIS SAN DIEGO SAN FRANCISCO SINGAPORE SYDNEY TOKYO

Elsevier Limited

First published 2004

British Library Cataloguing in Publication Data
A catalogue record for this book is available from the British Library

Library of Congress Cataloguing in Publication Data
A catalogue record for this book is available from the Library of Congress

ISBN 0 7506 5899 1

Typeset by Newgen Imaging Systems (P) Ltd., Chennai, India
Printed and bound in Great Britain

Contents

Introduction

The purpose of this book is primarily to give those new to fund management an understanding of the operational issues with which they will need to be familiar – whether as potential fund sponsors, new entrants to the third-party administration industry, regulators, legal advisors or in any other capacity.

However, the book is also intended to serve as a more permanent reference manual for those engaged in fund management and administration issues, especially where they may be involved in a relatively specialized area such as fund accounting and would benefit from a broader overview of the issues. It seeks to give an overview of the practical issues to be taken into account for a broad range of aspects of fund management – from set-up and licensing to pricing, distribution, dealing and so on.

The first part of the text takes readers from the start-up phase – indeed, pre-start-up – through to the selection of an appropriate jurisdiction, fund structure and team of advisers and service providers. The second section deals with ongoing operational matters. It also deals with a range of problems which may arise, the risks that sponsors and operators may run, and what do to when things go wrong. The third and final section of the book takes a look at some relatively recent developments, and compares the advantages and disadvantages of certain jurisdictions.

The focus is intended to be on international funds, although reference is made to various domestic regulatory and tax regimes. The range of jurisdictions is of necessity not comprehensive, but aims to give readers a flavour of the material differences in how funds can be operated in various territories, and to provide a roadmap for making the right selection.

Part 1

Principles of Fund Management

1 The concept of collective investment schemes

1.1 What is a FUND?

It is worth spending a few moments considering what we mean by the term 'fund', since the term is used by different people in different ways and can cause confusion. Defining our terms will allow a potential sponsor then to take the next step – where he determines whether a fund is in fact a suitable vehicle for his purposes, and if so what type is most appropriate.

A fund is simply a vehicle which permits the pooling of assets by a group of investors with a *common investment objective* (Figure 1.1). This objective will be to invest their money in (for example) securities or other assets, with the aim of generating a specific type of return – for example, capital growth, income, or some balance of the two. The pooling effect means that each investor participates – has a part share – in a large portfolio of securities or other assets, along with many other investors. No single asset in the underlying portfolio is attributable to any one investor – that is, we do not say 'the shares in ABC plc relate to Catherine Turner, whilst the shares in XYZ are Joe Singer's.'

The term 'fund' is often used interchangeably with the phrase 'collective investment scheme', and we will do the same in this text; 'c.i.s.' will also be used as an abbreviation for 'collective investment scheme'.

The above (fairly simple) definition is not where it ends, though. There are many vehicles which fall into it, and which most people would refer to colloquially as funds,

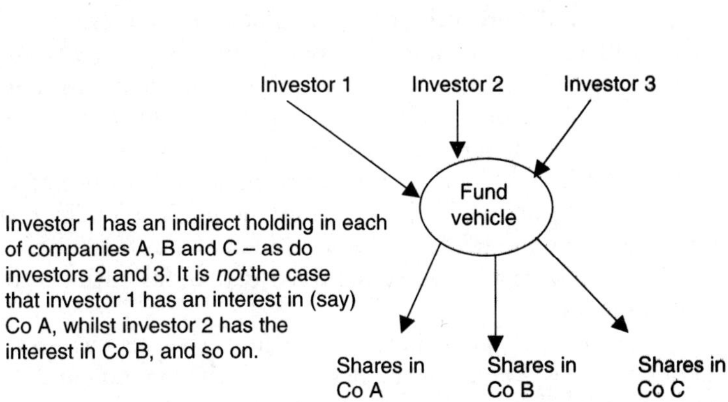

Figure 1.1 Schematic of a fund vehicle.

but which do not meet the *regulator's* definition of what constitutes a fund or c.i.s. – and where the arrangements consequently do not have to comply with any specific regulations applicable to either funds themselves, or to those who operate or promote and distribute them. For example, in many jurisdictions 'closed-ended' schemes are not regarded as funds for regulatory purposes, despite the fact that investors and sponsors alike see them as a means of satisfying their pooling requirements.

Further, definitions of what constitutes a fund for regulatory purposes are usually quite broad; a whole host of arrangements may technically meet the definition, whilst being of such a nature that it would be unnecessary and unreasonable to regulate them. For example, the definition of a pooling vehicle is usually drafted widely enough to capture almost any sort of arrangement where several people throw in their lot with one another, such as franchises and investment clubs, and where the income and profits or losses are shared *pro rata*. The definition therefore needs some fine-tuning if it is to exclude those arrangements which the regulator does not, or should not, want to capture. This can be done in one of two ways:

- by having a wide definition of what *is* a fund, and then defining some specific exclusions, or
- by having a narrow and specific definition of what a fund is, in which case no exclusions are necessary.

In practice, the former approach is more common, although examples of the latter still linger on in some countries. The former approach is, in essence, 'if it looks like a fund, it's a fund; but here are the exclusions' as opposed to the more unwieldy, 'if it meets this set of criteria it's a fund; but also if it meets this set, and this one, and this.... '

A major advantage of the former approach is that it makes it much easier for a regulator to adapt to the changing environment. Regulators are usually keen to limit the opportunity for people to wriggle through their 'regulatory net', by setting up new arrangements which escape regulation because they were simply never contemplated when the law was drafted. Where a definition is wide and turns on a set of broad characteristics, new schemes are unlikely to escape capture because of some technical nicety.

These matters may sound more theoretical than practical, but they can be important. Depending on a fund sponsor's intentions, it may suit him to set up his arrangements so as not to fall within a particular jurisdiction's definition – in which case a whole range of regulations may simply cease to apply. The sponsor should consider not only the definition which applies in the jurisdiction(s) where his fund is to be established and operated, but also that in any country into which he intends to promote it. This is because, again, one set of rules may apply to the promotion of a foreign fund into that country: and another – or none at all – to the promotion of non-fund investments. This is an issue we will revisit, once we have explored the 'definitions' theme further, by way of some specific examples.

First, we will take a look at the definition of a collective investment scheme as it is set out in Isle of Man legislation. This model is relatively common and derives from that which was established in the United Kingdom under the Financial Services Act 1986 (now superseded).

Section 30(1) of the Financial Supervision Act 1988 of the Isle of Man ('FSA88') defines a collective investment scheme as:

> '...any arrangements with respect to property of any description, including money, the purpose or effect of which is to enable persons taking part in the arrangements (whether by becoming owners of the property or any part of it or otherwise) to participate in or receive profits or income arising from the acquisition, holding, management or disposal of the property or sums paid out of such profits or income.'

So far, this is a very wide definition, potentially capturing all sorts of business arrangements and partnerships. Section 30(2) of FSA88 helps to clarify matters a little further: it states that to be a scheme, these arrangements:

> '...must be such that the persons who are to participate ... do not have day to day control over the management of the property in question, whether or not they have the right to be consulted or to give directions...'

From this, it is now clear that if our vehicle is to be regarded as a fund (for regulatory purposes at least), its participants must be at one remove from the day-to-day management. This is helpful, as it rules out the kind of partnership arrangements where the parties operate their business between themselves: for our setup to be a collective investment scheme, someone else must be operating it.

Section 30(3) clarifies the definition even further. To be a scheme, the arrangement must have one or both of the following characteristics:

> (a) that the contributions of the participants and the profits or income out of which payments are to be made to them are pooled;
> (b) that the property in question is managed as a whole by or on behalf of the operator of the scheme.

Subsection (a) contains the pooling requirement which we have discussed earlier; and subsection (b) brings into the definition the concept of a scheme 'operator' – someone managing the assets and affairs of the vehicle, for its participants. This is the 'fund manager', whose role we will look at in detail in Chapter 4.

This is fine as far as it goes, but the definition we have so far is still very wide, and captures a number of arrangements which should not have to fall within the funds regulation regime. Therefore, and following the model of establishing a very wide definition and then carving out specific areas, subsections 30(5)–(7) of FSA88 then provide a number of specific *exclusions* from the scope of the definition – for example:

- Closed-ended companies
- Inter-group arrangements
- Employee share ownership schemes

- Franchise arrangements
- Clearing house arrangements.

The exclusion of closed-ended companies is important. If we establish our fund in the Isle of Man, or in any other jurisdiction with similar definitions, and if our scheme is closed-ended (i.e. has relative inflexibility in terms of the amount of share capital in issue) then it is not a collective investment scheme for regulatory purposes – and the c.i.s. regulations do not apply. That is not to say, of course, that other investment business or companies acts requirements do not apply – for example, the marketing of shares in the closed-ended company will still need to be carried out in compliance with applicable investment business regulations. Again, if our fund is quoted on a particular exchange, it will have to comply with any applicable listing requirements.

This limitation of the regulatory definition of a c.i.s. to open-ended vehicles is very common: for example, the definition of a mutual fund as defined under the Companies Act 1981 of Bermuda states that it is a company 'limited by shares and incorporated for the purposes of investing the moneys of its members for their mutual benefit and having the power to redeem or purchase for cancellation its shares without reducing its authorised share capital... .'

There are good reasons for having a much tighter regulatory regime for open-ended vehicles than for closed-ended ones, relating mainly to the need to provide investors with liquidity. We will look at these issues and the concept of open-endedness vs. closed-endedness in Chapter 2.

You might have noticed that under the Isle of Man definition we have been examining, we have not yet managed to completely exclude private arrangements – as, for example, where two people choose to pool their resources and have their money managed jointly by a third party, but have no reason to want their private arrangement to be regulated. In fact, the legislation in most jurisdictions does not *exclude* such arrangements from the scope of the definition – instead it *exempts* them from having to comply with the legislation and regulations, provided they are not promoted to the public and (often) provided they do not have more than a certain number of investors. So a private arrangement is still a scheme; it just does not have to be registered with a regulatory authority, or to labour under any regulatory constraints.

The difference between an arrangement being *excluded* from the definition of a scheme, and its being a scheme but *exempted* from the need to comply with c.i.s. regulations, might seem largely immaterial but it can have important ramifications for those providing services to them, which we will consider in Chapter 3 (The Regulatory Environment).

So far we have seen that in many countries, the definition of a fund is quite specific, and for regulatory purposes at least, usually excludes closed-ended schemes. We have, however, also said that in common parlance closed-ended vehicles which are used for pooled investment purposes are also referred to as funds. For a layman's description of a fund we could do worse than something along the following lines:

Definition: A fund is a form of *collective investment vehicle*, which is managed on behalf of investors and which allows them to *pool their assets* with the aim of achieving a *common investment objective*.

The types of assets which might be included in a fund's portfolio are as varied as investors' imaginations (although regulated funds are subject to some limitations in

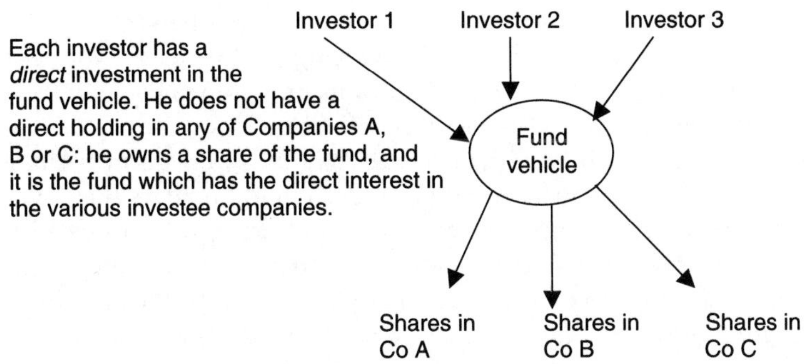

Figure 1.2 Each investor has a direct investment in the fund vehicle.

terms of what they can invest in; we will look at this in Chapter 3). The common underlying investments include:

- Equities
- Bonds
- Convertibles
- Derivatives
- Warrants
- Commodities
- Real property
- Deposits and near-cash assets in local and foreign currency
- Other funds.

More specialist or lightly regulated/unregulated funds may hold a much wider variety of assets, some of them relatively illiquid or difficult to value. For example, some – usually those aimed at sophisticated investors or those with specific interests in common – have been used to hold assets such as vintage cars, property ground rents, antiques etc.

Each investor has a direct investment in the fund vehicle, which holds the 'underlying' investments (Figure 1.2). He does *not*, however, usually have a direct investment in the underlying investments. It is the fund itself which has the direct interest in the underlying investment.

Investment via a fund is also therefore sometimes known as 'indirect investment'. The concept of indirect investment can be stretched somewhat where partnerships are used as fund vehicles, since with a partnership it is possible for tax authorities and others to look through to the individual partners and attribute interests such as tax liabilities/losses directly to them.

1.2 Capital structures

Funds may be 'closed-ended' or 'open-ended'. A company which is closed-ended will have a fixed authorized share capital – and a fixed amount of capital in issue at any point, with relatively little flexibility in terms of adjusting this (as, for example, with an ordinary company operating under traditional company law). An example would be the UK 'Investment Trust', a closed-ended company (and not a trust at all), established under the Companies Acts of the United Kingdom. Increasing or decreasing the number of shares in issue is a relatively laborious and potentially costly exercise and so the capital in issue is regarded as essentially fixed.

An open-ended vehicle, in contrast, has the ability to create new shares/units to meet demand from new subscribers, and to redeem and liquidate them when there is net disinvestment. Funds set up as unit trusts, partnerships, open-ended investment companies and purely contractual vehicles can be structured as open-ended vehicles.

Remember that, as we noted earlier, in many jurisdictions, the definition of a 'collective investment scheme' often excludes closed-ended vehicles: that is, the regulations which apply to regulated fund vehicles do not extend to closed-ended companies. Nevertheless, those businesses involved in establishing, managing and administering funds for third-party sponsors – known as 'third-party fund administrators' – usually have systems which can cater for both open-ended and closed-ended vehicles, and refer to both as funds or c.i.s.

We will look in more detail in Chapter 2 at the practical (as opposed to regulatory) implications of establishing a scheme as open-ended or closed-ended, and why a prospective fund sponsor might choose one option over the other.

1.3 Legal structures

When we discuss a fund's 'legal structure', as opposed to its capital structure, we mean the legal form it takes: that is, whether it is constituted as a company, a partnership, a trust or a purely contractual arrangement.

Depending on whether the fund is to be open-ended or closed-ended, some of these options may not be available: for example, a number of jurisdictions do not allow companies constituted under their laws to be open-ended, so only a unit trust structure can be used as an open-ended vehicle. Legislation facilitating open-ended investment companies is a relatively recent development in a number of countries.

Again, we will look at the practical implications in more detail in Chapter 2; at this stage, we will focus on acquainting ourselves with the general concepts.

1.4 The size of the funds universe

The variety of different legal and capital structures, and consequent definitions of a fund, means that industry estimates of the number of funds available worldwide vary wildly; at the time of writing, they ranged from under 40 000 to over 80 000 – depending on how a given commentator defined his fund 'universe'.

The picture is complicated in part because some agencies only capture open-ended funds in their statistics, whilst others include all vehicles intended to provide pooling benefits – that is, including closed ended vehicles. It can be further confused in terms of whether the agency includes only regulated funds, or both regulated and unregulated; and whether it registers an umbrella fund (a concept which we shall look at in Chapter 2) as a single fund or whether it counts all the umbrella's sub-classes as separate funds.

One of the other difficulties of assessing the size of the funds universe is the number of 'private' schemes which are established nowadays. Many funds are set up for the purposes of accommodating a handful of private individuals, or a specific institutional investor. They may not apply to, or need to, be regulated. Where this is the case there is often no easy way for the statistical agencies or regulators to capture them in their estimates. Further (and especially in the case of unregulated schemes), whilst the process of adding newly established funds to the statistics may be relatively straightforward, and is helped by the fact that sponsors may be willing to volunteer this information so as to attract investors, the process of removing closed funds can be a little more hit-and-miss. If a fund is unregulated and there is no legal reason for its removal to be flagged to the regulator, and if its managers are not inclined to provide performance data to any of the agencies measuring such data, it can linger on in the headcount statistics for some time after it has, in fact, ceased trading.

The different methods of defining the funds universe have also distorted the perceived success of different jurisdictions in attracting new funds business – some choosing to cite the headline numbers in terms of the widest possible definition, so as to improve perceptions of their success. Others are more rigid in their interpretations. When looking at cross-jurisdictional comparisons, therefore, it is important to delve deep enough to ensure you are comparing like with like!

Nonetheless, it is possible to emass meaningful statistics. At the end of the year, the size of the worldwide mutual fund market (that is, open ended schemes only) was estimated at just under $14 000 000 000 000 – some 23% upon the previous year. This estimate excludes funds-of-funds.

1.5 Origins: the first collective investment vehicles and the emergence of a funds industry

The fund industry is often said to have begun in the United Kingdom in the mid-1800s, when the Foreign and Colonial Government Trust was formed. However its roots in fact go back much further. The concept of collectivization of 'investment' interests can be traced as far back as 200 BC, by way of contracts which we would probably describe nowadays as life annuities. A European variation on this theme, the 'tontine', became a relatively common means of raising finance from the public in the Middle Ages; many of the principles then developed still inform today's fund industry, although it was not until the 18th century that true funds began to emerge.

Two developments in the capital markets also assisted in the development of a fund industry: these were:

- The development in the 18th century of securitization, which allowed private loan instruments (typically plantation loans to the West Indies) to be transformed into publicly traded securities;
- Stock substitution – that is, the repackaging of one security in the form of another with different characteristics which were more palatable to a particular investor market. The end product was essentially an early form of depository receipt.

Both of these developments led to new markets in instruments which had potential investor appeal – but which, in order to attract private capital from a risk-averse investor base, needed something more. This 'something' was provided in 1774, in Holland, where in that year the first '*Negotiatie*' of its type was formed by a local merchant named van Ketwich.

Van Ketwich solicited subscriptions for a new vehicle, which promised even smaller investors diversification at a low cost. This benefit – risk spreading, at accessible entry levels – is still a key selling point for collective investment vehicles the world over. The fund was called *Eendragt Maakt Magt* (literally, 'Unity Makes Strength' – an apt motto for the industry even today) and it invested in a range of bonds issued in countries such as Spain, Russia, and central and south America.

The fund was what we would today term a closed-ended fund, an equivalent to the UK investment trust: the concept of open-endedness had not yet arrived. At launch, some 2000 shares were issued at a par value of 500 guilders each, giving it an initial capital of some 1 m guilders. The fund was listed on the Amsterdam exchange, and a number of key investor protection concepts, surprisingly modern in their approach to corporate governance and the avoidance of conflicts of interests, were inbuilt:

- Van Ketwich himself was not involved in any investment selection. His involvement was limited to managing the fund's administrative affairs, and he was committed to providing an annual statement of account to the vehicle's 'commissioners'.
- The day-to-day investment management was delegated to two of the fund's directors, who were required to operate within a defined mandate.
- The company's prospectus restricted investment selections to 10 classes or groupings of bonds, and required that the investment managers spread the portfolio across these groupings so as to achieve the promised level of diversification.

The fund aimed to distribute a prescribed dividend of 4 per cent per annum. It was innovative in design: as well as its implicit benefits of diversification, van Ketwich built in a type of draw or lottery, such that each year a number of shares would be redeemed at slightly over par. Both of the shares which came immediately before and after a retired share in the register would receive a dividend in excess of the standard 4 per cent. This lottery concept was a not uncommon feature in the Dutch market of the time, but introduced an element of complexity which might be regarded as excessive in today's markets.

The fund was wound up in 1824, following difficult market conditions which took some of the shine off its initial success; nevertheless its early healthy returns and popularity had by then spawned a number of imitators, including others sponsored or administered by van Ketwich himself.

The concept of the investment trust took some time to travel abroad: it was not until 1868 that the first such fund was established outside the Netherlands. This was the Foreign and Colonial Government Trust. Established in London, it promised 'the investor of modest means the same advantages as the large capitalist, in diminishing the risk of investing in Foreign and Colonial Government Stocks, by spreading the investment over a number of different stocks.' The fund was again closed-ended – it was the first UK investment trust – and was closely modelled on its Dutch predecessors (including provisions such that shares would be retired from income during its defined life of 24 years).

As had been the case in Holland, once the concept was introduced the London market took to it with enthusiasm, and in the next decade a number of other trusts were established. It took until the 1890s for the idea to cross the Atlantic and for the first US investment trusts to be set up.

Despite its late arrival on the fund scene, credit for establishing the first open-ended is usually accorded to the United States. In 1924, three Boston-based businessmen pooled their cash to establish the Massachusetts Investors Trust, a mutual fund launched with assets of $50 000 (invested in about 45 stocks). It was so popular that after a year it had grown in size to nearly $400 000 and had about 200 participants. Many imitators followed and whilst the stockmarket crash of 1929 slowed growth, confidence was bolstered in the 1930s and 40s as Congress passed laws formalizing certain investor protections. The Securities Act of 1933 and Stock Exchange Act of 1934 required that mutual funds be registered with the Securities and Exchange Commission and that they provide a prospectus for prospective investors. The Investment Company Act of 1940 then introduced a regulatory framework for mutual funds, which still provides the basis for US fund regulation today.

Following these developments, the US mutual fund market grew rapidly in popularity over the 1940s and 50s. In 1940 there were fewer than 80 funds on the market, with total assets of some $50 million; by 1960 this had grown to 160 funds with around $17 billion and by the end of the 60s, some 270 funds and $48 billion of assets.

Subsequent landmarks have been the development of new categories of fund. In 1972 the United States' first money market mutual fund was formed, by way of the Reserve Fund, inc. and invested in money market instruments (i.e. cash and near-cash investments such as treasury bills, certificates of deposit and commercial paper) as opposed to longer-term securities. It offered investors an alternative to cash in the bank, with competitive returns and diversification across a number of deposit-takers. It began life with assets of some $300 000 and by 1975 had grown to around $390 million. From these beginnings the US money market fund industry exploded to some $80 billion by 1981.

In 1976, John Bogle was credited with the launch of the first retail fund to track a market index – the precursor of today's tracker funds. Now known as the Vanguard 500 Index Fund, Bogle's fund hit the $100 billion mark in November 2000 to become the then-largest mutual fund in existence.

Other developments and innovations have further fuelled the growth of the fund industry. Whilst space does not allow for a more detailed examination of the past, we will look at the emerging trends and likely future developments in Part 3 of this book.

1.6 Purposes, advantages and disadvantages of collective investment schemes

Why would an asset manager decide to offer his services packaged as a fund, rather than by way of direct investment portfolios? There are advantages and disadvantages to be considered, both from the perspective of the potential investor, and from that of the sponsor himself.

First, as we have noted, funds allow a group of investors to combine their resources with a view to achieving certain objectives. For retail investors, they can provide a useful alternative to direct investment, where the investor lacks any or all of the following:

- enough money to achieve a reasonable degree of diversification in his own right;
- sufficient investable assets to interest a professional fund manager running segregated client portfolios;

- the expertise to make the appropriate investment decisions;
- the time and inclination to do so.

The *advantages* to a retail investor of investing via a fund may include:

- *Economies of scale*. The combined weight of assets in a fund should mean that its manager can negotiate favourable commission and other charges, thus (in theory, at least) reducing the costs of investment to the individual investor. In addition a money market fund should, by pooling its investors' assets, be able to command the institutional rates of interest on the CDs, treasury bills etc. in which it invests, that any other substantial investor could obtain – but which would be inaccessible to the retail investor. At the least, it is arguable that these economies should partially offset the costs of running the fund itself.
- *Diversification (spread of risk)*. Diversification is the process of spreading investments across a number of different holdings, and potentially across different asset classes or markets. It has the effect of mitigating investment risk: if an investor has only a single investment holding, he will suffer considerably if that holding falls in value. On the other hand, if his portfolio contains several investments, the effect of any one of those investments falling in value is reduced. (Of course, the price to be paid for this risk reduction is that the positive effect of outperformance by any one of those holdings will also impact less on the performance of the portfolio as a whole.) A fund manager who seeks to deliver returns which do not diverge very far from the market norm is likely to have a well-diversified portfolio – that is, a large number of holdings in the underlying portfolio. One who is aggressive and confident in his stock selection skills, and whose fund is aimed at investors who can tolerate more risk will tend to a more focused approach: his portfolio will not be so well diversified, but if his selections are correct the impact of each one will have a correspondingly greater impact on the overall fund performance.

  An investor with a relatively small sum to invest, investing directly into shares or bonds, is unlikely to be able to achieve a meaningful level of diversification. That is, firstly he will probably not have sufficient money to invest in more than a handful of stocks; and secondly, if he does try to spread his money across a number of holdings, the costs of commission, stamp duty (if applicable), bank charges and so forth on each transaction will be disproportionately high and will reduce his net investment performance. By investing via a fund, the investor is gaining an indirect interest in a much wider spread of holdings.

  Many larger funds have far in excess of 100 underlying investment holdings – even the most focused funds rarely have fewer than 20 holdings (unless they are 'funds-of-funds' – see Chapter 2), and regulations usually require that retail funds observe minimum diversification requirements. We will look at the form these often take in Chapter 3.

  The degree of diversification achieved will depend not only on the number of holdings in a fund's portfolio, but also on the likely correlation between their individual returns. For example, a fund which focuses solely on the shares in US retailers may be diversified in terms of holdings in that sector, but it will be completely focused on a single industrial sector; if that sector suffers, the investor's fortunes will also suffer accordingly. We can therefore say that funds may offer diversification across not only individual companies, but also across a range of sectors, asset classes, countries and even investment styles.

- *Specialist investment expertise.* Normally, professional portfolio managers are only interested in providing services to those investors with substantial sums to invest. Investing via a fund allows many small investors to pool their resources, so as to collectively amass sufficient to be of interest to a professional manager. Thus funds provide access to specialist professional investment skills which would otherwise only be accessible to the very wealthy.
- *Eliminate administrative burden.* Even those investors who have sufficient funds to invest directly may not wish to take on the administration of a well-spread portfolio, with all that this entails. Investing via a fund means that it is the fund's manager/administrator, and its custodian, who will deal with issues such as the administration of investment transactions, settlement, dividend and interest collections, corporate actions and so on – and the record-keeping for all these activities.
- *Regulated status.* Not all funds are regulated, but many are – indeed many actively seek regulated status, because this can be a considerable comfort to investors. Investors may be encouraged to commit money to a fund because they know that it and its operators have been subject to scrutiny (by way of a licensing process) and that they are supervised on an ongoing basis and have to observe certain investment restrictions.
- *Access to foreign markets.* Certain of the world's stockmarkets are not open to private investors from abroad (although the number of markets where this is the case has fallen in recent years, as many countries have opened up to foreign investment). Others are theoretically open to private foreign investors, but the complexities and costs of dealing on them are such that most people would not want to incur them. Whereas a private individual may not be able to deal on a specific market, a fund manager may, on behalf of its fund (which is an institutional investor), be able to do so. Thus funds may offer individuals exposure to areas of the world which are difficult or impossible for them to invest in directly.
- *Access to products.* Some products are not available to retail investors, either for regulatory reasons or because of the product provider's policies. An example might be a hedge fund with high minimum entry levels, or one which has closed to new business but whose managers are willing to provide access to certain favoured institutional counterparties. Other examples might include sophisticated investment products employing derivatives, with the aim of achieving a specific risk profile. Individuals investing in a fund which itself uses such products or strategies can thus gain access to a portfolio with specific risk characteristics, which would otherwise not be available. Examples might include the many funds structured to offer capital protection coupled with an element of exposure to the stockmarket's upside.
- *Tax efficiencies.* Where an investor is resident in a jurisdiction which has capital gains taxes (CGT) or the equivalent, a fund can achieve significant tax deferral or mitigation: indeed many private funds are established to protect a family's wealth, for exactly this reason.

  An investor resident in a country with CGT, and who holds a portfolio of direct investments, will (subject to any CGT allowances) be liable for tax on the gains he realises when trading that portfolio. Even if he has other losses against which these gains can be offset, the administrative burden of doing so can be reasonably substantial.

However, if his investments are held indirectly – that is, through the medium of a fund – then it is the fund which realises the gains. Many types of fund incur no, or low, tax liabilities on gains realised on their underlying portfolio.

This means that a fund can act as a tax 'shelter' for gains on underlying transactions; the investor pays no capital gains tax until he realizes his holding in the fund itself. He may thus obtain significant cash-flow advantages through the deferral of CGT; indeed, he may be able to permanently avoid the tax in part or in full, by realizing his fund holding at a time when his overall CGT liability is low – for example, when he has other losses against which to offset it.

The *disadvantages* to the investor of investing via a fund may include:

- *Costs*. The costs of operating a fund offset some of the economies of scale. They include management and administration charges, custody costs, stock brokerage, legal and audit fees, printing and publishing costs and the like. The costs involved for some funds can be extremely high, and may outweigh any anticipated benefits. Investors are well advised to investigate the Total Expense Ratios (TERs) of funds they are considering buying. TERs are published by many funds directly; in other cases they can be obtained by referring to surveys published by agencies which specialize in calculating them. An example would be Fitzrovia (available at www.Fitzrovia.com). We will look at the various costs incurred in operating a fund, and how these are borne, in Chapter 4.
- *Lack of control*. Some investors like to be highly involved with their investments, and do not appreciate the fact that they cannot instruct the fund's manager as to what holdings to buy and sell – in fact in the case of a retail fund they are unlikely to have much, if any, contact with their fund manager at all. Certain managers whose funds are aimed at, and tailored to the needs of, very wealthy or sophisticated investors are happy to engage in discussion with their clients – but the communication is likely to be one-way; whilst an investor may be kept informed, he is unlikely to be able to influence investment decisions unless the fund is one which has been established specifically for himself and his family/close associates.
- *No guarantees*. Specialist investment expertise does not guarantee good performance, as many investors can attest; so an investor may end up paying substantial costs, but still suffer from an investment performance well below that of the market as a whole.

  Of course, certain funds *do* come with 'guarantees' attached; but these sometimes need close examination. Certain regulators exercise controls over the use of the word 'guarantee' in product descriptions; but where funds are established in countries where this is not the case, the 'guarantee' could be close to useless. In some cases they are limited to the guarantees attached to the underlying bonds or other investments in which the fund invests; in others, they are issued by a subsidiary of the fund sponsor group which has little or no substance.
- *Tax inefficiencies*. Whilst funds can provide a useful shelter for income and gains realized on their underlying holdings, they can also be inefficient in some circumstances. This is particularly the case where they are established in jurisdictions which do not have double taxation treaties with the countries in which they invest. This is quite often the case with 'offshore' jurisdictions, which – because of their tax regimes – may have difficulty in negotiating treaties with onshore authorities. Such

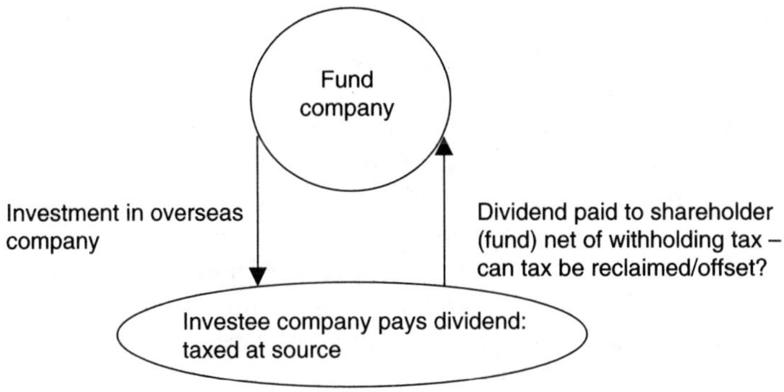

Figure 1.3 Tax inefficiencies.

funds may find it impossible to reclaim withholding taxes deducted on dividend or interest income on their underlying investments (Figure 1.3).

- *Lack of depositor protection.* Whilst many regulated funds, including those in certain offshore jurisdictions (e.g. Authorized Schemes in the Isle of Man) benefit from investor protection schemes of one form or another, this is not the case with every jurisdiction or class of fund. In some locations investors will benefit from more effective or comprehensive depositor protection under a bank deposit protection scheme, than they will when investing in a mutual fund operated in or from that jurisdiction. For example, investors in a US Mutual Fund are essentially uninsured against loss, whereas an individual with his money in a savings account would have the benefit of the Federal Deposit Insurance Corporation protection scheme, to the tune of up to $100 000 per account.

For the fund sponsor, the advantages of offering his services by way of a packaged product (a fund) are:

- *Ease of administration.* The sponsor can (for a cost) outsource the administration of many aspects of the investment function – including portfolio valuations, the maintenance of individual investor accounts, dividend/distribution calculation and so on. This means that the sponsor can concentrate on its core competencies, whether these be investment selection, macro-management or marketing and distribution.
- *Homogenization.* The sponsor does not have to cater to the differing requirements of a number of investors – all of his customers have accepted standardized terms and conditions, both in terms of an investment mandate and in terms of administrative functions such as reporting, etc., by way of the fund's offering documents.
- *Distribution.* Depending on the regulatory status of the fund, it may be possible for it to be distributed widely by tied sales agents, independent financial advisers, fund supermarkets and as fund-links to life products. Increasingly, the use of Contracts for Differences ("CFDs") is also being used as a way for investors to gain exposure to certain funds.

The potential disadvantages are:

- *Inability to personalize services.* The sponsor's offering to all of its investors will be relatively homogeneous; there will be no opportunity to tweak portfolios, or administrative features, to appeal to the needs of specific potential clients. This constraint is mitigated to a degree, if the sponsor's client base and fund range is big enough that he can offer:

  - different share classes with different features (such as feeder funds with a currency hedging overlay, or classes with different fee structures); or
  - a sufficiently large range of sub-funds from which investors can construct a tailored portfolio of funds, so as to meet a specific investment objective.

- *Cost.* The various costs of administering a fund, both in terms of paying its service providers and in meeting any regulatory costs, must be borne – either by the provider, or by the fund itself. If the provider meets the costs, its profit margin will be reduced; if the fund meets them, its net returns will be reduced, its investors will be less satisfied and it will find it more difficult to market itself on the basis of performance.
- *Regulatory and product constraints.* Depending on the regulatory status of the fund, there may be considerable constraints in terms of:
  - Obligation to diversify;
  - Limits as to the size of influential holdings in investee companies;
  - Limits on holdings in illiquid or unquoted investments;
  - Restrictions to certain 'eligible markets';
  - Inability to borrow or hedge, and controls on the ways in which hedging instruments may be used.

1.7 The market for funds – institutional, retail, specialist

Funds are typically grouped by the category of underlying asset in which they invest, or by the nature of the returns they are intended to generate. However, they can also be broken down into groupings according to the type of investor they are aimed at.

Retail investor funds are aimed at the general public; they typically have relatively low entry levels, and are subject to the most stringent regulatory controls in terms of their investment policies and how they are managed, administered and promoted. Individual investors may make their own decisions about which funds to buy, or they may be guided by a financial advisor.

Managed clients are often medium-to-high-net worth individuals, with sufficient investable funds to have their money professionally managed – albeit not in a portfolio of directly held shares. Their wealth may be managed by a specialist investment house, or a stockbroker or bank offering wealth management services. Portfolios will comprise a number of different funds. Managers targeting this category of investor may structure their funds so as to appeal to investment houses which will hold their clients' assets in the name of a single nominee, sub-segregating individual client portfolios on their own in-house systems. They tend to operate on a non-certificated basis, and may have a relatively high minimum entry level, which relates to the aggregate holding of the investment house as opposed to the positions of its underlying investment clients.

Wholesale investors include institutions such as life insurance companies, pension funds and so forth – organizations with large pools of surplus wholesale cash, on which they need to generate a return. The institutional market has grown significantly in recent years, in part because of developing pensions and trust legislation which has allowed greater freedom of investment to pension fund managers and trustees. Whilst trustees are now able to invest assets in a wider range of instruments than was once the case, they have also generally been burdened with an increasingly explicit duty of care – in terms of matters such as how they invest money, when they should take external advice or engage external managers, and what degree of diversification they should employ. Products such as funds have grown in their appeal as the providers of packaged solutions to many of these issues.

1.8 The role of funds as a node between the investing public and the capital markets

We have already noted the advantages that funds can offer investors, in providing access to areas of economic opportunity which might not be available to them (or at least, not on attractive terms) as direct investors.

The concomitant benefit of this is that funds play a role of huge importance in fuelling a developed economy. They do this by collecting investable capital from private and other investors, converting its form through the vehicle in which it is packaged, and then bringing it to those businesses and markets which need it, but which cannot easily accommodate direct investments.

Many products and markets are – for regulatory reasons, or for reasons of economies of scale – only accessible to substantial or professional investors. This would exclude most private individuals, but might well include the majority of funds. Further, whether they can access those markets or not, retail investors might well stay away from them simply because they do not have the knowledge, experience or access to information to engage with them, or because they do not have the ability to employ the strategies which will optimize the risk/reward characteristics of their exposure to them. By pooling together the individual sums of many individual investors, and channelling this into equity, debt and other offerings, fund managers provide much-needed funding to the capital markets.

Examples include:

- Venture capital funds, many of which benefit from tax favourable treatment – a means for governments to encourage private investment into startup businesses or businesses operating in economically disadvantaged areas.
- Pension funds investing via specially established fund vehicles (which may well not be available direct to the investing public).
- The various forms of partnership vehicle which are used in some jurisdictions to facilitate investment in film financing, a type of activity which might be unpalatable to many if it were not 'packaged' in this way.

Of course, fund managers have a particular agenda in mind: and that is to achieve sufficiently good performance to keep attracting new money, either for their existing funds or for new ones. The demands of this agenda are not always consistent with the needs of the investee companies. A fund manager investing in startup vehicles may be supplying it with much-needed capital: but it may be looking, in return, for any or all of:

- A quick move to profitability, and a return on capital which will be crystallized by the fund manager's withdrawal of his capital.
- High levels of dividend payouts, preventing the investee company from reinvesting as much of its profits as it would like.
- Management decisions which favour the short-term interests of the shareholders at the expense of long-term growth.

The company on the other hand, whilst it is undoubtedly capital-hungry, may be hoping for the type of investor who provides:

- stability of capital;
- a long-term investment horizon and a level of patience which can only be offered by a private investor or one who does not labour under the obligation to demonstrate a good investment performance to his clients;
- potentially, management expertise which will benefit the investee company.

This mis-match between the requirements of investor (fund) and investee (business) can make for certain tensions. Further, the propensity of even specialist fund managers to adopt a herd mentality and to have similar aims and outlooks means that the effect of one manager withdrawing support for a business or sector can be amplified as his peers do likewise. Thus, from the perspective of an underlying investee company, product provider or even an economy, funds can in some circumstances be as great a force for evil as for good. This is particularly so for those funds which are lightly regulated, or completely unregulated, and which therefore have the flexibility to act quickly and decisively in moving money around.

Numerous studies have been carried out on the 'herding effect' of fund-based investments on share prices, with a view to establishing just how destabilizing the effect is. The subject is not an easy one to deal with, especially since the villains of the piece are usually seen as being unregulated or lightly regulated hedge funds, whose managers are notoriously coy about revealing their funds' positions. However, enough robust data appears to have been obtained to make certain deductions – in particular confirmation of what one might intuitively have suspected: that past investment returns tend to be greatest in those stocks bought by 'herding' funds – funds with a propensity to copy their peers, in a sort of 'follow-the-leader' approach, rather than choosing stocks on a truly independent or random basis. It was also lowest in those stocks sold by herding funds. This implies that the trading behaviour of funds can trap investee companies in a vicious (or virtual) cycle of disinvestments (or reinvestment); and further, there are indications that the effect is greatest amongst small-capitalization companies – that is, those most in need of stable investment.

The reasons for this type of behaviour on the part of fund managers are not entirely clear, especially given the proportion who cite their independence of view as being the chief propellant of their performance. Most of the possible answers seem to indicate that this independence of view is, in fact, less common than many managers would like to admit:

- In practice it appears that many, if not most, funds trade on the basis of a positive feedback strategy. That is, they tend to buy stocks with a good past performance. Given the finite investment universe, this means that many funds will buy many of the *same* past winners.
- Similarly managers display a tendency to sell stocks which have recently fallen in price (this tendency may be particularly exacerbated in managers whose strategies are momentum-driven).
- Many managers have a particular aversion to the shares of small companies, those with low liquidity or those with unfavourable volatility or risk/reward histories. If they do invest, they react in a more risk-averse way to any perceived sell-signals.
- Reputational fears appear to play a large part in decision-making, with managers in many cases apparently ignoring the results of their own in-house research to copy the trading activity of other managers. This indicates that they prefer the risk of 'getting it wrong' with the general herd than that of getting it wrong alone.
- It may also indicate that rather than copying the trades of the wider fund community, simply for reputational reasons, they are looking at the trades of other managers whom they regard as better-informed, inferring their rationales from the trades they have undertaken and copying them in certain cases – selective herding, but herding nonetheless.
- It may however also indicate that their in-house research is actually strongly correlated with the in-house research of their peers as a result of being based on the same indicators.
- Herding activity appears to be strongest amongst those managers with a growth-oriented style, as opposed to amongst value-style managers; and among specialist managers and focused funds, as opposed to generalists.

As we have noted, the actual measure of herding activity is difficult to assess, particularly among less regulated and less transparent vehicles, although there is cause to believe it exists to a greater extent in some types of fund than in others. This tendency has led on a number of occasions to funds – and in particular hedge funds – being castigated as the 'tools of economic chaos'; because they are a means by which sophisticated investors can move money quickly into and out of particular assets or markets, they are blamed – often correctly – for sharp swings in currency, commodity and share prices. Those on the receiving end of these swings (and those responsible for ensuring orderly markets and economies) often characterize this behaviour as profiteering: witness the comments of former Malaysian Prime Minister Dr Mahatir at the time of the Malaysian economic crisis in 1997/8 (Dr Mahatir placed the blame squarely at the door of hedge fund managers), or the press comment in 2001 which blamed a small number of hedge fund managers for the sharp decline in the value of the South African rand.

There is undoubtedly an element of truth in this view: the larger hedge funds (and indeed the mass of smaller funds, when exhibiting herding characteristics) exert real influence on markets and currencies as well as on individual stocks. Without doubt managers will apply – indeed, have a duty to apply – strategies which will benefit their funds, regardless (within reason) of whether these are at the expense of companies and economies. But any criticism of them should be balanced with their capital-raising and liquidity supplying role and the fact that in a free market they are often the clearest means of allowing investors to vote with their feet (or indeed their pockets).

Hedge funds – even where they invest primarily in derivative products as opposed to the underlying assets – perform a particularly important capital-raising function for the less-liquid markets. Where derivative products have been developed and are offered by a particular market, they exist to provide a risk management and capital-raising mechanism for various economic operators; and in buying and trading them, hedge funds provide essential components of the market's capital and liquidity in them, by acting as counterparties.

In addition, because they are not bound by the liquidity and other constraints of highly regulated funds, and typically have relatively long 'lock-in' or notice periods for redemptions, hedge funds are also major investors in (and therefore major providers of funding to) many new ventures in which there is little or no market at all. Their fleetness of foot in moving money around, as facilitated by their freedom from regulatory investment restrictions, is counterbalanced by the relative stability of their investors' commitments.

1.9 Listed funds

In addition to determining what degree of regulation his fund should be subject to, a prospective sponsor should also consider whether there are advantages to listing it. If so this should be borne in mind early on, so as to ensure that the structure of the fund does not preclude its being listed on the most appropriate exchange, or necessitate an unwieldy and expensive restructuring.

The advantages are mostly related to increased investor appeal:

- Many institutional investors are bound by law or regulation only to invest in listed investments.
- The 'visibility' of a fund's shares may be increased significantly.
- Shares can be traded at any time when the exchange on which they are listed is open – not just once a day, at the fund's dealing point.
- A fund which is listed may be attractive to investors who wish to employ a wider range of strategies – for example, placing stop-loss or limit orders.
- Listing may also allow investors to buy on margin or short-sell, so as to hedge the risk in his portfolio.
- Some listed funds such as Exchange Traded Funds (ETFs) now have options on their listed shares. Again, this can provide investors with a wide range of strategies which would otherwise not be open to them.
- Investors will pay reduced costs for their buy and sell transactions (i.e. there will be no initial charges or redemption fees for them to pay).
- Where an exchange provides for settlement through a central agency, such as Crest or Eurocelar's FundSettle, this can be particularly attractive to institutional investors.

There can also be benefits from the sponsor's perspective – for example, in terms of investment performance. Listed funds such as ETFs do not have to hold cash in anticipation of investor redemptions (because the exchange is facilitating liquidity in the shares); this can reduce performance drag in times when market conditions favour a fully invested portfolio. Sponsors have also claimed that they regard the 'quality control' imposed upon them by virtue of a listing as being a useful internal discipline and means of promoting good governance.

There is no particular reason for a fund to be established in the same jurisdiction as that in which it is listed, although there may be economies in doing so. Managing listings across multiple jurisdictions, and the need to engage agents and legal advisers in other countries, can cause costs to escalate and increase the administrative and regulatory burden.

In order to obtain a listing, funds will generally be required to meet certain criteria. These differ from exchange to exchange, and may include minimum subscription levels, limits on the legal form which listed funds may take, and minimum disclosure requirements. A typical list of requirements is given in Table 1.1.

As well as entailing different requirements, listings on different exchanges will afford different benefits – some being regarded more favourably by investors of a specific type or in a particular location than others, and some being regarded as having a better reputation and general credibility than others. For this reason, it is important to have a clear idea of the needs and wants of your intended investor base at the outset, and to take advice on whether listing is likely to be of advantage – and if so, where.

For example, after taking advice a fund sponsor may decide that it would be advantageous to list a fund on one of the offshore exchanges, which may have less demanding criteria than onshore exchanges. At the same time, however, it may be advised that in order to meet the requirements of its target investor base, it should choose one which is recognized or designated by the US Securities and Exchange Commission or the United Kingdom's Financial Services Authority.

A comprehensive comparison of those offshore/international exchanges on which funds may be listed is beyond the scope of this text: however the following examples illustrate just a few of the considerations which a sponsor might bear in mind.

- *CISX*. An example of an exchange which can accommodate offshore/international funds in the offshore British Islands would be the Channel Islands Stock Exchange (CISX). The CISX has obtained recognition by the UK Inland Revenue under s841 of the Income and Corporation Taxes Act 1988 of the United Kingdom. This is a requirement for certain types of issuer and affects the UK tax treatment of securities listed on the CISX, including their ability to be held in certain UK 'tax wrappers' such as Individual Savings Accounts, Personal Equity Plans and Self-Invested Personal Pension Schemes; so, of course, a fund sponsor who saw the UK retail investment market as a primary target might see listing on such an exchange as attractive, because a fund which can be held in a tax-advantageous way will have a clear advantage over one which cannot. The CISX has also been accorded the status of a 'Designated Offshore Securities Market' by the US Securities and Exchange Commission, as provided for by rule 902(b), under 'Regulation S' of the Securities Act 1933. This regulation deals with sales of securities made outside the United States where there is no registration under the Securities Act 1933. The CISX will accommodate listings of funds set up as protected cell companies, and those established as limited partnerships.

Basic Requirements for Listing	Yes/No
Fund itself must be locally approved, incorporated in a jurisdiction acceptable to the relevant exchange on which listing is sought, or be otherwise acceptable to the exchange	
Fund must have appointed an independent auditor	
Fund units/shares may have to be held through a named depository/ settlement agent	
Fund may be required to be of a prescribed minimum size (if already established) and there may be a requirement for a minimum tranche per affected class to be listed	
Fund must be able to provide timely calculation of its Net Asset Value (NAV) to the Exchange periodically	
Exchange will require that the fund's directors accept responsibility for contents of the listing documents	
Exchange will require that directors can demonstrate adequate knowledge, skill and experience in the management of funds – both in general and in the context of the type of fund which is to be listed	
Fund's Investment Manager (if one is appointed) must be able to demonstrate appropriate knowledge, skill and experience	
The various functionaries and service providers must disclose any conflicts of interests	
Shares/units in the fund must be freely transferable and capable of being traded on an equal footing (shares in the same class must rank *pari passu)*	
Annual accounts may be required to conform to International Accounting Standards, or to US or UK 'Generally Accepted Accounting Principles'	
Contents of Listing Documents	
General details	
All basic details – name, address, domicile, legal constitution of the fund which is applying to be listed	
Directors' 'Responsibility Statement'	
Declaration that an application has been made for listing	
Nature, amount, means of valuation and issue price of the tranche to be listed	
Arrangements for conversion between classes, if any	
Statement as to the potential for cross-class liabilities to arise, if any	
Auditors and other functionaries/service providers	
Disclosure of any pending legal proceedings	
Management	
Details of the fund manager, investment manager and any advisers	
Details of service and other material agreements, and remuneration	
Details of directors' remuneration	

Table 1.1

Basic Requirements for Listing	Yes/No
Investment policy	
Statement as to the fund's investment objectives, policy and strategy	
Disclosure of material risks	
Specific disclosure requirements may be prescribed where a fund is able to make investments off-exchange/on an 'over the counter' basis, etc.	
Information regarding financial position	
Where a fund has been in existence for 12 months or more at the listing date, audited annual accounts	
Interim financial statement made up to a period of (say) no more than 3 months prior to the date of the listing document	
Where a fund has been in existence for less than 12 months prior to the listing date, an audited statement of its NAV as at a period of (say) no more than 3 months prior to the date of the listing document	
The makeup of the fund's investment portfolio as at a date no more than (say) 3 months prior to the date of the listing document	
If the fund is new and the above statements are not applicable, a declaration to that effect	
Any other material financial information	
Other information	
Information as to dividend/distribution policies	
Procedures for buying and selling	
Information as to costs of investment	
Ongoing Obligations	
Annual accounts (audited), and interims, to be sent to the exchange and to shareholders within a prescribed date (usually 6 months) from the close of the period to which they relate	
All NAV calculations to be notified to the exchange immediately on their finalization	
A file of all marketing material to be maintained, and provided to the exchange's officials on request	
All material changes, new developments or operational changes to be advised immediately to the exchange	
All price-sensitive information, material changes in performance or financial position to be notified immediately to the exchange	

Table 1.1 Continued

- *Europe*. Examples of exchanges with listing regimes for funds in the Eurozone include Dublin, Luxembourg and London; listing on these exchanges can be advantageous for funds with particular interest in being marketed into Europe. At the time of writing, one interesting trend was that of sponsors allegedly willing to pay the listing, legal and other fees necessary to get their fund listed on such exchanges, at least in part because of the 'due diligence' benefits this afforded them. That is, investee companies, banks and other counterparties which have to comply with detailed anti-money laundering requirements may, in many jurisdictions, be permitted to regard an entity listed on certain European exchanges as having been subject to sufficient 'due diligence' already. Consequently, they will not require full and up-to-date evidence of the identity and residential addresses of the fund's directors and key shareholders. The costs of listing may seem quite a high price to pay to remove what is essentially no more than an administrative burden, but for an investment company with numerous counterparties, and coupled with the other benefits we have already noted, it appears to be a realistic solution.

- *Other*. Other regional exchanges accommodating funds listings would include the Cayman Islands Stock Exchange (available at www.csx.com.ky) and the Bermudan Stock Exchange (available at www.bsx.com). As with several other exchanges accommodating funds, the Cayman Islands exchange now accommodates settlement of funds via Euroclear's 'FundSettle'.

1.10 Fund categorizations

There are a number of ways in which funds can be categorized; one is by target investor type, as we saw in Section 1.7. Another means of categorization is to group them according to their underlying investments.

In some cases, this type of fund categorization is prescribed by the regulatory authorities in the countries in which the fund is authorized; for example, in the United Kingdom the Financial Services Authority distinguishes between:

- Securities Funds – those funds investing in securities such as shares and debt instruments.
- Funds-of-Funds – those funds investing in the shares or units of other funds. We will look at funds-of-funds in greater detail in Chapter 2.
- Feeder Funds – those funds which invest solely in the units or shares of another fund, and whose NAV will therefore vary in approximately direct proportion to that of the underlying fund. Again, we will look at feeder funds in more detail in Chapter 2.
- Money Funds – those which invest in money market instruments such as certificates of deposit, commercial paper, bankers' acceptances, treasury bills, short-term government securities or quasi-government securities, repurchase agreements and the like. The precise definition of what is considered a 'money market security' differs from jurisdiction to jurisdiction, and so investors should ensure that they understand the true nature of the fund they are contemplating investing in (similarly, sponsors would be well-advised to articulate their investment policy clearly so as to obviate the potential for mismatched expectations).
- Futures and Options Funds; those which can invest in covered futures and options to a prescribed extent.
- Geared Futures and Options Funds; those which can employ uncovered futures and options to a prescribed extent.
- Property Funds; those funds which can invest in a mix of real property and shares in property companies: the maximum and minimum exposures to real property will be determined by regulations.

However, each of these categories is quite broad – its only purpose is to provide a framework on which the regulator can hang more specific regulations relating to investment restrictions. It would not necessarily help an investor compare funds with a particular industrial or thematic focus; for example, the UK regulatory grouping of 'Securities Funds' will include:

- a fund which invests solely in government stocks (gilts);
- a funds which tracks the UK main market index (the FTSE100);
- a fund which invests in a broad range of UK corporate bonds and shares with the aim of generating a balance of income and growth; and
- a highly focused fund which invests solely in (say) media stocks or start-up companies and which aims to generate high levels of capital growth with no income objective.

Because of this, other categorizations are laid down by industry bodies such as the UK's Investment Management Association (IMA). These are considerably more useful for the prospective investor, since they aim to make it easy for him to compare 'like with like' – either in terms of funds with a specific focus (e.g. UK Large Cap Equity Funds, or Emerging Markets Funds) or in terms of specific objectives (income funds, growth funds etc.). At the time of writing, the IMA maintained 31 main categories of fund, with a number of different methods of sub-categorization (see www.investmentuk.org).

1.11 Matching investors' objectives

How does a sponsor come to the decision to establish a fund? This is something of a chicken-and-egg question:

- In some cases, it is the fact that he has investment expertise which comes first. Having considered the options, he may decide he can best capitalize on this expertise if it is packaged as a fund, administered by a third party and marketed to investors.
- In others, the driver is the investor's need (and not the sponsor's requirement to find some way of commoditizing his skills). That is, a sponsor will see a captive investor base with unsatisfied investment needs, and will put together a product aimed at satisfying these needs. In this case, the sponsor may need to hire in the requisite investment skills by appointing an external investment manager or adviser.

Where it is investor need that is the driver, the prospective fund sponsor needs to take into account a variety of requirements – not just the basic requirement for an investment return, but features such as tax efficiency, income distribution capability, legal form and so on. Sometimes, a sponsor will need to structure a fund so as to accommodate different investor objectives, especially where the target market comprises different investor types (retail, institutional etc.) and investors in different jurisdictions. Such structuring can involve the use of different fund classes, or of feeder/hub-and-spoke arrangements so that offerings have the required features and charging structures and meet regulatory requirements for a number of different target investor bases.

We have already seen that – whatever the complexities of measuring the funds universe! – there is a vast array of fund-based offerings to choose from. This means that in theory the right choice is available to the investor, if only he knows where to look; but it also means that making the right selection can be a daunting prospect. The peer groupings and performance rankings which we noted above in Section 1.10 support comparisons of funds of similar types from the perspective of pure performance: but this stage is only of value once an investor has ascertained his own objectives, and then selected the group of funds from which he will ultimately choose an investment. The following headings set out some of the considerations which an investor will (or at least, should) consider when making a fund selection – and therefore the issues a sponsor should consider when investigating investor appetite for a proposed new fund launch.

Investment objective

One of the most basic questions will be '*what is our target investor base's investment objective, and what therefore must be the investment objective of a fund which will meet their needs?*' The question may sound so basic as to be facile, but fuzzy thinking at the outset, a failure on the part of management to articulate a fund's objectives and strategy clearly and thoroughly, and a tendency to allow strategy to drift rather than keeping these objectives in mind are between them perhaps the biggest causes of investor/manager tension in the fund industry.

The way in which a fund manager selects and uses the fund's underlying investments should be informed at all times by the fund's *investment objectives*; that is, the *type of return* which it aims to generate, and by its *risk profile*. It is important that the investor understands these, because his primary task is to select a fund with objectives and a risk profile which accord with his own.

The 'investment objective' of a fund refers to the type of returns it aims to generate for its investors. The types of return are, in the broadest terms:

- Capital growth – the fund will invest in order to increase the *capital value of its assets* without generating much, if any, income. Funds of this type often invest in low-yielding growth stocks.
- Income – the fund may invest in (for example) bonds and other fixed interest securities, or perhaps cash or high-yielding equities, to generate an *income for investors*; but without a substantial level of capital growth, and perhaps at the expense of some capital erosion.
- A combination of the two (a '*balanced*' fund) – a mix of equities and bonds may be used.

Of course, a variety of other assets may be used to achieve the objectives stated above and they are provided as examples only.

It may be worth considering what we mean by the words 'income' and 'capital'; although these are terms which most people take for granted they can be hard to define. Further, some fund product development and marketing departments (and the tax authorities) may take a different interpretation to that which you might intuitively assume.

Generally speaking, *income* is a form of return which is relatively regular: and which when taken does not result in the erosion of the capital base from which it is generated. *Capital* is more one-off in nature, and when it is taken reduces the value of the investment providing it, either in part or in total. Some relatively straight forward examples are given in Table 1.2 – and some of which are more complex, in Table 1.3.

Nature of return taken	Income or capital?
Interest	Income: the cash deposit or bond is left intact and will continue to pay interest regularly until its maturity date
Dividends	Income: the company will continue to pay dividends regularly whilst profits and cashflow permit
Rent	Income: the value of the property is not diminished by taking rents, and rent will continue to be received whilst paying tenants are *in situ*
Partial realization of profits on a shareholding	Capital: the value of the shareholding is reduced by the amount of profit taken out

Table 1.2

In addition to the distinctions between different types of return, a fund services provider should determine the means by which such returns are to be measured. That is:

- Is the fund intended to provide positive returns compared to some other benchmark – for example, one synthesized from the performance of the markets in which it invests, or the performance of its peers? In this case, it will be described as targeting *relative returns* – returns which are positive relative to the performance of that benchmark. By this definition, a fund which rises 10 per cent over a period in which its benchmark rises 6 per cent will be described as having achieved a positive return of 4 per cent relative to the market. A fund which falls by 8 per cent over a period in which its benchmarks falls by 12 per cent will also be described as having achieved a positive return of 4 per cent relative to the market. An example of a fund targeting relative returns would be one whose stated investment objective is 'to outperform the MSCI World Index by at least X per cent per annum.'
- Is the fund intended to provide positive returns, regardless of the direction of the markets in which it is invested (or indeed of any other benchmark)? If so, it will be described as targeting *absolute returns*. An example would be a fund whose stated investment objective is to achieve 'an absolute return of in excess of 12 per cent per annum, regardless of market conditions and within a controlled risk framework.'

Fund policy: how will the fund's managers attempt to achieve its objective?

Every fund will have an investment policy – the strategy by which it attempts to attain its stated objective, and the geographic, sectoral or other investment focus that the portfolio will maintain. This policy will determine the types of asset in which the fund can invest, and helps potential investors determine whether the fund is appropriate to their situation.

Some examples of investment focus are given in Table 1.4.

Of course a given fund may have an investment policy and focus which combines several of the above elements – for example, one investing UK biotechnology stocks is specific in terms of geographic focus (the United Kingdom), asset class (equities) and sector (biotechnology).

Nature of return taken	Income or capital?
Dividend reinvestment schemes on fund holdings (see Chapter 9)	Many investors who have dividend reinvestment on their fund holdings mistakenly believe that they are benefiting from capital growth – they see the value of their fund holding increase by the value of the reinvested dividend each year and do not realize that this is the result of a dividend payment, the proceeds of which have been reinvested However the taxman's view in most jurisdictions is generally that the investor has received a dividend (income), which is taxable, and has simply chosen to spend it on buying more shares in the same fund
Returns on zero coupon or 'deep discount' bonds	Some bonds are issued in non-interest-bearing form, or pay very low levels of interest; instead, the investor receives his return by way of the difference between the discounted purchase price of the bond and its eventual redemption price. These are known as deep-discount or zero-coupon bonds Again, the tax authorities in most jurisdictions have long regarded such instruments as potential tax- avoidance vehicles, and in many cases have issued rulings or practice notes stating that a proportion of the return over the period will be deemed to be income. The holder will then be assessed to income tax on the increase in value, either in full at the redemption date or, in some cases, on a *pro rata* amount each year (despite the fact that the investor has received no cash flow from which to fund the tax)
Returns on rollup funds	Many funds which invest either directly or indirectly into income-yielding assets such as bank deposits, interest-bearing bonds and high-yielding stocks do not distribute the income they earn on these underlying investments by way of distributions or dividends. Instead, the income stays in the fund's bank account and is eventually invested in other assets. It 'rolls up', and boosts the NAV of the fund as a whole over time On the face of it, this allows an investor to gain exposure to stable, income-producing assets without actually receiving income in his hands. Instead, he receives the income accruals by way of what is, to all appearances, a capital gain on his holding in a fund. This may, for many investors, appear more tax efficient – for example, some live in jurisdictions which have income tax regimes but no capital taxes; others have capital gains tax allowances which can be offset against any liabilities In many jurisdictions, however, the local tax authorities have issued practice notes or rulings stating that they regard investments in income-producing assets via rollup funds as being potential avoidance techniques. They therefore assess resident investors in rollup schemes (whether domestic or overseas) on the proportion of the overall gain on redemption which is deemed to have arisen from income-producing assets. This may be taxed on eventual redemption, or annually, based on a notional return

	An example of this is the United Kingdom's 'Distributor Status' regime for overseas funds. UK investors buying overseas funds which distribute substantially all of their income, and which comply with certain investment restrictions, will pay income tax each year on the dividends or distributions actually received. Those who invest in non-Distributor Status funds will be taxed on the entire capital gain upon redemption as if it were income tax, thereby losing the ability to offset 'true' capital gains against any capital gains tax exemptions or capital losses from other sources. At the time of writing, this regime was under review, but it provides a good example of the way in which a revenue authority can seek to prevent investors 'recharacterizing' income as capital growth and thereby mitigating their tax liabilities.
Definition of interest under the EU Savings Directive	The EU Savings Directive introduces a new regime for the tax of interest income earned by residents of the Union. It seeks to help national tax authorities collect tax due to them, where their residents have invested in products issues in another jurisdiction which is subject to the regime. It is intended that member countries, and certain 'third countries' will undertake to ensure that their local interest 'paying agents' identify those depositors or investors who are resident in the European Union. Depending on the local arrangements product providers will either withhold an amount of tax on certain 'interest' receipts, a proportion of which will be remitted to the tax authorities of the investing individuals; or alternatively, information relating to the interest income earned by an EU resident individual will be sent back to his local tax authority by the tax authorities in the interest paying agent's country. The wording of the directive is widely drafted; whilst it captures interest payments made to individuals, the wording defines 'interest payments' so as to capture distributions, and proceeds of redemption, from funds investing in debt instruments – whether directly or, in the case of a fund of funds, indirectly. This is another example of revenue authorities finding ways to drill down to the true source of an investment return, and characterize it according to its original source. Again, the detail of how the process will work in practice is yet to be finalized at the time of writing, as the details will need to be drafted at national level.
'High income' funds	Many funds promise a very high (sometimes guaranteed) level of 'income' to their investors. However, closer inspection of the offering documents may show that the promise is to make a set level of *payments* to the investor – whether or not the fund has earned sufficient income to support the level of payout. If the fund has not made capital gains to make up any income shortfall, then the value of the investor's holding will be eroded.

Table 1.3

Example of potential fund focus	The fund will only invest in (e.g.). . . .
Single industry sector	Technology stocks Financial services
Single country	UK equities only US equities and bonds only
Capitalization	Large-cap, 'blue-chip stocks' Start-up ventures and smaller capitalization shares
Wider geographic area	Investments selected from the Pacific Basin Companies listed on the stockmarkets of Europe excluding the United Kingdom
Single asset class	International equities Bonds
Market type	Emerging markets
Other	Ethical funds

Table 1.5

Entry levels: how much will investors be able to place?

Many funds impose a minimum investment figure, for example, \$10 000 or currency equivalent. In some cases, this is prescribed by regulation; for example, Isle of Man Professional Investor Funds must specify a minimum subscription of \$100 000, whilst Isle of Man Experienced Investor Funds had, until recently, to impose a minimum of \$15 000. (Both types of fund must also require that investors meet other criteria: see Chapter 12.) Managers of these types of funds are at liberty to impose higher minimum subscription levels if they so choose; but they cannot impose lower minima.

There is currently something of a trend away from the use of high minimum subscriptions, as a regulatory tool to screen out unsophisticated investors. This is in part because of an increasing acceptance that wealthy investors are not necessarily the most sophisticated (or vice versa). In addition, however, there has been a recognition that requiring a high minimum entry level to more complex, illiquid or risky funds may actually increase an investor's risk since if he is determined to invest, he has no option but to commit a large amount to the fund (whereas he may in fact have been content to subscribe much less if the option had been available).

Where funds are listed on a stock exchange, that exchange may also prescribe a minimum initial subscription: there are however a number of other exchanges which do not prescribe any minimum at all (e.g. the Channel Islands and Bermudan exchanges, excepting for certain types of fund). As noted in Section 1.9, this may be a factor in selecting an appropriate exchange on which to list.

In some cases, where listing requires that investors meet a minimum subscription, this can be addressed through the establishment of a feeder fund investing directly in the listed underlying vehicle. This allows those investors (perhaps institutions required to limit their holdings to listed vehicles) who can meet the minimum subscription level to invest directly in the listed fund. Smaller investors, provided they are not constrained by a requirement to invest only in listed vehicles, can subscribe their

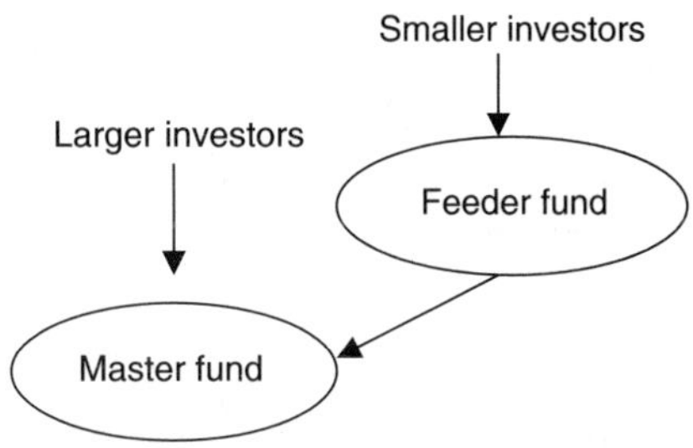

Figure 1.4 Feeder fund as a vehicle to accomodate smaller investors.

smaller sums via the feeder fund (Figure 1.4). The feeder therefore serves two purposes:

- Provided it meets the minimum subscription level itself, it acts as a vehicle to 'box up' those smaller investors and provides them with an entry route into the underlying fund.
- It may also provide a mechanism for differential pricing, with the direct institutional investors only suffering the charges levied within the listed fund and the smaller investors potentially being charged an additional layer of fees at feeder fund level.

Regulatory and listing requirements aside, a fund manager will in any event wish to impose some minimum initial subscription level; he should also impose minimum additional subscriptions, and minimum residual holdings to be maintained subsequent to any partial redemptions. This is necessary to screen out investments which are uneconomic in size; that is, those on which the management fees, adjusted for the costs of administration, will not turn a meaningful profit.

The level at which these minima should be set will depend upon the size and 'shape' of the fees charged by various functionaries. One factor which is increasingly affecting this process is the growing burden of 'due diligence'. We will look at this issue in more detail in later chapters; for now it is sufficient to note that many third-party fund administrators have discovered, on analysis, that where their agreement with the sponsor is such that the third-party administrator's staff collect identity verification documentation from the client fund's investors, so as to comply with anti-money laundering legislation, the regulations have changed to such an extent that they now need to reprice their services. An alternative is for the administrator to agree that it will carry out a certain amount of work in requesting investor due diligence, but that after that and if it fails to receive the appropriate documentation, it will be entitled to decline the subscription or (if the subscription has been processed), forcibly redeem the holding. This is clearly unattractive for the fund sponsor and in some cases, especially where the sponsor is itself involved with the distribution process and/or the fund is essentially aimed at a private, known investor base, the sponsor is now taking the collation of due diligence on itself.

Lump sum or regular contribution

Most funds accept only lump sum investments. However some, typically retail funds, offer a regular investment option which can make them accessible to investors who

Date	Amount invested	Price per share	Shares purchased
January	100	50	2
February	100	40	2 ½
March	100	30	3 ⅓
April	100	30	3 ⅓
May	100	40	2 ½
June	100	50	2
July	100	60	1 ⅔

Over seven months, the fund's average price per share was £42.86. However, an investor employing pound cost averaging would have paid only an average of £40.39 per share.

Table 1.5

have not yet amassed the minimum lump sum, or who are seeking the self-imposed financial discipline of a regular payment. The inclusion, or otherwise, of a regular payment option will, of course, have cost implications as the administrator is required to deal with a large number of relatively small subscriptions. Many third-party administrators simply do not have the capacity to deal with regular contribution funds; those which do generally rely on highly developed and efficient systems and relationships with their banks. A sponsor who wishes to add regular payment options at a later stage should enquire of his proposed administrator at the outset, since changing administrators so as to accommodate this could be unwieldy and expensive.

One benefit which is often 'sold' to retail investors is pound-cost (or dollar-, or euro-cost) averaging; this relies on the fact that an investor who is subscribing the same amount each month will receive more shares/units when the fund's NAV is depressed, and fewer when it is high. The effect is that the investor pays a lower portfolio average cost per unit/share purchased, than the average unit/share price in the fund over the period. It can be illustrated as shown in Table 1.5 – our investor will subscribe £100 per month in the same fund.

The average unit cost to a monthly investor can therefore be shown to be lower than the average fund price over same the period.

What is the investor's time horizon?

In most cases, both sponsor and investor alike should take the view that the longer the term, the better. From the sponsor's perspective, the longer an investor's funds are tied up, the greater the management fees and the less administration involved in terms of applying newly subscribed, or liquidating newly redeemed moneys. A sponsor will therefore prefer to target an investor base whose money, once invested, is relatively inert – rather than one which may be high volume but high-turnover.

As regards investor needs, the conventional wisdom is that a 5-year time horizon is the minimum to which the investor should be able to commit, before buying an equity-based fund. Three years is the minimum often cited for bond funds, and as little as one year for cash funds. Sponsors should bear in mind, however, that whilst the above time frames are commonly quoted, they are also nowadays probably too simplistic.

For example, fund managers establishing cash and near-cash funds for certain types of institutional client may find that their target audience's time horizons and liquidity needs merit a much closer analysis than the indicative timeframes set out above. Captive insurance managers, in particular, will usually have a detailed understanding of the likely incidence and scale of any potential claims their client captives are likely to suffer (potentially necessitating redemptions from any cash fund in which they are invested). A fund manager who ensures that he has a clear picture of both the maturity and risk profile of his clients' portfolio from an investment/claims matching perspective may find that he is able to make use of longer-term instruments – and thereby potentially achieve a significant performance uplift – than would otherwise be the case. The same will be the case for any fund aimed at meeting the needs of an asset/ liability matching client – pensions, insurance or otherwise.

Under the heading of time horizons, a sponsor should also consider the frequency at which the proposed fund will deal, and any required notice periods which investors must give prior to redemptions. Considerations to be borne in mind include:

- *Regulatory requirements:* Highly regulated and retail funds are generally daily dealers: and indeed in some jurisdictions this is a requirement. Funds subject to lighter, or no, regulation may be able to operate with more infrequent dealing periods.
- *The nature of the underlying assets*, and how easy they are to liquidate to meet redemptions. For example, a fund which invests in other, infrequently dealing funds (e.g. a fund-of-hedge-funds investing in hedge funds which are mostly monthly dealers) is unlikely to be able to offer a dealing period of less than one month, and may need to prescribe a one-month notice period as well so as to enable redemption money to be raised. Many funds dealing in illiquid assets such as property have very lengthy inter-dealing and notice periods.
- *Investor expectations*, and whether the fund will be less appealing to investors if they perceive it as offering restricted access to their funds. In practice, investors in relatively retail offerings often see no material difference between a daily dealing fund and a weekly dealer. Investors in specialist funds, with illiquid underlying holdings, are (if the fund has been properly distributed) normally sufficiently sophisticated to understand the limitations on their investment's liquidity.
- *Cost.* The process of calculating an NAV on a daily basis (and if necessary, of publishing this) can push costs up considerably, and weekly dealing may enable the administrator and manager to levy a significantly lower annual management charge.
- *Impact on investment portfolio.* Where a fund manager can collate a weeks' worth of investor transactions and process all those received prior to the cut-off date on one weekly dealing day, instead of placing many small deals on a daily basis, life can be considerably easier for the investment manager and the portfolio may be subject to much less disruption. For one thing, the investment manager should receive better advance notification of significant net inflows or outflows, and can consider how best the portfolio should be positioned. For another, the reduced dealing frequency reduces the amount of tinkering which has to be done to raise or absorb liquidity on a daily basis, which may keep underlying dealing costs down; and the netting-off of a week's subscriptions and redemptions can mean that the number of underlying portfolio transactions which are necessitated purely for liquidity purposes may be reduced or eradicated all together.

- *The administrator's capability.* Many third-party fund administrators (particularly those in the offshore environment) do not have the systems and staffing to accommodate daily dealing funds and will either decline to take them on, or will quote terms which effectively price daily dealing out as an option. Sponsors who intend to launch a fund on a weekly-dealing basis on cost grounds, with an eye to moving to daily-dealing when critical mass permits, should check whether their administrator will be able to cope.

Where a manager is forced, for operational reasons (e.g. the illiquidity of the underlying assets) to impose an infrequent dealing cycle there may be other ways in which investors with particular liquidity needs can be accommodated.

These can include the interposition of a 'manager's box' or 'marketmaker' facility with the ability to undertake transactions in between formal dealing dates. In such cases, care must be taken to ensure that both investor and manager understand the basis on which the interposed marketmaker will price the asset, and where the risk lies between the marketmaker's dealing date and the fund's next dealing date.

In many cases, listing a fund is a means of providing such liquidity but for fund managers who cannot or do not wish to meet the requirements for listing on an exchange, a proprietary marketmaker can often provide this facility – depending on local regulatory requirements. The marketmaker may be the management company itself; alternative structures include establishing a separate vehicle which may may hold out as willing to deal in the shares of one or more funds. The marketmaker itself may be subject to some form of regulation.

In some cases, a marketmaker vehicle which is itself a subsidiary of the fund in which it provides intra-dealing day liquidity can be advantageous, in that it can assist in managing the fund sponsor/manager's position risk; where the sponsor/manager owns the marketmaker itself, it will either need to assume the risk of price changes in the fund between dealing dates, or to draft the sale agreements between marketmaker and investor in such a way as to remove this risk – an arrangement which some would regard as artificial. However, where the marketmaker is established as a subsidiary of the fund, care must be taken in terms of:

- the marketmaker's own regulatory status;
- the avoidance of conflicts of interest;
- the nature of the disclosures made to investors (both in connection with sales through the marketmaker, and in connection with the status of the marketmaker as an asset of the fund); and
- any regulations relating to self-investment.

Charging structure: investor expectations and transparency

The issue of an investor's time horizon leads us on to consider the use of charging structures as a potential tool for encouraging investor commitment. So, for example, sponsors should consider whether exit fees are a viable alternative to initial fees. This has implications in terms of cash flow (especially where the sponsor or manager has to fund intermediary commissions up-front and there is no initial fee to provide the cash for this). Further, not every third-party administrator has the systems capability to accommodate exit fees – especially where these are to be levied on a staggered basis (i.e. 5 per cent on any redemption in the first year after investment; 4 per cent in the second year, and so on). This is because the administrator has to be able to identify the agedness of a given holding on redemption and apply the appropriate exit charge. Where they are able to do this, administrators may nevertheless charge a higher fee for the extra administration burden. This will need to be borne either by the fund or individual existing investor, impacting on performance, or by the manager, impacting on profitability.

The inclusion of a performance fee element is now commonplace for certain types of fund (typically hedge funds). There are conflicting views on their merits: many investors are happy to see a manager incentivized to perform well on their behalf. Others feel that it encourages the manager to take risks which he otherwise might not – particularly if the performance fee is supplemented by a relatively high 'basic' annual management fee. We will look at some of the issues arising in the calculation of performance-based fees in a later chapter.

It is worth noting that investors are, nowadays, considerably more fee-savvy than they used to be. In part this is a result of better investor education, and in part because of greater regulatory demands for transparency on the part of product providers. As we have noted above, TERs are now published by professional agencies and it is relatively simple for a prospective investor to determine how competitive a fund is in terms of its charging structure.

Fund management group

Before selecting a fund on the basis of its individual merits, an investor will usually also consider whether the management group to whom he is entrusting his funds meets various criteria. In some cases, there will be little the sponsor can do to address any concerns arising from these considerations, but in others there may be some options:

- *Track record:* Some fund management groups have better records than others, and an unknown fund sponsor may find that he benefits more from an alliance with an established fund group than from going it alone.
- *Ownership:* The fund management industry has been subject to much merger and takeover activity. Investors and advisers will usually be concerned that the management team within a recently merged group may be suffering from a lack of focus, or that there will be changes within the investment team as economies are sought.
- *Investment style:* By investment style we mean the investment manager's approach to selecting investments. The differences in various styles merit a text in themselves, and are beyond the scope of this book. However, at different times and in different market conditions, those managers who favour a 'value'-oriented style will perform better than those pursuing a 'growth' style. In addition, investors and their advisers will also have their own views as to which style is preferable. For a description of the value style of investing, we could do worse than to look back to van Ketwich, introduced in Section 1.5. After the success of his first investment trust, van Ketwich introduced a second in 1779 (named *Concordia Res Parvae Crescunt*: 'Little things grow by consent'). Instead of specifying the groups of securities in which this fund could invest, this time his prospectus simply specified that the fund would invest in 'solid securities and those which, as a result of a decline in their prices, merit speculation and may be bought at below their intrinsic value ... which it

would appear reasonable will result in benefit.' Put very simply, value investors buy securities which appear undervalued when they are assessed on the company's fundamentals – its cash flow, NAV, dividend cover and so forth. Growth investors are less interested in fundamentals and more in the momentum of a given stock or sector.

- *Geographic resources:* Some fund houses have a real presence in the countries in which they invest, and understandably will cite this on-the-ground ability to stay in touch with the market as a reason to expect them to outperform. Others rely on a desk-based analysis of third-party research and other data, and may believe that technology and the speed of modern communications renders an *in situ* presence an unnecessary expense. Again, investors and advisers will have their own views as to which approach is better.
- *Internal management style:* Many investment houses have individual managers with strong reputations, and have used these individuals' track records to attract business. However, people are prone to moving from one job to another, and reliance on the reputation of a single individual can leave the investment house vulnerable if that individual is poached by another house and investors switch holdings in order to follow him. Many houses nowadays avoid the culture of the 'star manager' and prefer to promote their team approach and overall investment philosophy.
- *Regulated status:* Investors may take comfort from the fact that a fund management group is regulated; however this is only really meaningful if the regulator itself meets certain standards. This generally means its having statutory status (as opposed to its being an industry-sponsored body of which membership is voluntary, or which has little in the way of sanctions); and that it is a member of, or adheres to the standards of, an internationally recognized body such as the International Organization for Securities Commissions (IOSCO). Where a fund manager is regulated by such a body, its investors have the comfort of knowing that it has been subject to a vetting process at the outset, and that it should also be supervised on an ongoing basis. In a few jurisdictions, the element of ongoing supervision is non-existent or cursory; some regulators place most of their reliance on financial reporting and on notifications from the business' auditors; in a number of others it is largely focused on anti-money laundering practices, with low levels of supervision in terms of investor protection. In addition, the existence of a statutory compensation scheme, and/or an industry ombudsman, can be a valuable investor protection benefit and thereby a meaningful marketing tool, despite the additional costs associated with them. Whilst many investors will not appreciate such niceties, awareness is increasing rapidly, partly aided by the efforts of the international financial press and of those jurisdictions which do impose such requirements.

Taxation

Sponsors should consider the tax status of their target market, and any requirements which may arise out of this. Specialist advice should be taken, in connection with:

- The tax treatment of income distributions and redemption proceeds in the investor's hands. A number of offshore jurisdictions are currently reviewing the likely impact of the EU Savings Directive on their funds industries since it is clear that both distributions and redemptions on certain types of funds will be affected. These include all of those jurisdictions which are a part of the European Union (such as Ireland), but also those which are not member states but whose status has some dependency on another member state (such as the Isle of Man, the Channel Islands, and the Cayman Islands).

- Tax treatment of the fund itself. In many jurisdictions, international funds (i.e. those not targeting local residents) are not subject to local direct (income, capital or corporation) taxes or indirect taxes such as value added tax (VAT); in others, tax is levied, albeit at a relatively low level.
- Tax treatment of the underlying investments; where the fund is to invest in foreign instruments on which withholding taxes are levied, are double taxation agreements in place which will allow for the reclamation of those taxes? As we have seen, this may not be so if the fund is established in an offshore jurisdiction since these locations often have difficulty in negotiating treaties with their onshore neighbours.

Taxation matters will be important in selecting not only the correct jurisdiction in which to establish and/or operate a fund, but also its legal form: for example, funds established as partnership vehicles may be more attractive from a tax perspective where applicable legislation allows income, gains and/or losses to be attributed on a *pro rata* basis to the relevant investors. A number of jurisdictions, including the United Kingdom, United States, Isle of Man and Channel Islands have enacted legislation permitting partnerships viable as fund vehicles.

Past performance

Whilst it has become a commonplace to say that past performance is no guarantee or indicator of future performance, it is a rare investor or adviser who will not take account of a fund manager's track record in deciding whether to place funds with him. In recent years, regulators in a number of jurisdiction have become increasingly concerned about investors' reliance on past performance, on the grounds that:

- Certain surveys appear to have confirmed the lack of correlation between past and future performance; and
- The investment teams within a given fund management house can, and do, change, taking with them the skills and experience which have stood the house in good stead.

In some cases, regulators have sought simply to impose regulations which standardize statements of performance (so that investors can compare like with like), and which place increasing focus on transparency in terms of charging structures and on full disclosure of material risks. In others, there are indications that they are keen to go further, seeking to prevent managers from advertising on the basis of track record at all.

Whilst there may be merit in their arguments, and it is true that investors should not assume that a fund which has performed in the top quartile for the past year will continue to do so, it is unlikely that past performance will cease to be a material factor in decision-making. It may be fair to say that a fund which has consistently been a top performer will not necessarily continue to be so: however, it is also likely that most investors and advisers would prefer to avoid a fund which has been a consistently poor performer – unless there are very persuasive reasons for doing otherwise!

Fund managers can do nothing to change history: however what they can do is ensure that any performance measurements of their funds position them fairly, against relevant benchmarks and/or peer groups and that the NAVs and distributions represented are accurate. A sample of prices quoted in independent fund pricing/performance measurement agencies can reveal a frighteningly high number of inaccuracies. There may not be a great deal that the manager can do to obtain redress, other than ensuring that those price feeds over which it does have control (e.g. because it pays for their publishing) are accurate.

Risk profile

Just as every investor should have a clear picture of his investment objective, so as to be able to identify a fund which has similar objectives, so he should have a clear idea of his risk tolerance so as to be able to select a fund which has a similar profile. Whilst many institutional investors can articulate their risk tolerance accurately, unfortunately many private investors have a much hazier idea of their own tolerance: time and again advisers struggle to explain that the potential for reward will almost invariably be correlated to the level of risk incurred.

Many managers, and indeed some third-party distributors such as fund supermarkets and life companies offering third-party fund links now offer 'risk ratings' to try and assist investors in choosing appropriate investments for their needs. These may use models along the lines of a scale, from 0 to 5, where:

0 = the fund is regarded as virtually zero-risk (its capital is protected by a third-party guarantee given by an institution with a strong credit rating);

5 = the fund is regarded as highly risky and whilst its objective is to obtain high levels of capital or income, there is a significant possibility that the investor may lose some or all of his capital.

It is important that where a fund manager provides his own risk profiler, this is as accurate as is possible; and that where he becomes aware that his funds are included in another business' risk profiling he raises any concerns as to the accuracy of the rating with that business promptly:

- An inappropriately high risk rating could deter investors for whom the fund is, in fact, appropriate.
- More seriously, an inappropriately low rating could result in investors taking on a level of risk they had not intended to. In the event of losses this could, conceivably, lead to claims for compensation on the grounds that the fund's riskiness was misrepresented.

Certain regulators have considered, or are considering, introducing their own risk rating models but progress in this regard is not brisk: in part because of difficulties in agreeing risk rating methodologies and in part because of concerns over liability to investors in connection with any inaccurate ratings.

2 Different fund structures

2.1 The different capital structures: open- vs. closed-ended schemes

Before proceeding further, we will build on the brief acquaintance we made, in Chapter 1 in Section 1.2, with the concept of 'open-endedness' and 'closed-endedness', and what this means in terms of the practical operation of a fund. We will revisit some of these concepts in more depth later: at this stage it is important only that we grasp the broad concepts.

Open-ended funds are those where:

- The capital structure is flexible: it expands to accommodate new investors' subscriptions, and contracts when there is a net outflow of funds.
- By 'new investors' we mean, here, people who are placing new money into the fund – they are not buying shares or units 'second hand' from an existing investor, but direct from the fund manager. The cash which they pay for their holding ultimately finds its way into the bank account of the fund, so in simple terms we can see the fund itself as issuing them with shares and receiving the consideration into its portfolio of assets – thus increasing the fund's total Net Asset Value (NAV). Similarly, investors exiting the fund have the effect of shrinking its total available investment capital – because they sell their holdings back to the fund, and the fund pays them the proceeds of that sale out of its assets. It may have to sell underlying investment holdings to realize the cash to make this repayment.
- As we proceed, we will see that this simple approach can be complicated by the interposition of intermediaries such as a manager's box or marketmaker, and that listing a fund can provide a secondary market in the fund's shares or units; we will consider these mechanisms in Chapter 7 when we look at dealing processes; for now, we will stay with the basic process above to establish a few basic principles.
- The price of a share/unit in an open-ended fund is, broadly, calculated by reference to the total value of the fund, divided by the number of shares/units in issue. As we shall see later, there are a number of adjustments which may be made to this calculation – but for now, again, the basic principle will suffice.

As an example, let us take the SJT Fund, which for the sake of argument we will say is an open-ended investment company. The SJT Fund is established when 30 people decide to put £10 000 of cash each into a pool, with the aim of establishing a collective investment vehicle. This means that they have a combined pool of (£30 × £10 000) = £300 000.00 in total.

The fund company's share capital of £300 000 is divided into 3000 shares of £100 each, that is, 3000 × £100 = £300 000.

Each subscriber therefore receives 100 shares, being worth £100 per share initially: this reconciles back to their initial subscription, that is, 30 people × 100 shares × £100 = £300 000.00.

On Day 1 of the fund's life, its available cash is used to buy investments:

Investment	Price	Value
30 000 Gemtronics Ords	£5.00	£150 000.00
30 000 Pizza Warehouse	£3.00	£90 000.00
15 000 British Bank plc	£2.50	£37 500.00
		£277 500.00
Uninvested cash		£22 500.00
NAV @ close of Day 1		£300 000.00

To work out the price of each share in the SJT Fund, we use the following formula:

$$\text{Price per share} = \frac{\text{NAV of the fund}}{\text{Number of shares in issue}} = \frac{£300\,000.00}{3000 \text{ shares}} = £100.00$$

On Day 2, the prices of the fund's investments move;
Gemtronics Ords shares go up to £5.20;
Pizza Warehouse shares go down to £2.50;
British Bank plc go up to £2.70.

Investment	Price	Value
30 000 Gemtronics Ords	£5.20	£156 000.00
30 000 Pizza Warehouse	£2.50	£75 000.00
15 000 British Bank	£2.70	£40 500.00
		£271 500.00
Uninvested cash		£ 22 500.00
NAV @ close of Day 2		£294 000.00

To work out the price of each share in the SJT Fund we use the same formula again:

$$\text{Price per share} = \frac{\text{NAV of the fund}}{\text{Number of shares in issue}} = \frac{£294\,000.00}{3000 \text{ shares}} = £98.00$$

What would be the value of the fund if the investment prices moved as follows at the end of Day 3? (Try this one yourself using the underlying share prices below and then check them against the answer, to ensure you have absorbed the concept.)

Gemtronics shares go down to £4.85;
Pizza Warehouse go up to £3.20;
British Bank go up to £2.90.

Investment	Price	Value
30 000 Gemtronics Ords	£4.85	£145 500.00
30 000 Pizza Warehouse	£3.20	£96 000.00
15 000 British Bank	£2.90	£43 500.00
		£285 000.00
Cash		£ 22 500.00
NAV @ close of Day 3		£307 500.00

To work out the price of each share in the SJT Fund:

$$\text{Price per share} = \frac{\text{NAV of the fund}}{\text{Number of shares in issue}}$$

$$= \frac{£307\,500.00}{3000\ \text{shares}}$$

$$= £102.50$$

From the above exercise, we should have absorbed the key point that:

- the value of shares or units in an open-ended collective investment scheme is driven by changes in the value of the underlying investment portfolio; and
- *not* by supply and demand for them, as would be the case with shares traded on a stock exchange.

We can also see why a part of the manager/administrator's function is to generate portfolio valuations on a regular basis – so that investors can buy and sell shares/units at an accurate price. We will look at the valuation process, and what happens if prices are incorrectly calculated, in a later chapter.

Changes in the value of the underlying assets are not, however, the only events which will occur in the life of a fund. Among the others are:

- new investors will buy into the fund (they will 'subscribe' for units/shares);
- investors will sell out of the fund (they will redeem their holdings);
- investments will be bought and sold for the fund's portfolio;
- income may be received by the fund, by way of dividends/interest etc.;
- income may be paid out to investors from the fund, by way of distributions/dividends;
- fees will be paid by the fund to those involved in running it, and for costs and services such as audit, legal fees, printing, publishing of prices etc.

As we move on through other chapters, we will see how all these things impact on the fund and its pricing. For the time being, we will continue exploring the concept of open-endedness on our funds. We have seen what open-endedness means in terms of unit/share pricing. Now, let us consider what the impact of new investors has on the fund as a whole, and on the existing investors. We need to satisfy ourselves that when new investors buy shares (or exiting ones sell them), the existing investors in our fund are not affected.

Example
Fund ABC has a portfolio valued at £3 million.
It is made up of 1 000 000 shares.
Therefore the NAV per share is (using the formula we applied above)
£ 1 000 000/1 000 000 = £3 per share.

New investor John Smith has £150 000 to invest.
How many shares will this buy him?
Shares are priced at £3 each so it will buy him 50 000 shares.

Two things happen to the fund:

- It gains £150 000 in assets.
- 50 000 more shares are created to give John Smith his interest.

The number of shares in the fund is therefore 1 000 000 + 50 000 = 1 050 000.
The assets of the fund are £3 000 000 (the original portfolio)+ £150 000 (new cash paid by John Smith for his shares = £3 150 000

The NAV per share is therefore £3 150 000/1 050 000 = £3 per share – that is, unchanged by the introduction of a new investor.

So when new money is introduced into an open-ended fund, two things happen: the fund issues new shares, and the fund's assets grow (by way of its bank account absorbing the subscription price of the new shares). Because of the way in which share prices are calculated for an open-ended fund, the effect of these two events broadly cancel each other out: an existing shareholder's interest is diluted as a percentage of the fund (he now holds a slightly smaller percentage of the fund because new shares have been issued) – but that smaller percentage is worth the same as it was before the new shareholders were admitted (because it is a now-smaller percentage *of a now-larger fund*).

The same is not true for closed-ended funds, such as investment trusts (as they would be known in the United Kingdom and some other jurisdictions; a somewhat confusing names, as they are not trusts at all). Such vehicles essentially operate just as any other company established under 'traditional' company law, although because of the nature of their business they may be subject to additional regulations such as:

- listing requirements, if they are quoted on an exchange;
- financial services legislation, if they are required to comply with local investment business regulations; or
- investment restrictions which may be imposed if they are to receive certain tax concessions.

They will have a fixed share capital in issue at any given time, as for any company with a traditional capital structure. This means that the number of shares in issue can only be increased/decreased by application to the relevant companies registry/the courts, and it can be a fairly time-consuming and (if stamp duties or similar taxes are involved) a costly process. It would certainly not be undertaken on a regular basis to accommodate the ebb and flow of investor demand.

Because of this, investors in closed-ended funds do not have the option of dealing direct with the fund in its shares in the way that we saw for open-ended funds. The exception is of course when the shares are initially issued, or when some fairly major capital restructuring is being undertaken. Instead, investors wishing to buy shares must find an existing holder willing to sell, and vice versa. Thus, investment trusts are usually listed on a stock exchange, which provides a secondary market in the shares and an exit route for investors wishing to realize their holding.

Because of this, shares in an investment trust are not dealt in at a price related directly to their NAV, but instead by reference to market forces and investor supply and demand. Of course, it is perfectly possible to calculate an NAV – indeed it will be necessary to do on a regular basis for reporting and investment management purposes, and changes in the fund's NAV will affect investors' perception of its appeal and therefore their demand for the shares. However, the fact that dealing prices are arrived at through the action of market forces means that they can often be significantly over or (more commonly) under the actual NAV per share. This is termed 'trading at a premium', or 'at a discount', as the case may be. Where an investment trust is established with a limited life, that discount or premium will narrow as the winding-up date of the trust approaches, since the terms of the company will be such that its assets are to be distributed in accordance with a predetermined formula (after payment of any costs, prior charges and so forth).

As well as the ordinary share capital, which makes up the majority of their funding, investment trusts can issue different classes of shares, and indeed loan stock and warrants – just as any ordinary company can. This can allow a range of investments to be issued which have appeal to different types of investor.

We will look at the mechanics of fund pricing, and the adjustments which may have to be made to ensure fairness to incoming, outgoing and remaining investors, in Chapter 5.

2.2 Legal structures: corporate, trust-based, partnership and contractual vehicles

Funds can be established using a variety of legal structures – depending on the statutory provisions in the jurisdiction in which the fund is to be constituted. The alternatives open to a particular sponsor will depend on:

- The capital structure required – that is, open-ended or closed-ended. Some legal forms cannot be established as open-ended vehicles in certain jurisdictions.
- The intended nature of the underlying investment assets – funds investing in less liquid assets may be better structured as closed-ended vehicles, so that the manager does not have the distraction of needing to raise cash to meet investor redemptions. This may influence the choice of legal form, as noted above.

- The intended investment strategy – closed-ended vehicles are generally subject to much less in the way of regulatory investment restrictions, if any. They can gear (borrow) and are usually able to use derivatives and have greater concentration of investment than are open-ended vehicles. Again the situation will vary from jurisdiction to jurisdiction.
- The legislative framework in the jurisdiction in which the fund is to be established. Some jurisdictions do not have the statutory framework to provide for the sponsor's preferred fund vehicle.
- Tax considerations, both at fund and at investor level.
- Regulatory considerations. These may relate to the different ways in which fund vehicles themselves are regulated (e.g. restrictions on pricing formulae, distribution and promotion etc.). They may also be related to the target investor market and the types of instrument in which it is permitted to invest.
- Listing requirements – some exchanges only allow corporate entities to be listed, whilst others allow for trust-based vehicles also to be listed.
- Marketing considerations and investor preference; in some countries there are cultural and investor educational hurdles to marketing certain types of vehicle, even if there are no regulatory or tax barriers.

Open-ended vehicles may be established as:

- *Unit trusts*. These are the longest established open-ended vehicles. As the name suggests, the vehicle is constituted as a trust, with a trust deed, trustee and beneficiaries (the investors). The management of the unit trust is generally entrusted to a separate management company.
- *Open-ended investment companies (OEICs)*. Where a fund is constructed as an OEIC, the investors hold shares in it as they would with any 'traditional' company structure. However, as we have seen in Section 2.1, the means of determining the value of their shares, and the way in which they invest and redeem will be driven by the NAV of the underlying portfolio: the precise method will be dictated by the terms of the constitutional and offering documents. In most cases, the OEIC will issue a flexible number of participating shares which are held by the investors, and which carry rights over the assets of the fund. A management company will normally hold a separate class of 'management shares', which are termed 'non-participating' shares because they do not carry rights over the fund's portfolio. However, certain jurisdictions provide for OEICs to be self-managed, with responsibility for the fund's management resting with its directors.
- *Limited liability partnerships*. Increasingly, a number of jurisdictions have passed new partnership legislation (or amendments to existing partnership) to facilitate their use as open-ended investment vehicles. In some cases, this has meant removing restrictions on the maximum number of partners. In most cases, the legislation is such that there are a number of limited partners (the investors) and a general partner, whose liability is unlimited and who is responsible for the management of the fund; the general partner can therefore be seen as broadly equivalent to the manager of a unit trust or OEIC.
- *Quasi-OEICs*. The Isle of Man, Jersey and Guernsey are all examples of jurisdictions which – whilst they have to all intents offered the option of OEICs as fund

vehicles for many years – in fact do not yet have 'true' OEIC legislation. Instead, the open-endedness of a fund (i.e. its ability to create and redeem shares or units with participation rights on demand) is simulated by the use of nominal shares. These are 'activated' by converting their status, so that they become participating shares and acquire a value relating to a proportion of the fund's portfolio: this equates to the creation of new units in a truly open-ended vehicle. On redemption by an investor, the shares revert to their nominal status, shedding value which is used to repay the redemption proceeds. Whilst this can work well in practice, it is theoretically somewhat ungainly, requires some extra accounting work, can in theory present difficulties in times of net redemptions and can present a hurdle – real or imagined – to prospective sponsors.

Various countries which provide for 'quasi-OEICs' have passed legislation to try and ameliorate some of their perceived disadvantages. For example, legislation enacted in the Channel Islands now provides for the issue of shares with no par value (NPV): in Jersey this is by way of the Companies (Amendment no. 6) (Jersey) Law of 2002 and in Guernsey by way of the Companies (Shares of No Par Value) Ordnance 2002. These developments allow for companies in those jurisdictions to issue shares which have no 'par', or 'nominal' value, either alone or along with issues of other share classes which have a par value. All subscription money received for NPV redeemable preference shares is credited to the fund company's share premium account, so that on redemption shares, there is no need to fund their nominal value out of profits or a new issue: the entire redemption proceeds can be funded from the share premium account and/or retained earnings.

This makes the accounting exercises which have to be undertaken on redemption of participating shares significantly simpler, by obviating the need to issue nominal shares to satisfy the redemption of par value. Appropriate conditions must be included in the fund company's memorandum and articles (M&As), but it is possible – subject to the satisfaction of various requirements – for an existing company to take advantage of this development and amend its M&A so as to permit the issue of shares of NPV. Whilst this means that Jersey and Guernsey funds can now be set up with more similar characteristics to funds established in the United States, United Kingdom and many other European countries, they are still – in theory at least – at a slight disadvantage to competitor jurisdictions where 'true' OEICs are permitted, and where shares can therefore be created and liquidated on demand.

- *Contractual vehicles*. In some jurisdictions, open-ended funds are established by way of contractual agreement; this may not sound too different from a unit trust, and indeed it is not. This means of establishment is common in jurisdictions where the concept of trusts is not accepted, whether in law or in investor culture.

We will look at the role of the various functionaries to these vehicles – manager, trustee and so forth – in the next chapter.

The concept of an open-ended company is a relatively recent development – in some jurisdictions at least. In the United Kingdom, for example, the option of using OEICs was only introduced in January 1997, by way of the Open-ended Investment Companies (Investment Companies with Variable Capital) Regulations 1996 (the ECA Regulations). These were the United Kingdom's means of implementing certain EU legislation, which was necessary because of the United Kingdom's EU membership.

A collateral benefit was, however, that the development also met demand from the UK fund industry for new vehicles allowing it to compete more effectively in the European investment arena. Prior to this, the only form of UK open-ended vehicle available was the unit trust – arguably, not such an easy structure to market to investors in countries which did not recognize the concept of a trust. Other countries, too, have recently recognized the benefit of a pooled investment vehicle which combines the capital flexibility of a unit trust with the legal personality of a company. South Africa, for example, brought in its Collective Investment Schemes Control Act in 2002 – again, prior to this unit trusts were the only available option for open-ended vehicles in that jurisdiction.

Closed-ended vehicles are also known as *investment trusts* (ITs): this term is used in many English-speaking countries, and we shall use it in this sense in this text. The legal form is corporate, and the fund operates under what we might call 'traditional' company law, with a fixed authorized and relatively stable issued share capital.

Whilst the legal form may on the face of it be relatively simple, investment trusts can become quite complex – offering a range of different types or 'classes' of shares, the different classes carrying different rights and benefits. These ITs are known as 'split capital' investment trusts or 'splits', and they are generally formed for a limited timespan. Split capital investment trusts are designed to appeal to many different types of investor. One of the main motivations for a manager to operate a split capital investment trust has been the attraction of new funds into the fund, without causing it to suffer from the typical discount. (We will deal with IT pricing discounts in a later session.)

On an agreed date, the split investment trust is usually wound up and the assets are divided according to a set formula; in some cases, there may be provisions for the shareholders to vote on whether or not to wind up the trust on the specified date. This provides them with the opportunity to realize the fund's portfolio if they wish, or to keep it going if they believe that the prospects merit it. A typical example would be a split established with an initial life span of 10 years, but with the built-in provision (at the investors' option) to extend this lifespan by (say) 3 years at a time.

Where an investment trust is set up on the simplest basis – with a single class of shares – these ordinary shares will normally be entitled to all the income and capital of the trust, subject to any borrowings that have a prior charge.

In the case of a relatively basic 'split capital' trust, there may instead be two classes of shares:

- income shares, which pay out broadly all the income received by the investment trust, and receive a predetermined and relatively low capital return when the fund is wound up;
- capital shares, which pay no income at all – but which benefit from the bulk of the assets on the fund's wind-up.

Normally, income shares are purchased by investors who have ongoing income requirements and who do not find this form of return unduly tax-inefficient. The capital shares, on the other hand, will be bought by investors who find capital gains more tax-efficient. Tax may not be the only determinant, however, since the two classes of share may also have markedly different risk characteristics and investors should ensure that they have considered this aspect of their investment properly.

Since their origin in the United Kingdom in the 1960s, splits have become significantly more sophisticated and offer a wide range of different types of shares. A few variations are set out below:

- *Income shares* – there are several different types of income shares, with significant differences in capital entitlement. It is important to distinguish between these, because certain shares can give rise to substantial capital losses at redemption.
  - Traditional income shares give investors a right to distributions of the fund's income, and a fixed redemption price on the wind-up of the fund – subject to there being sufficient assets remaining in the fund, after repayment of debts and other preferred classes of shares. This requirement for a sufficiency of assets if capital is to be returned introduces a real element of risk, and one which investors don't always appreciate.
  - Many split capital issues have included income shares which are rather closer to an annuity in form. They pay out a relatively high level of income, but may provide for only a nominal redemption amount (e.g. 1p for every 100p share).
  - Some split capital issues have combined a fixed redemption price, with a share of any remaining capital at redemption – thereby providing a known 'base level' of capital return.
- *Capital shares* are the natural counterpart to income shares, in that they generally pay no income whatsoever to their holders.
  - Investors buy them with a view to a capital return: they receive the bulk of the investment trust's assets when it is finally wound up.
  - Because of their nature, capital shares can be highly geared and the returns on them tend to be volatile.

These are the simplest types of shares which a 'split' will offer, but there are a number of other variations:

- *'A' shares* are ordinary shares which carry no voting rights; they will often have dividend rights over and above those of ordinary shares. 'A' shares are not generally popular with regulators or listing authorities, on the grounds that the absence of any voting rights may be contrary to the principles of good governance and may undermine the interests of the investors who are carrying the bulk of the risk.
- *Zero-dividend preference shares* (or 'zeros'). These pay no income, but offer a predetermined rate of return when the trust is finally wound up. Their shareholders have a priority claim over the company's assets when it is wound up.
  - The return on zeros is not guaranteed (there may be insufficient assets left at wind-up, after all) but there is a strong likelihood that the return will be paid because of their prior claim on the trust's assets. Holders of other classes of shares will receive nothing until the zeros have been paid out their full entitlement.
  - The redemption value of a zero at the liquidation date will be calculated in accordance with a stated formula. This will be such that the zeros are issued at a price based on an initial asset value, rising by a compound growth rate to reach the intended final value.
  - The returns on zeros are taxed as capital growth rather than income, and they are particularly attractive to investors who are not resident in jurisdictions which

have capital gains taxes, or who are resident in such countries but have an available exemption.

- *Stepped preference shares* have an income entitlement, which grows at a predetermined rate and provides a predetermined maturity value. They are relatively rare, but have obvious advantages for investors who need to know their future income and capital returns.
- *Income and residual capital shares* (formerly known as 'highly geared ordinary shares'). These are designed to give a highly geared return in terms of both capital and income – which is to say, the returns will be volatile as a result of the company's borrowings.
- *Package units.* Some split capital trusts bundle together 'packages' of capital, income and zero preference shares to create what is (almost) the equivalent of an ordinary share. In some cases, this is beneficial in reducing or eliminating the discount which may apply to the ordinary share alone.
- *'C' shares* were initially introduced in the United Kingdom in the 1990s, as a means of enlarging the capital base of an investment trust without the attendant drawbacks of a traditional rights issue. These are that:
  - existing holders who choose not to take up the rights issue may be disgruntled, perceiving their investment to have been diluted by the new inflow of money;
  - existing holders have to bear the costs of the rights issue, which may be poorly received; and
  - in any event, the manager of the investment trust may have specific reasons for wishing to bring in new shareholders.
- C shares allow the company to raise new capital as follows. Money received from the new issue is *initially allocated to temporary C shares*. The funds so raised are then invested, and the C shares exist alongside the original class of shares. In due course, the C shares are then converted, on the basis of the relative NAVs, into the original class of shares.
- The benefit of this approach is that it avoids flooding the existing portfolio with cash, which could unfairly dilute the short-term performance of the existing shares to the disadvantage of the existing shareholders.
- *'S' shares* are a means of launching a new investment trust whose strategy is close to, but not identical to, that of an existing fund. They have not been heavily used but were employed for a small number of funds in the 1990s.
- S shares relate to rights over a separate portfolio from that to which the ordinary shares relate, and this portfolio remains separate throughout the life of the investment trust.
- S shares will therefore have a different NAV, and be quoted at a different price, from the company's ordinary shares. They have been described as 'perpetual C shares'.
- The rationale for issuing S shares as opposed to launching a completely new and separate fund has generally been the speed of issue, and cost containment.
- *Convertibles in ITs.* Like other companies, investment trusts can issue convertible loan stock. This offers investors the right to convert their fixed interest loan stock issued by the investment trust, into a set number of the issuing company's ordinary shares at a predetermined rate and on or between predetermined dates.

- One attraction for investors is that convertibles often offer a higher running yield than the income return which would be earned from dividends on the ordinary shares of the issuing company.
- In certain market conditions (typically rising markets), the price of a convertible will vary with the price of the ordinary shares into which it can be converted. However, when the market falls below a certain level, the convertible's pricing will reflect its status as a fixed interest security (i.e. it will be valued on the basis of its yield, duration to maturity and credit rating).
- Investors wishing to convert must ensure that they do so before the specified conversion date, since after that date the convertible will lose any conversion 'premium' attached to it and will be valued simply as a fixed interest security.

2.3 'Onshore' vs. 'offshore' vs. 'international'

If you have picked up this text because of its title: *International Funds – Their Establishment and Operation*, it may well be that it is the international element which attracted you. The term 'international' can, however, mean different things to different people:

- In the context of fund offerings from a particular jurisdiction, the term 'international fund' may be used to denote one whose underlying investment portfolio comprises securities issued outside that jurisdiction. So a domestic UK fund, established, operated and regulated in that jurisdiction, but investing in foreign securities might be included in the Investment Management Association's 'international equity funds' peer grouping.
- In the context of this text, however, the term 'international' is intended to denote the scope of distribution of a fund, as opposed to its underlying asset mix; that is, the fact that it is intended to appeal to an international client base, and that it is likely to be established in a jurisdiction other than that of the intended client base. So a fund which is incorporated in (say) the BVI, managed and administered in the Isle of Man and which was to apply for approval to solicit investments in South Africa would meet our criteria for an international fund.

Until relatively recently, the term used would have been 'offshore'. However this term has fallen into disfavour over the past decade, since it is perceived – rightly or wrongly – as carrying connotations of tax evasion (as opposed to legitimate tax planning). In any event, most jurisdictions – even those perceived as having traditional onshore-type tax regimes – are 'offshore' to someone; further, the tax advantages which used to be offered by some 'offshore' jurisdictions have been eroded – both by anti-avoidance provisions enforced by the domestic tax authorities where the investors are resident, and by steps taken by the 'offshore' jurisdictions themselves in the face of pressure from bodies such as the OECD and European Union. To a large degree, then, the change in usage is perhaps no more than a reflection of the increasing internationalization of the financial services industry, and signals the changing rationale for such international structuring.

In this text, where the term 'offshore' is used it will denote those countries which typically have tax-friendly or tax-neutral regimes and flexible regulatory/legal frameworks, with a focus on attracting international business; and the term 'onshore' will be used to indicate those countries which have the more traditional taxation regimes and generally a more rigid regulatory infrastructure.

2.4 'Umbrella fund' structures

'Umbrella funds' are not of themselves a separate legal form: rather, they are a development of the capital structure of open-ended vehicles, which can (in most jurisdictions) be adopted by any of the legal forms which open-ended schemes are allowed to adopt. So, for example, in a number of jurisdictions an umbrella fund may be constituted as a unit trust, an OEIC or a limited partnership. In some others, umbrella structures may be adopted only by OEICs.

One benefit of this structure to the management group is that – in theory at least, the umbrella fund's overheads are lower than would be the case for a set of discrete funds. This is because an umbrella fund only requires one set of accounts and documents for the entire scheme, rather than separate documents for each sub-fund, and there should also be economies of scale in terms of things like audit and legal fees and, in some cases, regulatory fees: there should be some marginal advantage when they are shared across the different sub-classes. These economies can be passed on through the fund's charging structures. Thus, whilst one of the advantages of an umbrella structure to investors is that there may be a wide range of different investment opportunities within one fund, another is that the charging structure is usually set so as to make the cost of switching between sub-funds low. This should further benefit the fund manager, since it should encourage investors to stay within the same management group when changing investment focus, rather than switching to another group.

An umbrella fund is a family of sub-funds established as a single legal entity (Figure 2.1). The fund company or trust is divided into a number of sub-funds, each with:

- its own discrete portfolio of underlying assets;
- its own investment objectives, intended to appeal to differing types of investor;
- a separate class of shares relating to it.

Valuations of each share class are carried out (broadly) as if for a separate fund, and in theory the assets and liabilities of one sub-fund are separate from those of other sub-funds. In practice, however, the law in some jurisdictions is not entirely clear as to whether this separation is sufficient to prevent the insolvency of one sub-fund from having an impact on the assets of other sub-funds, and sponsors are well advised to ensure they have taken appropriate legal advice if this is an issue.

It is quite possible for each of the different sub-funds of one umbrella fund to have a differing regulatory status from the others, so that one sub-fund might be marketable to the retail public in a particular jurisdiction whilst other sub-funds of the same umbrella are not; or for different sub-funds to be targeted at different types of investor, with differing fee structures.

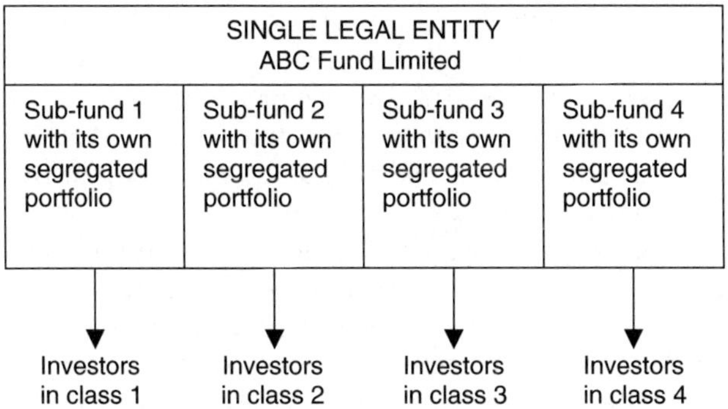

Figure 2.1 A family of sub-funds.

2.5 Protected Cell Companies

Protected Cell Companies (PCCs) can be seen as a further development of the umbrella concept, as it manifests itself through the legal form of a company (Figure 2.2). PCCs are generally established under separate companies legislation, such as the Protected Cell Companies Ordnance 1997 of Guernsey. They are dealt with here, since in most locations they are used as a form of umbrella OEIC; however in some countries, including Guernsey, the legislation has also been extended to closed-ended companies (e.g. investment trusts).

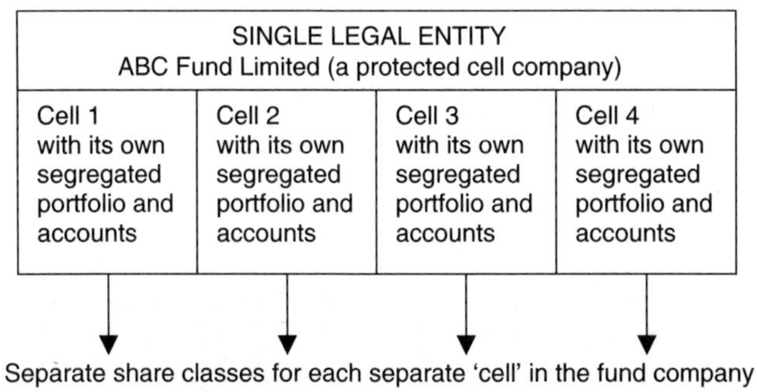

Figure 2.2 Protected Cell Company.

PCCs are an attempt to remove some of the uncertainty as to whether the insolvency of one sub-fund could affect other sub-funds. That is, the provisions for statutory PCCs generally allow assets and liabilities to be attributed to two or more separate 'cells' within the same company, in such a way that should one of those cells become insolvent, the other cells are protected from contagion and are not liable for the debts of the insolvent cell. The cells may be regarded as analogous to the sub-funds of an umbrella fund.

When a PCC issues shares, it can elect whether those shares are attributable to a particular cell; if so, the proceeds of that issue will form part of the cell's assets and if not, they will form a part of the PCC's non-cellular assets. Where a PCC has a liability to some third party who has contracted with a particular cell (e.g. an investor in the sub-fund to which that cell relates, or a service provider to that cell), then that third party will have recourse in the first instance to the assets of that cell, and thereafter only to the PCC's non-cellular assets. The legislation allows that the third party will have no access to the assets in the PCC's other cells.

PCCs are seen – especially in those jurisdictions which have implemented legislation to accommodate them! – as removing much of the uncertainty surrounding the insolvency of a traditional umbrella fund. However sponsors should be aware that there are still varied opinions as to their efficacy in this regard, especially where a claim against a PCC established in one jurisdiction arises in a foreign jurisdiction where assets of the PCC are held, and where the courts may not recognize the concept of segregated cells. Again, specific legal advice should be taken if sponsors are contemplating such structures.

In those jurisdictions which do not accommodate umbrella funds set up as PCC legislation – either because there is no statutory provision for PCCs at all, or because the statutory regime does not at the time of writing extend to the funds industry, PCC funds may still be 'synthesized' by appropriate drafting in the fund company's constitutional documents, and with the use of appropriate disclosures in its offering documents.

2.6 Feeder funds

A feeder fund is a fund of which the only underlying investment is a single other fund (Figure 2.3). Generally, both feeder fund and underlying fund are open-ended, and so the value of the feeder fund will rise and fall almost directly in relation to the rise and fall in value of the underlying vehicle.

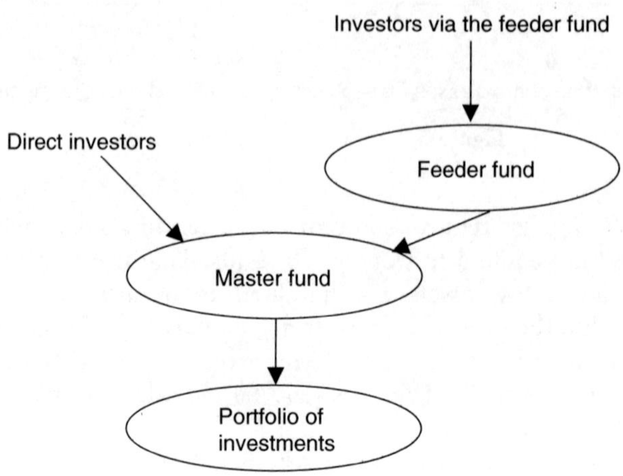

Figure 2.3 Feeder fund.

The rationale for interposing a feeder fund between the underlying fund and the investor may not be immediately apparent – but it becomes so when considering a diverse, international investor base with varying needs:

- A common reason is that the structure of the existing underlying fund suits certain investors, but not others; this might be for legal, regulatory or tax reasons. For example, let us imagine that the ABC Unit Trust is established in the Isle of Man, its target market being investors in the United Kingdom. The managers have considerable success marketing the fund into the United Kingdom, but after a period determine that there is also a viable market for it amongst institutional investors in another country. Their research indicates that there would be good investor appetite for an investment with their fund's investment objectives and policies: and that the fund management group itself has good brand awareness. However, their key institutional investor target base – the providers of domestic pensions products in a highly regulated jurisdiction – is subject to investment restrictions such that it is only permitted to invest in corporate shares, corporate debt and government debt. There is no provision for investing in trust-based vehicles. ABC's managers do not wish to establish a second, stand-alone fund; and it would be impractical to seek agreement from the existing unit-holders to convert the fund from a unit trust to an open-ended investment company. Instead, the managers establish a separate feeder fund, incorporated as an open-ended investment company (Figure 2.4). Thus, the target market's requirements are met: institutional investors invest in shares in the new open-ended investment company, whose NAV per share varies in direct proportion with the unit price of the underlying unit trust. Some small distortions may arise, but these are usually very minimal and are often prescribed by regulations. In such cases, the fund manager may decide not to deduct charges at both underlying and feeder fund level; if the feeder vehicle is established with its own fee structure, fees on either the underlying or the feeder fund may be largely rebated to investors.

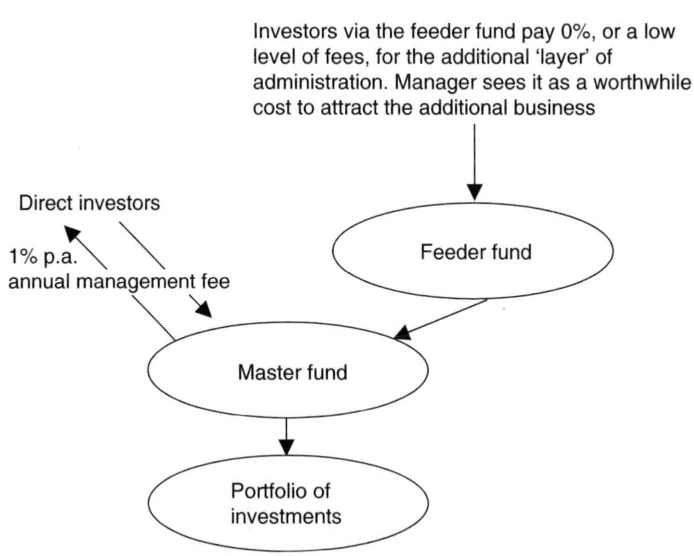

Figure 2.4 Feeder fund, incorporated as an open-ended investment company.

- Feeder-type structures may also be used where managers wish to establish a fund offering which offers access both with and without a currency hedge (Figure 2.5). Investors who so choose may be able to invest directly in the underlying fund without the currency hedge overlay; alternatively investors who want exposure to the underlying assets, but not to the foreign exchange movements inherent in the relevant markets, may invest via a feeder which also superimposes a currency hedge, constructed with the aim of removing much of the currency risk.

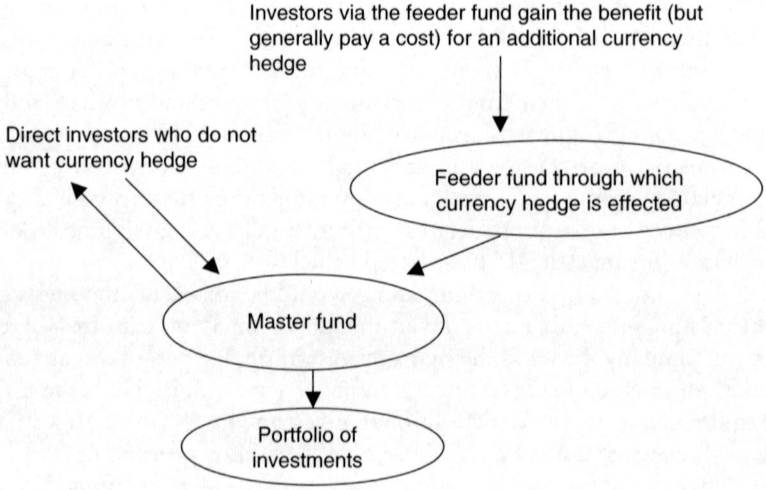

Figure 2.5 Feeder-type structure offering access with and without a currency hedge.

- A third reason for using a feeder fund structure is where the manager wishes to be able to apply differential pricing, depending on the size of the investor (Figure 2.6).

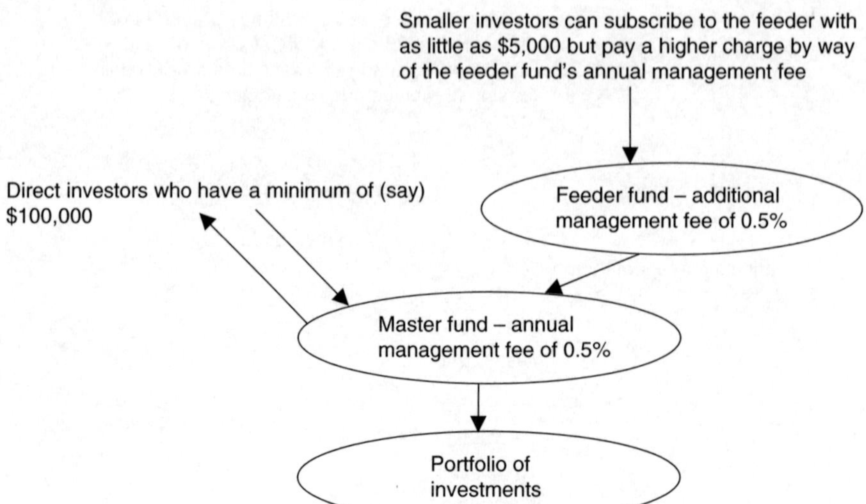

Figure 2.6 Feeder fund structure with differential pricing.

For example, institutional investors placing a minimum of (say) $500 000 may be permitted to invest directly in the underlying fund on which a relatively low level of fees is suffered. Investors placing less than this sum may be required to invest via the feeder, suffering an additional layer of charges.

- Fourthly, a feeder fund may be established where the underlying fund is listed on an exchange which requires a high minimum initial subscription per investor. Larger investors who can meet the requirements of the listing authority may be able to invest directly in the underlying fund, whilst smaller ones may be required to invest via a feeder.

2.7 Funds-of-funds

A fund-of-funds is a fund whose only, or main, underlying investments are other funds (Figure 2.7). It is not a separate capital or legal structure, but is included here because of the frequency with which funds-of-funds are confused with feeder and umbrella funds.

Why invest in a fund which simply invests in other funds – rather than investing in those funds direct? The fund manager's selling proposition is that he is able to add value by choosing the most appropriate mix of underlying markets or asset classes in which to invest, and by identifying the individual fund managers who are best able to deliver value in these markets. He then combines these in what he believes to be the optimum mix to achieve the fund-of-fund's investment objectives.

Example 1 ABC fund managers determine that their real expertise lies in macro-economic analysis: that is, determining the most appropriate mix of geographic markets and asset classes in the light of the current economic environment.

Their skills do not lie in picking individual stocks; they have a view as to how well the Japanese economy will perform, for example, but would not be close enough to the market to select individual companies in which to invest. They do believe, however, that they have the skills to allocate the correct percentage of their clients' assets to the Japanese equity market. Further, they believe they have the ability to select and

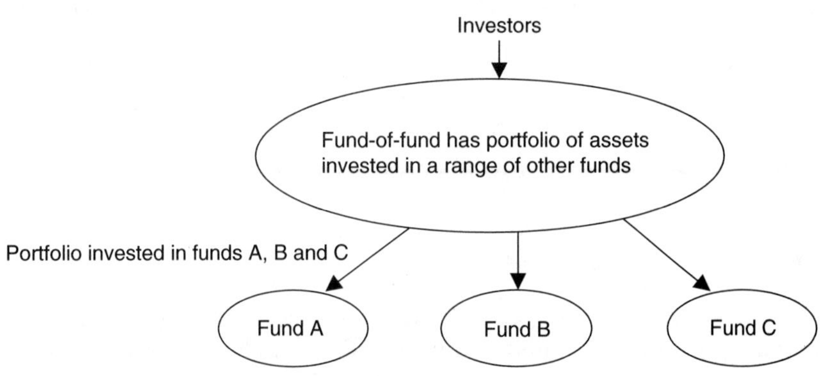

Figure 2.7 Fund-of-fund.

monitor the performance of a good specialist Japanese fund manager from the range available. Similarly, they believe they can do the same in other markets.

In essence, ABC fund managers are providing a highly standardized, 'multi-manager' global equity portfolio management service to their retail clients – who would likely be unable to make these selections unaided.

Example 2 An area of considerable growth in recent years has been the fund-of-hedge-funds. Here the fund manager seeks to combine the various differing strategies of a range of individual, underlying hedge fund managers, in order to achieve an optimal balance of risk vs. potential rewards. This is a strategy commonly employed by fund-of-hedge-fund managers, where they are pursuing 'absolute returns' – a concept we looked at earlier – by combining uncorrelated strategies so as to insulate returns from the direction of the markets.

Example 3 A fund house has a range of in-house, specialist fund offerings. It offers an equity and a bond fund in each of the United Kingdom, United States, Continental European, Asia-Pacific and various other markets – each with a minimum investment level of \$10 000. Its investors have appetite for a more balanced offering than is available through any one of its focused funds; but few have sufficient money to construct a portfolio with more than two or three holdings, at the entry levels described above.

The manager may decide to establish an additional fund – a 'managed fund' providing investors with appropriate objectives and risk profile with exposure to all of the specialist funds, in a mix determined by the fund house from time to time. The entry level to this fund-of-funds may be set at (say) \$10 000 or perhaps even higher: the benefit is that:

- it allows individual investors to gain exposure to the specialist funds without needing to meet the minimum subscription for each;
- it allows the fund manager to increase the volume of money flowing into the specialist funds without their needing to lower their subscription levels (the specialist funds' 'client' or investor is the managed fund-of-funds);
- it allows the fund manager to provide added value through an asset allocation overlay, for which it can charge at the level of the managed fund-of-funds.

As we have noted, in contrast with a feeder fund, a fund-of-funds invests in *more than one* underlying fund; regulated funds-of-funds are usually required to include at least a specified minimum number of underlying funds (typically, this is set at a minimum of five investee funds).

The rationale, from a regulatory perspective is that investors do not invest via a fund-of-funds to obtain some structuring benefit (as they do in the case of a feeder fund). Rather, they do so in order to increase the level of diversification in their portfolios – and therefore to reduce their risk.

2.8 Exchange traded funds

Exchange traded funds (ETFs), are a relative newcomer on the funds landscape. They are structured as open-ended mutual funds, and, like index or tracker funds, track a particular stockmarket index.

ETFs are listed on a stock exchange, and so new buyers can purchase shares from redeeming holders on-exchange. In some cases, they may also be able to buy the ETF through a designated broker-dealer, who will then deal direct with the ETF: in this case the transaction will result in a creation/redemption of shares. This normally happens in predetermined block-sizes known as 'creation units' – standardized block amounts of shares. It is this open-ended nature which ensures that the ETF's share price as quoted on the exchange tracks its 'NAV' per share with relatively little divergence.

In contrast with a traditional mutual fund, which trades only once a day, ETFs trade throughout the day. Whilst investment trusts and other closed-ended vehicles have always offered this advantage, ETFs avoid the distorting effects of the discounts and premiums to NAV which closed-ended funds suffer from (although of course, some investors actively seek such distortions for arbitrage purposes).

Ongoing management fees on ETFs tend (as with any tracker fund) to be noticeably lower than those for actively invested funds. However, this advantage has to be weighed against entry costs. An ETF can cost the investor more to buy than a comparable no-load tracker fund, because of the impact of brokerage. Further, ETFs will (like any listed stock) have a bid–offer spread, which should be regarded as an acquisition cost.

The number of ETFs has grown significantly, in line with increasing investor understanding and enthusiasm: the range available now includes Barclays Global Investors' iShares range, tracking a number of different equity and bond market indices, and numerous industry sub-sectors; 'QUBEs', which track the NASDAQ and are so called because of their trading symbol (QQQ); 'Spiders', the Standard and Poors Depository Receipt trackers (SPDRs); and Vanguard's Vanguard Index Participation Receipts or 'Vipers'.

3 The regulatory environment

3.1 Recap: the regulatory definition of a fund

In Chapter 1 we saw that what is regarded as a 'fund' in common – and indeed industry – parlance may not be treated as one for regulatory purposes. In this chapter, we will consider the implications or regulated status, and exemption from it, and the rationale behind certain regulatory requirements.

We saw in Chapter 1 that in many jurisdictions only open-ended funds are caught within the detailed 'regulatory net'. However, developing this theme:

- Even in those jurisdictions which regulate open-ended funds, some funds may be excluded from the net.
- Where closed-ended fund fall outwith any locally applicable funds regime, they may still need to comply with investment business legislation in terms of the marketing and distribution of their shares, any listing requirements to which they are subject, and, in some countries, with any restrictions imposed by the revenue authorities in order to obtain favourable tax treatment.

In addition to this, we saw that regulators normally take steps to exclude from the regulatory net those arrangements which are essentially private, or which for other reasons should not be supervised.

It is important to remind ourselves of the distinction between an exemption and an exclusion:

- An arrangement which is *excluded* from the regulatory definition of a fund, therefore does not need to comply with the regulations *because it is not a fund*.
- One which is *exempted* does not need to comply with the regulations because of that applicable exemption: it is still, however, a fund – it is just exempt from the need to comply with a certain set of rules. This may have certain ramifications for its tax treatment, or regulatory consequences for its functionaries.

Examples of the kinds of exemptions which have been implemented in various jurisdictions are:

- Those for funds which are not promoted to the public anywhere, and which do not have more than a prescribed number of investors. This is a model in common use in many jurisdictions: for example, the Isle of Man's 'Exempt International Scheme' regime.

- Those for funds which accommodate investments only for groups of investors who are clearly closely linked and may be regarded as a private group: for example, the regime for 'Family Trusts' operated in the British Virgin Islands.

Examples of other arrangements which are typically excluded from the definition of a fund – but there are many others – are:

- Those arrangements which are made between members of the same corporate grouping (e.g. treasury operations).
- Arrangements made for commercial purposes (e.g. franchise arrangements).
- Employee share schemes.

3.2 Regulation of schemes, and applicable exemptions

Once a scheme is deemed to fall within the regulatory net, which for these purposes will usually mean that it is open-ended, it will be subject to regulations. The level and nature of these will depend on the jurisdiction in which it is regulated and the category into which it falls (see below), but they will in any event generally cover its constitution, operation and promotion. It is worth noting that a fund may well be regulated in more than one jurisdiction at once – for example, if it is incorporated in one jurisdiction but operated and administered in another.

Many jurisdictions operate a two-tier regime; that is, a fund is either:

- regulated and has to comply with reasonably comprehensive rules (the nature of which we will discuss below) – but may then be able to be promoted relatively freely to the public in that jurisdiction; or
- unregulated, in which case it does not need to comply with any regulations but is likely to be subject to promotional restrictions.

Many traditional, 'onshore' fund regimes operate in accordance with this model. For example, UK funds are either 'authorized', in which case they must follow the Financial Services Authority's detailed regulations but may be promoted freely to the UK public; or they are unregulated, in which case they are not subject to any regulations themselves, but their distribution may only be carried on in accordance with a separate regime governing the promotion of unregulated schemes. We will look at the UK regime for funds in more detail in a later chapter.

Most offshore jurisdictions, recognizing the international nature of their fund industry, operate multiple fund categorizations so as to accommodate a more diverse investor base. For example, in the Isle of Man a fund may be:

- Highly regulated (an 'Authorized Scheme'), in which case it must comply with a comprehensive set of rules – but may be promoted freely to the public in the Island, and subject to relatively swift recognition processes, direct to the public in the United Kingdom (on whose schemes regime the Island's is modelled), Jersey, Guernsey and Bermuda, all of whom have similar regimes for this category of scheme.

- An intermediate level (an 'International Scheme'), in which case it has to comply with a much more flexible range of regulations and guidelines. There is the proviso that such schemes must also comply with the regulatory regime in any overseas jurisdiction into which they are to be distributed. The 'International Scheme' category is itself subdivided into a number of sub-categories allowing for sponsors to select the vehicle which most nearly meets their target market's requirements in terms of the balance between investor protection, on the one hand, and flexibility, on the other.
- Unregulated (an 'Exempt Scheme'), in which case it need not comply with any regulations. The regime is intended to accommodate private schemes, where there will be no public offering anywhere in the world and where the number of investors will be limited.

We will look at the regulatory regime for funds in the Isle of Man, in more detail in Chapter 11.

Typically, the regulatory regime for the more highly regulated classes of open-ended scheme will cover the following matters:

- provisions as to how such funds may be constituted. For example, it is likely that the scheme will be required to be constituted in the jurisdiction itself; and the provisions will deal with the legal form permitted for a scheme of this category (unit trust, OEIC etc.);
- provisions as to what title to units/shares will involve, and how it may be transferred;
- the powers and duties of the scheme manager, trustee (if a unit trust) or custodian (if an OEIC or partnership) and directors (if it is an OEIC);
- provisions relating to the distribution of income by the fund;
- the content, frequency and timeliness of reports to investors;
- the means by which, and frequency at which, valuations of the fund's property will be carried out;
- the procedures for the creation and cancellation of shares/units;
- the procedures for the sale and repurchase of shares/unit;
- any investment restrictions which must be observed. These will generally be highly specific and will deal not only with investment parameters but also with borrowing powers, and with the types of assets which are acceptable as scheme property;
- provisions in connection with investors' meetings;
- procedures to be observed upon terminating the scheme;
- procedures in connection with the service of notices and documents.

There may also be other more specific rules. For, example, if the jurisdiction provides for umbrella funds to be established as 'retail' (i.e. generally the most highly regulated) category funds, these will be dealt with.

Further, there may be a requirement that any scheme within the highly regulated category falls within a formal system of classification determined by the nature of its underlying assets (e.g. money market fund, securities fund, property fund). The regulator will generally then apply certain specific investment restrictions to each such classification of scheme, and we will look at these (and the rationale behind them) in Section 3.11. The point here is that certain types of fund, because of the nature of the assets in which they are to invest, will be required to observe certain rules so as to ensure they have access to sufficient liquidity: that is, they can always turn a reasonable proportion of their assets into cash quickly enough to meet the liquidity needs of their investors – an essential feature of an open-ended scheme.

So a fund investing 100 per cent in real property would have difficulty in meeting this requirement, since buildings can take a very long time to sell and do not lend themselves to partial disinvestments (e.g. it is not usually commercially viable for a commercial property investor to sell one flat in a block or development, or one or two rooms of a large residential property, in order to raise cash to meet small redemption requests – he must sell the entire property or not at all).

The investment classifications available for the more highly regulated type of scheme usually include the following categories:

- securities schemes (including, for example, funds investing in public securities),
- money market funds,
- umbrella funds,
- funds-of-funds,
- feeder funds.

As you will note, the above list is not exhaustive – it does not cover every possible type of underlying investment (e.g. derivatives, precious metals).

Thus there will be certain kinds of scheme that cannot, by definition, fall into the most highly regulated or 'retail' category:

- because they will invest in things which do not fall within one of these classifications; or
- because their constitution or terms do not meet the detailed requirements of the regime in the relevant jurisdiction.

They will therefore not have the promotional advantages of this category. However, this does not necessarily mean that such funds cannot be operated at all: in some jurisdictions they will simply be seen as unregulated schemes, and must only be promoted in accordance with the relevant rules for such vehicles. In other jurisdictions operating the 'three-tier' approach discussed earlier, they may either be unregulated schemes, or they may fall within some intermediate regime (such as the Isle of Man's 'International Scheme' regime, or Guernsey's Class B regime – which we will look at in more detail in a later chapter).

3.3 Regime for functionaries, and applicable exemptions

Where a scheme itself is to be regulated, the preconditions for authorization will normally include the requirement for both its manager (if it has one) and its trustee/custodian to be licensed. In most jurisdictions, a scheme falling into this category must have a trustee/custodian which is a locally authorized bank.

Thereafter, any proposed change to the scheme must normally be notified to the regulator in writing, and in advance.

3.4 Compensation schemes

Many jurisdictions operate compensation schemes – either in connection with all regulated schemes operated in or from the jurisdiction, or (more commonly) for just the most highly regulated tier. Examples of such compensation schemes are those operated:

- in Member States of the European Union, in connection with Undertakings for Collective Investments in Transferable Securities (UCITS) schemes;
- in many of these member states, in connection with locally recognized but non-UCITS schemes. The United Kingdom itself operates just such a regime; and
- in those jurisdictions which have obtained 'Designated Territory Status'(a form of regulatory recognition accorded by the United Kingdom) and which need to maintain the scheme in order to demonstrate equivalence of investor protection with the United Kingdom to maintain this status.

Compensation schemes are generally intended to ensure a level of compensation for retail investors, in the event that a manager cannot repay them the funds they ought to be due on liquidation of their investment.

Whilst most compensation schemes are operated by the government regulator in the jurisdiction to which they relate, many are not funded by the government. This is especially the case in those smaller jurisdictions, which might struggle to muster the resources to pay compensation in connection with a large fund. Instead, the schemes are usually unfunded, unless and until a compensation claim arises: at that point, the regulator (in its guise as compensation scheme operator) will usually make a levy on those other fund managers in the jurisdiction – typically based on the size of the total claim, and *pro rated* in proportion to the scale of each manager's operations in connection with that class of scheme.

Membership of statutory compensation schemes is generally compulsory for those managers (and often also trustee/custodians) who operate funds in the relevant category. Managers of funds which are not covered by the compensation scheme (e.g. unregulated funds) will not generally be required to contribute.

There is normally a maximum payout from such schemes. This is usually set at a relatively low level, because such schemes are usually intended to provide a safety-net for retail investors and not institutional investors. This aim is also reflected in the requirements for eligibility for compensation: most statutory compensation schemes, in defining which investors may be eligible for compensation and which will not, specifically limit the class to individuals (not companies). Many also specifically exclude payments to 'professional investors', 'experienced investors' or 'business investors' – and the definitions of these terms may or may not be the same as the definitions used in connection with the marketing of funds. (Remember that in some jurisdictions, there are provisions for funds targeted specifically at professional or experienced investors.)

A sponsor considering establishing a scheme in a particular jurisdiction should consider:

- whether the existence or absence of a statutory compensation scheme for funds will be a marketing "plus" in the context of the fund he plans to launch (i.e. is the type of investor he is targeting likely to draw comfort from the presence of such a scheme, or will it be of little or no consequence); and
- whether the existence or absence of such a scheme might have cost implications for him, for example, if another manager fails and the industry is called upon to fund the scheme. Of course, if the prospective sponsor's operation is likely to be relatively small in the context of the relevant industry sector as a whole, then any required contribution is likely to be small – the bigger industry participants bearing the lion's share of the burden.

3.5 Advantages and disadvantages of regulated status

Whilst a highly regulated scheme must operate under some fairly rigorous constraints, as we saw above, there are compensatory advantages (if there were not, no one would opt for this route!):

- Chiefly, these relate to distribution. Generally, a jurisdiction which operates a highly regulated regime (such as the United Kingdom or Isle of Man's Authorized Schemes, or the UCITS schemes of individual EU member states) will permit such schemes to be promoted direct to the public in their home country. This is not normally the case for 'second-tier' or unregulated schemes.
- In addition, the promoters of such schemes will usually find that they have 'fast-track' access to approval or recognition for promotion direct to the public in other jurisdictions, or indeed that there is no approval process required at all.
  - For example, this would be the case in connection with UCITS schemes established in one EU Member State, which may be promoted in another EU Member State subject only to a notification process in that second state.
  - The United Kingdom's 'Designated Territory Regime' allows for overseas schemes operated in a handful of other countries, which are operated in accordance with similar rules to those in the United Kingdom, to be promoted direct to the public in the United Kingdom subject to a relatively simple process of notification under s270 of the Financial Services and Markets Act 2000.
- The advantages of being able to distribute a fund direct to the public may be greater for those promoters with the brand recognition and distribution capability to capitalize on it (i.e. they may be able to offer their fund through established branch networks, advertizing in the national press and on billboards etc.). This may, for some, be a more effective – and cost-effective – route than marketing through intermediaries, who may want commission from the fund company.
- In addition, of course, the fund will have a wider appeal and its promotion need not be restricted to any particular category of investors (e.g. those who are high-net

worth, sophisticated investors or experienced in the particular underlying assets in which the fund is to invest).

- A more minor benefit may be the discipline imposed by a stricter regulatory regime. Some managers have said that operating within a restrictive scheme regime is:
  - Simpler in that it removes the need to make decisions in a number of areas. The contents of many documents are prescribed, as are most of the operational features; and
  - Beneficial from a risk management perspective, since it imposes a number of investor protection and general governance mechanisms which might otherwise be absent. In turn, this can protect the manager from potential claims and losses.

Second-tier schemes (those which are operated from jurisdictions which have an intermediate or 'light touch' regulatory regime) are generally subject to a much more flexible set of rules. For example:

- whereas a highly regulated scheme may be required to observe strict limits on its maximum exposure to the securities of any one issuer (e.g. 10 per cent), second-tier schemes may be subject to much more relaxed limits;
- whereas a highly regulated scheme may not be able to borrow, second-tier schemes may be permitted to borrow to quite a significant extent;
- whereas a highly regulated scheme may not be permitted to use derivatives excepting for 'Efficient Portfolio Management' purposes (see Section 3.12), second-tier schemes may again be able to use them to a significant extent.

The caveat to this increased flexibility is generally as follows:

- the second-tier schemes cannot (as we have already seen) generally be promoted direct to the public in their home jurisdiction – although their distribution may be permitted in accordance with certain rules. These may include provisions such that, for example, the fund may be sold to an investor provided the sale is arranged through an appropriately authorized adviser who takes account of the investor's circumstances;
- they may be promoted direct to the public elsewhere, *provided that in doing so they comply with any applicable requirements in the jurisdiction into which they are being sold;* and
- the lack of product prescription is balanced by an emphasis on disclosure.

A second-tier scheme might therefore be appropriate to a sponsor whose offering is non-retail, and which is intended to invest in a portfolio which could not be accommodated within the first-tier regime. Funds which are subject to this intermediate level of regulation may be able to gain 'recognition' (see Chapter 10) from the regulatory authorities in those markets in which they are to be sold, on the grounds that they are subject to a certain level of supervision in their home country and/or their operators are also supervised. The effect of recognition is to allow a foreign scheme to be promoted direct to the public in a particular country.

So, for example, a fund sponsor who was considering establishing an international scheme for promotion into South Africa might choose to establish it as an Isle of Man

'International Scheme' – the 'second-tier' category in that country. He would then apply for it to be recognized by the South African regulators, so as to allow him to solicit business for it in that country:

- As an International Scheme, the fund would not be required to comply with the detailed investment requirements needed for a scheme targeting the Isle of Man public.
- As a scheme applying for approval to market in South Africa, from the South African Financial Services Board, the fund would need to comply with the requirements laid down under applicable South African legislation.

Second-tier regimes therefore have the key advantage that the sponsor can select the parameters which are appropriate for his target investor market – and need not be constrained by the parameters which would apply if he were marketing the scheme in its 'home' country.

Unregulated schemes may generally invest in whatever they wish; they are not subject to any regulatory constraints at all. The price of this limitless flexibility is the constraint on their distribution.

3.6 Applying for a license, and applicable exemptions

Various functionaries associated with a fund will generally require appropriate licenses. The precise requirements will depend on the regulations in the relevant jurisdiction, and on the regulatory category of the scheme. However, it is likely that the following will require some form of approval:

- *The fund manager.* In certain jurisdictions, a manager need not be licensed if it manages only one, or a very small number, of unregulated funds which are not promoted to the public, since the essentially private nature of its activity means that the same level of investor protection is not necessarily appropriate. In addition, certain jurisdictions will permit the manager of certain 'second-tier' schemes to operate without a license provided the management company is itself managed and administered by a fully licensed third-party fund administrator. For more retail (and therefore more highly regulated) funds, however, a manager will require a license and will therefore need to be able to demonstrate that it meets the 'fit and proper' criteria.
- *The fund administrator.* Where a fund administrator provides services to many funds from different groups (a 'third-party administrator') it is likely to have to meet particularly stringent licensing requirements, since it is responsible for the administration of many funds – and therefore the interests of very many investors.
- *The trustee and/or custodian.* In many jurisdictions, the trustee/custodian of a first-tier scheme is required to be a licensed bank. For second-tier schemes, a licensed investment business may be permitted to act as custodian.
- *The investment manager and/or adviser.* Jurisdictions vary in their approach to investment advice: in some it is a regulated activity and requires a license, whilst in others it is not – or is only licensable where the advice is being provided to funds.

In any event where an adviser is appointed the manager will generally remain liable for investment decisions, and will almost certainly also need to be licensed.

- Where any of the management or administration functions are delegated by the manager to a third party (e.g. a specialist share registrar) there is a possibility that this third-party will be required to be licensed. If there is any uncertainty as to whether a particular activity is licensable, advice should be sought.
- The fund itself may require a specific approval or authorization. Whether or not this is to be the case generally depends on its target audience and the means by which it is intended that it should be distributed.

Before undertaking any form of regulated activity, then, it may well be necessary to make an application for a licence or authorization. This will generally include the completion of a detailed application form, plus additional forms for all key individuals and controllers of the applicant. Individuals will normally be required to provide full curriculum vitae and regulators may seek bank and employer references, and carry out police checks on them as well. In most cases, regulators will also require a business plan for the applicant entity, setting out its intended activities, the target market and its distribution strategy, how its operations will be staffed and managed (including appropriate segregation of duties) and so forth. For an applicant such as a fund manager, the business plan will usually also include projected figures for the first 3–5 years, so that the regulator can assess the likely robustness of its solvency over the period. The application usually needs to be accompanied by drafts of any relevant agreements, and by an application fee to the regulator (which is normally non-refundable).

The licensing process can, from initial discussions with the regulator, take anything from a few weeks to four months, or sometimes more – depending on the jurisdiction, how demanding the regulator's requirements are, whether approvals are governed by a set cycle of meetings and how well prepared the applicant is. Where an applicant and the key individuals associated with it are already known to a regulator, the process may be smoothed because the regulator may already hold sufficient references and other details.

On receipt of an application for a license, the regulator's staff will review the business plan and details of proposed staffing. They may discuss the details with other regulators with whom the key individuals have had dealings and take references where necessary. Where the applicant is a fund, that fund is unlikely to have operating staff: but references will still be taken on its directors in the same was as they would for the staff of a fully staffed entity. The regulator's staff will then generally make a recommendation to their board, chief executive or minister as to whether they feel a licence ought to be granted and what, if any, conditions are felt to be appropriate.

A recommendation is generally no more than this, and the board or other decision-making body within the regulator will discuss the application and the staff's recommendation, together with any separate representations that may have been made by the applicant. It will then generally withdraw to consider its decision, which will be forwarded to the applicant in writing, along with any conditions, 'subject to' requirements, or reasons for refusing a license. 'Subject to' requirements are conditions subject to which a license will be granted, and in the absence of which it will not.

Provided an applicant can satisfy the regulator's staff that it has met the 'subject to' requirements, it will not need to formally reapply.

If an applicant is aggrieved by a decision not to issue it with a license, then in many cases a regulator will offer some form of review or appeal process; increasingly, governments and the international bodies which review national financial services regulators are insisting on their being subject to some form of review and subject to a degree of accountability.

3.7 'Fit and proper' status – sponsors, service providers

When assessing an applicant for a license to carry on funds business, including fund management or advice, a regulator's main concern will be the safety of investors. The financial health and well-being of a fund services provider, and the quality of service it offers to its customer base (whether this is the fund itself, or its investors) will depend upon the integrity and competence of the management and of those to whom management is accountable – that is, the directors, shareholders and anyone else exercising control over the entity. Most regulators' licensing policies are therefore based around what is known as the 'fit and proper' test.

Regulators generally apply the 'fit and proper' test both at the outset, when a business applies for a license – and on a continuing basis, in light of the ongoing conduct of the business and its relationship with its regulator(s). The onus will be on the applicant to satisfy the regulator that it is 'fit and proper', and the provision of false or misleading information when applying for a licence is normally a criminal offence.

Regulators will usually apply the 'fit and proper' test not only to the business entity itself which is applying for a license (e.g. the fund management company, administrator, investment advisor or custodian); they will also usually apply it to the applicant's directors, significant shareholders, management and 'key staff'.

Whilst there is generally no formal definition of the term 'fit and proper', most regulators take it to comprise three main criteria: integrity, solvency and competence.

- *Integrity* is generally taken to mean the track record of a business, its management and its controllers in behaving honourably and honestly towards its customers, its creditors, its counterparties and any regulatory bodies with whom it may have dealings. However, in assessing integrity, a regulator will not limit its view to the applicant's conduct in connection with its business: it may also take account of that applicant's behaviour in relation to the wider community.

  In assessing integrity a regulator may take account of an applicant's past record of behaviour, including running police checks on their background. Misdemeanours which imply that the applicant is dishonest (e.g. theft or misleading investors) will generally be considered more seriously than those which might imply a lack of judgement, but which do not necessarily imply dishonesty (e.g. a conviction for drink driving).

  An applicant might be able to remedy his failure to meet other elements of the 'fit and proper' test – for example, someone who has been insolvent in the past may be restored to solvency; competence can be learned, or – in the case of a corporate applicant, gained by hiring appropriately qualified staff; poor judgement may be improved with age and experience. However, generally speaking regulators appear to take the view that integrity is an inherent characteristic which cannot be learned, and a poor record of integrity is therefore likely to be a significant barrier to licensing.

A key element in assessing integrity will be the applicant's track record of openness and honesty in its dealings with the regulator – for example, whether the applicant has been proactive in drawing the regulator's attention to any matters which it might reasonably be expected to want to know.

- *Solvency*, in the context of the 'fit and proper' test, usually has a rather wider interpretation than its technical definition in, say, insolvency law. So, for example, a regulator's solvency criteria will normally include a 'capital adequacy' test which requires the maintenance of a surplus of net assets, and a 'liquidity test', which requires that the business can show that it has sufficient liquid capital to meet its liabilities as they fall due. The solvency requirements will generally go further than these basic tests, and require that a licensed business maintains a level of capital and liquidity which will enable it to survive tough periods – for example, if markets are depressed for prolonged periods, or if there is a dearth of customers for a while.

  Where a sponsor's plans involve establishing a licensed fund manager or investment manager/adviser, it will need to consider the solvency requirements in its chosen jurisdiction – both at the outset and, based on the projections in its business plan, on an ongoing basis (i.e. taking account of the timings of cash flows, and the impact of potential downturns in the markets or in business).

  Most jurisdictions want to attract funds business and recognize that they are in a competitive environment. Capital requirements therefore tend to be pretty similar from one place to another as each regulator tries to set them at a level which is sufficiently high to protect investors' interests, but not so high that fund sponsors will be deterred. Nonetheless, there are variations, particularly where a jurisdiction's regime provides for the establishment both of highly regulated (retail) schemes and a second-tier, more lightly regulated category.

- *Competence* at applicant level will be assessed by considering the range of individuals employed (in particular the management), taking into account anything that is known of the applicant's track record as a business to date. The regulator will consider what knowledge and experience of the proposed business the new applicant has, how efficient and reliable it has proved to be in the past, and whether its business plan demonstrates appropriate organizational arrangements and controls. It will also look at the applicant's history of compliance with laws and regulations, and in some cases with any voluntary industry codes of practice.

  For key individuals, regulators will have regard to qualifications and experience. In some jurisdictions, there are mandatory 'benchmark' qualifications which an individual should hold before being appointed to a given position, and even where this is not required by law or regulation, it is not unknown for a regulator to require that an individual passes a particular exam before permitting his appointment to a proposed role.

Competence in one area of the industry does not necessarily indicate competence in another: so an applicant which can demonstrate competence as (for example) an investment adviser to a fund might well not have the skills to be competent as a fund administrator.

Not every jurisdiction applies the same rigour to its licensing requirements and 'fit and proper' tests. It is worth a sponsor considering the different regimes when deciding on where to establish the fund and what functionaries to appoint to service it. The existence of a robust licensing regime may well give comfort to the sponsor – and indeed to prospective investors in the fund.

An individual who is a prospective fund sponsor may well find that the 'fit and proper' requirements are applied to him personally, for example, if he is to be appointed to the board of the fund company. Sponsors also frequently establish companies to act as dedicated fund managers or investment advisors, which will provide services to the fund and act as a fee vehicle; again the 'fit and proper' test is likely to be applied to these entities, and to their management, controllers and owners.

3.8 Ongoing supervision

Once a business has gained its license it will generally be subject to ongoing supervision – licensing is not a 'one off' process. This varies from jurisdiction to jurisdiction – some regulators taking a very 'hands on' approach, and carrying out supervisory visits on their licenceholders regularly. Others rely on desk-based supervision (if indeed they do anything at all), for example, by requiring periodic notifications and compliance returns from their licenceholders, coupled with copies of reports from the licenceholder's auditor. A fund manager based in a jurisdiction such as the Isle of Man could expect to find itself subject to the following supervisory techniques on the part of the Island's Financial Supervision Commission:

- Off-site supervision, whereby the Commission will require written information from the business and its auditors. This will include periodic financial returns, compliance returns, statistical information and notifications of certain events.
- Annual review meetings, in which the Commission's staff will look to meet with the business's management to discuss any regulatory issues or concerns and ensure the Commission's understanding of the business plan is still current.
- *Ad hoc* meetings at the request of either the Commission or the business, to discuss any matters that have arisen during the year – for example, proposed restructuring of the fund management group, any particular areas of concern from a compliance perspective, or the development of new areas of activity.
- Periodic on-site visits, where the Commission's staff will spend time in the business' premises reviewing its activity. The frequency of these visits will generally be based on the Commission's 'risk-rating' of the licenceholder – riskier businesses generally receiving more frequent visits. Their point is to enable the regulator to assess whether the licenceholder continues to meet the 'fit and proper' requirements, to assess compliance with the regulations, and to assess whether there are any weaknesses in its internal controls or procedures.

The regulator will normally have a range of statutory powers to assist it in its task of supervising the licenceholder. These vary from country to country but usually include:

- powers to request information from a licenceholder (and, usually, also former licenceholders – so as to facilitate investigations where a business has had its licence revoked);

- powers to enter the licenceholder's premises and to inspect its books and records, including taking copies of these;
- powers to revoke or suspend a license, or to attach conditions. An example which is sometimes used to good effect is the condition that a licenceholder may not accept any further new business until it has taken certain steps. For example, where a fund administrator's systems are somewhat out-of-date or involve much manual intervention, it might be give the condition that it may not take on any further funds unless and until it upgrades them;
- powers to make recommendations and/or to issue directions to licenceholders. The law usually makes it an offence not to comply with a direction;
- in many cases, fining powers, and the power to make public statements ('naming and shaming') when things have gone wrong.

3.9 Investor due diligence requirements

Few in the financial services industry can be unaware of the rapidly increasing requirements in terms of investor due diligence. Prior to 11 September 2001 the focus was principally on verifying to the identity and residential address of customers. The events of that day prompted the world's regulators to increase their emphasis on 'Know your Customer' (KYC) – or as it is increasingly termed, 'Customer Due Diligence' (CDD). This new focus has had ramifications for the financial services industry as a whole, not least the fund management sector. Much of the impetus for this new emphasis is driven by the Financial Action Task Force (FATF).

FATF is an inter-governmental body which aims to develop policies at international level to combat money laundering (you may also see its name written as GAFI – *Groupe d'Action Financiere sur le Blanchiment de Capitaux*). Established in 1989, at the time of writing it had 29 member countries, including the United Kingdom, France, Germany, Italy, Australia, Ireland, Iceland and South Africa. However, many of the financial services regulators in countries which are not FATF members also try to adhere to its recommendations, with the aim of supporting the fight against money laundering (and in many with the additional goal of achieving membership).

These include many of the territories typically used as bases for international funds – for example, the Isle of Man, Jersey and Guernsey. The rationale for doing so is not always entirely altruistic; applying FATF's often demanding standards imposes a high administration and cost burden on the local industry – but FATF recognition of a jurisdiction can mean that its local service providers benefit from improved access to markets, which may be critical for any international offering.

FATF is not a regulator: rather, it is an international body which works on the one hand to establish policies which it believes regulators at national level can use to fight money laundering. On the hand, it works to create the political will needed to bring in legislative and regulatory reforms to combat money laundering. In 1996, it issued the FATF **'40 recommendations'**, which set out principles for the combating of money laundering.

FATF, together with other bodies such as the International Monetary Fund (IMF), monitors member countries' progress in meeting its recommendations. It also reviews the ways in which launderers are developing new techniques, and considers appropriate responses. When FATF was formed in 1989, it was intended that it would continue its work until 2004; and thereafter it would only continue if its members agreed that this was necessary.

The terrorist attacks on the World Trade Centre brought about a rapid consensus that FATF's remit should be widened to include not only pure money laundering activities, but also to the financial issues relating to terrorist financing. In June 2003, FATF issued a revised set of Recommendations, many of which specifically focus on terrorism. The full detail of these changes are too lengthy to deal with in this text: however a number will impact directly on international fund sponsors and managers. They include recommendations that at national level, governments and regulators should:

- *Specify a list of crimes ('predicate offences')*, the proceeds of which may be deemed to be the proceeds of crime for money laundering purposes. This is important because in certain countries, crimes such as tax evasion are not predicate offences and so need not be reported by financial services institutions to the local law enforcement authorities. There is considerable pressure for governments to align their schedules or definitions of the predicate offences, in part because where there is tax evasion there is often also some other, more serious but undetected crime. In part, too, this is because initiatives against money laundering lend themselves to furthering other agendas, such as the OECD and EU 'Harmful Tax Competition' initiatives: making tax evasion a reportable crime may potentially increase the flow of useful information to tax authorities in the evader's home country.
- The expansion of the customer due diligence process for financial institutions, including fund managers and administrators. This includes increasing obligations on managers to monitor their investors' account activity on an ongoing basis, in order to prevent money which may have appeared 'clean' when it was initially invested from being used to finance terrorist activities. This added dimension requires a different set of skills and systems from those which were needed for simple investor identification, and may prove to be one of the more costly developments in the industry.
- *Enhanced measures for higher risk customers and transactions*, including correspondent banking and politically exposed persons (PEPS). Where a fund sponsor is considering establishing a fund specifically targeting such people (e.g. a fund intended to act as an investment vehicle for a prominent family) it should ensure that this is fully discussed with the fund's proposed functionaries and service providers to ascertain their approach.

  Many service providers approach the issue of politically exposed persons pragmatically, accepting that these people may in some cases be more vulnerable to (or have more opportunity for) corruption than others, and simply adapt their CDD procedures accordingly. This may mean asking more searching questions than would be the case for 'lower risk' investors, and seeking documentary evidence of the source of the invested fund/investor's wealth. One or two service providers, however, have chosen to go far beyond the regulatory requirements and guidance (and arguably beyond the intention of the FATF), by simply refusing to accept investments from PEPs altogether, or by placing such onerous CDD requirements on them that investors opt for alternative investments.
- *The extension of anti-money laundering procedures to various non-financial businesses and professions* (e.g. real-estate agents, dealers in precious stones and metals,

accountants, notaries and legal advisers). This may have implications for the fund itself, for example, where it is looking to invest in precious metals or real estate. For a regulated fund, evidence of its (or its functionaries') regulated status and the fact that it is operated from a FATF-member country may well be sufficient for the broker placing the fund's money.

Where the fund and its functionaries are not regulated, or are not based in FATF-member countries, brokers (including property and commodities dealers) have been known to request information on the fund's underlying investors – despite the fact that their client is, technically, generally the fund itself. There have been instances of such dealers declining the business if this information is not forthcoming. This can prove difficult if there are not good statutory grounds enabling the fund operator to make such disclosures: especially where the investor's consent to such disclosures is unlikely to be forthcoming. Again, sponsors may need to bear this in mind when considering what jurisdiction their fund should be located in, what regulatory status it should apply for and who its counterparties will be for the purposes of underlying investment activity.

- *Greater transparency on the owners, beneficiaries or controllers of companies and trusts*. Again this can prove tricky where investors hold their units or shares through companies or trusts and in some cases third-party administrators (TPAs) have been known to insist on a greater degree of disclosure than is strictly necessary under applicable legislation. This can be particularly the case where the TPA is a member of a multinational organization which has chosen to apply common standards across all the jurisdictions in which it operates, and there have been cases where a TPA has issued forced redemption notices to investors in client funds who have been unwilling to make the requested disclosures. Again, sponsors need to consider carefully their choice of jurisdiction and TPA, and to ensure that their investors understand and are happy to accommodate the degree of disclosure which will be required.
- *The extension of the requirements to cover terrorist financing*: a trend which is placing increasing duties on fund managers and administrators to monitor the patterns of their investors' disinvestments and the recipients of their proceeds, and to identify and report any suspicious patterns.

FATF member countries are currently implementing most of the updated recommendations, as are a number of other countries. Most regulators are handling the process first by a detailed study of the recommendations coupled with industry consultation on the likely impact of any new measures needed.

In the long-term, these changes may prove to be critical in terms of the costs of taking on new investors to a fund, renewing CDD on them periodically and monitoring their patterns of investment and disinvestment activity. Indeed, in a number of cases it has resulted in the closure of funds altogether, as investors or fund sponsors have declined to acquiesce to a particular TPA's requirements.

In some cases, there can also be cross-border complications, as where the ultimate beneficiary of an investment held through a trust or other arrangement is not disclosable under applicable confidentiality laws (Switzerland, Luxembourg) without the beneficiary's consent: this consent may be difficult or impossible to obtain, especially if the beneficiary is (and is intended to remain) unaware of his/her status.

Other complicating factors can arise in connection with pension funds, where death benefits are to be paid to a spouse or other nominee – a factor which may be an issue where a fund has been established specifically as the underlying investment option for a money purchase scheme. In other cases, regulators may require evidence of CDD which the beneficial owner or other parties simply do not possess; for example, consider those older investors who have never held a passport and do not have a driving license, or those for whom all utility bills are in their spouse's name, who live where the local post is so poor that post-office boxes are always used, or who are resident in a care-home.

Some regulators who had, prompted by the FATF and IMF initiatives, brought in increasingly demanding CDD regimes are now recognizing the difficulties in implementing them at industry level, and are adapting them by introducing guidelines tailored to the needs of the funds industry. Others have to date declined to tailor guidelines reflecting the differing sectors of the financial services industry, on the grounds that to do so would be unnecessary, would be administratively burdensome, and might create an un-level playing field.

From this it should be clear that sponsors should, in assessing their potential fund structuring options, consider:

- the applicable AML requirements in the jurisdiction or jurisdictions in which the fund is to be operated;
- their own group policy in connection with CDD. This will depend in part on the business' appetite for risk, and may vary from doing the 'bare minimum' required to remain compliant, to a much more stringent regime;
- the internal group policies of the TPAs and/or managers they are considering using, and how compatible these are with the sponsor's own approach;
- the additional requirements which any funds trustee/custodian may impose on top of the above; and
- any difficulties which may arise in satisfying these, where investors are likely to invest via non-transparent structures, or to be located in countries with rigid confidentiality legislation.

Certain jurisdictions allow for investor introductions through appropriately regulated and supervised intermediaries to be subject to less stringent requirements. Usually, this means that the fund manager/administrator will still require the name and residential address of the beneficial owner of an investment in a client fund, but that verification of this need not be sought except in cases of suspicion.

Such intermediaries are known by differing names in each jurisdiction; for example, 'Eligible Introducers' 'Reliable Introducers', 'Qualified Intermediaries', but the principles are usually the same. The fund manager/administrator will be permitted to rely on the introducer's verification of identity and address provided:

- the intermediary is regulated and supervised by a statutory authority; this has presented problems for some Swiss intermediaries, since many are members of non-statutory associations;
- the intermediary itself should be subject to FATF-consistent CDD requirements;

- the intermediary must generally disclose the name and residential address of the 'ultimate beneficial owner' (a term itself subject to many interpretations);
- the intermediary must undertake that it holds the requisite verification documentation, that it will hold it for a prescribed period and that it will pass it to the fund manager/TPA upon request.

Thus, eligible introductions do not really reduce the CDD obligation: they do, however, reduce the paper trail in terms of certified verification documentation. As noted earlier, some TPAs will not apply investors' funds until their AML requirements have been satisfied, and if a sponsor or its sales intermediaries are not properly prepared this can cause anger and confusion. Others will apply funds, but should their requirements not be satisfied within 30 or 60 days will forcibly redeem the investments. Still others are looking into introducing additional charges for the time and effort spent on chasing down CDD documentation. From this it is clearly essential that all parties understand what is expected of them at the outset, and where the responsibility and expense of meeting these growing requirements will lie!

3.10 Recognition regimes for foreign schemes

Regulators do not only have an interest in approving and supervising the schemes operated in or from their own jurisdiction: they will also wish to oversee foreign schemes distributed in that jurisdiction, and how this is done. The process is usually referred to as 'recognition' (though other terms are also used).

In determining whether an overseas fund should be recognized, the regulator will assess it against the benchmark of its own regime for approving or authorizing local schemes. For example, it may assess foreign schemes against the criteria set out in Section 3.2, with some flexibility allowed in recognition of the differing overseas laws and terminology.

Where a regulator has agreed common standards with its counterpart in another jurisdiction, there is often some 'fast track' process. Provided the foreign scheme manager can demonstrate to the local regulator that the scheme falls within a particular regulatory category in his home jurisdiction, and is therefore required to comply with equivalent provisions and is supervised on an ongoing basis, the local regulator will generally not subject that scheme to the detailed scrutiny which it would otherwise apply.

An overseas fund which is not recognized in a given jurisdiction may not generally be promoted direct to the public in that jurisdiction. Local distribution – if it is permitted at all – will normally have to be carried out in accordance with the regime for unregulated schemes. This may mean that it can only be promoted:

- to existing participants in the scheme or (in some cases) to investors who can be shown to be participating in schemes with similar investment objectives and risk profile, or who have done so in the recent past;
- to other licensed or authorized investment businesses. Depending on the licensing regime in that jurisdiction, this may mean that the scheme can be promoted to

(for example), intermediaries such as financial advisers, discretionary portfolio managers and stockbrokers;
- to high-net worth or sophisticated investors.

In other jurisdictions, the promotion of unrecognized schemes may be entirely prohibited. The jurisdictions in which foreign schemes can be promoted without any regulatory requirements at all are few and far between.

It is therefore extremely important that a prospective sponsor thinks hard about the jurisdictions into which he hopes to promote his fund, and researches the local recognition regime so as to ensure that the way in which the fund is set up, its investment parameters and so forth will not prevent its achieving the required recognition.

3.11 The rationale for investment restrictions

The manner in which a fund's assets may be invested will be governed by regulatory constraints, the conditions laid down in its constitutional documents and any further restrictions imposed by regulations (which will depend, of course, on the fund's regulatory status). In this section, we will examine the general investment restrictions which a sponsor can expect to find, and the rationale behind them.

In most cases, the regulatory position will be that:

- The investments which any fund may hold *must* be consistent with the category of fund to which the scheme belongs. For example, a 'money market fund' should invest predominantly in deposits and other money market instruments, but not into equities, derivatives and so on.
- Any relevant upper limits which applicable regulations impose, in connection with single investments, issuers or classes of investment must be observed. For example, in many jurisdictions (including the United Kingdom, Isle of Man, Jersey, Guernsey, Bermuda and much of Europe), securities funds may invest a maximum of 10 per cent of their NAV in transferable securities which are not 'approved securities'. (We shall look later at the concept and definition of an 'approved security'.)
- Any additional restrictions included in the trust deed or scheme particulars are regarded as having *the same power as if they were included in the regulations.* Thus, a breach of the restrictions laid down in the scheme particulars will usually be regarded as being as serious as a breach of the regulatory restrictions – and similar liabilities, and regulatory sanctions, may arise.
- Regulated, open-ended schemes (such as retail or 'authorized' unit trusts, OEICs and the European 'Undertakings for Collective Investments in Transferable Securities') have very limited *borrowing* powers.

The categories into which open-ended funds are grouped for the purposes of investment restrictions are broadly based on the nature of instruments in which they invest. They include:

- Securities funds
- Money market funds

- Feeder funds
- Funds-of-funds
- Property funds
- Futures and options funds and geared futures and options funds
- Money market funds.

Before looking at the restrictions on the various different categories of regulated open-ended scheme, it is worth mentioning that in general, such schemes cannot borrow – excepting in very limited circumstances, and generally only for purposes of funding redemptions. They cannot generally 'gear' – that is, borrow against their portfolio so as to invest further in the markets. The rationale is one of investor protection, in that gearing amplifies both good and bad investment decisions; so whilst it may enable a vehicle to capitalize on rising markets, it can greatly increase the risk in a portfolio in falling markets or where poor investment decisions have been made.

Probably the most rigorous set of constraints is applied to 'securities funds'.

3.12 Typical restrictions on securities funds

Limitation to transferable securities

This category of funds includes equity schemes (typically growth funds, equity funds or smaller companies funds), but also funds investing into certain types of fixed interest securities. All such funds are limited to investing in transferable securities, within specific limits which we will look at shortly. *Transferable securities* are, in simple terms, those securities whose title can be transferred from one holder to another; thus they can be given away, or more importantly bought and sold, rather than the holder having to retain them until maturity or redemption by the issuer. An example of a transferable security would be the ordinary shares of a public limited company; but most private company shares are also transferable (albeit sometimes on restricted terms). However, some private company shares are not freely transferable to new holders, and certain local government/authority bonds issued in a number of countries are non-transferrable; the holder must hold them until their redemption date. Further, more and more funds invest in synthesized securities – for example, over-the-counter derivatives for which there is no ready market.

The reason regulators require that a regulated open-ended fund invests only in transferable securities is clear when you consider the actions that the investment manager will have to take if he has substantial net redemptions (we will look at the redemption process in more detail in a later chapter; for now we can summarize it as follows).

Investors exiting a *closed-ended fund* can generally sell their fund holdings to other investors willing to buy at a mutually agreed price. The shares, and the consideration for them, changes hands between the old and new investors, usually via a broker or other counterparty. There is no cash impact on the fund itself, and so the investment manager does not need to raise cash to repay the exiting investors, nor to receive the consideration from the new investors and apply it to the fund's investment portfolio.

In contrast, where an investor exits an *open-ended fund*, he generally sells his holding directly back to the fund or its manager; his shares or units are liquidated and the proceeds are paid to him out of the fund's assets. Where there are net redemptions (i.e. more sellers than buyers by volume), the fund manager will therefore need to liquidate sufficient underlying investments to repay the redemption proceeds to those exiting investors; it is consequently critical that the fund is invested in assets which can themselves be turned into cash – and this within a timeframe which is appropriate bearing in mind the frequency at which the fund itself deals. For this to be the case, it must be possible for the assets to be sold by the fund at any point before their maturity date (if they have one). This would rule out, for example, substantial investments in the types of local government bond or illiquid security we have looked at above.

Most regulators will therefore require that all, or all but a very small percentage, of a securities fund's assets are invested in transferable securities. The rationale is to ensure that the fund manager can meet its commitments to investors, in terms of redemptions; the regime therefore aids investor protection by helping ensure adequate levels of liquidity.

'Approved securities' and 'eligible markets' regimes

For the purposes of this text, we shall use the terminology used in the United Kingdom – but bear in mind that similar concepts and restrictions apply in other jurisdictions, albeit often using slightly different terminology.

An *approved security* is a transferable security which is officially listed on a stockmarket either within the EC, or on another *eligible market*, as agreed by the manager and trustee; however in many places the definition is also taken to apply to those securities which have been recently issued, and for which an application for listing will be made.

An eligible market is one which has either been prescribed as such by the regulator, or which is agreed by the fund's manager and trustee/custodian to meet the relevant criteria. These will include the market's regulated status, its open-ness to various types of investor, its integrity and robustness in terms of processing and settlement, and standards of liquidity and transparency in connection with securities listed on it.

Most regulators will require that a securities fund is either wholly or largely invested in approved securities: thus not only will its assets be transferable, but, being listed, there will be a ready market for them. Typically, a regulator will require that a securities fund may not hold more than 10 per cent of its NAV in unapproved securities. Again, this enables a fund manager to meet its liquidity commitments to its investors, and – equally importantly – ensures that there is a reasonably effective means of establishing a fair market value of the underlying investments, for valuation purposes. Once more, then, there are clear investor protection benefits to the regime in terms of liquidity and transparency.

Fund holdings

Where a fund is designated as a securities fund, a regulator will normally preclude it from investing in other funds to any great degree (a fund manager who wishes to do so may opt to establish a fund-of-funds instead). The maximum percentage of a fund's NAV which may be invested in other funds is typically set at 5 per cent, or thereabouts.

Diversification requirements

Most regulatory regimes will require that soon after a securities fund is launched, its manager and trustee must ensure that (as far as possible) the money taken into it is invested in a manner which will spread its investment risk. This is obviously difficult when a fund is still small and does not have the critical mass to diversify effectively, and so the rule is not generally applied from inception. However, after a given period (say 6 months) from authorization, or when the value of the fund exceeds a specified amount (e.g. £1 million), whichever is the sooner, the fund's managers must be observing specific limits relating to the spread of investments.

The point of the diversification rules is to protect investors from a fall in value of any one underlying asset; but they generally also reflect the fact that an event which affects (say) the shares in a given company may well also affect the price of other securities issued by that company. So, for example, serious concerns about the financial soundness of company ABC plc may result not only in a sharp fall or the suspension of its share price, but also in a downgrading of the credit rating, or even the default, of its bonds. Regulators therefore generally specify the diversification limits in terms of exposure to *issuers* of securities, rather than the individual lines of securities themselves.

The requirements are generally that:

- No more than 5 per cent of the NAV of the fund may be invested in securities issued by any one issuer; *except that*
- in respect of up to (and no more than) 40 per cent of the fund, that concentration may be increased to 10 per cent of the NAV of the fund.

Put another way, this means that up to 40 per cent of the fund may consist of securities issued by just four issuers, as long as each one is issued by a different issuer and accounts for no more than 10 per cent of the total NAV of the fund. Meanwhile, the remaining 60 per cent must be made up of holdings in securities issued by different issuers, none of which may account for more than 5 per cent of the NAV of the fund (Figure 3.1).

Again, the restrictions are prompted by investor protection considerations – in this case, ensuring that fund managers carry out what many see as one of the *raisons d'être* of collective investment, by securing a degree of diversification and risk spreading that would otherwise be unobtainable to many investors.

These restrictions have caused difficulties for managers of tracker funds, where one or more issuers are very dominant in the particular index which the fund is intended to track. It has happened, for example, that a particular issuer has accounted for more than 10 per cent of the UK FTSE100 Index by value, which has mean that those fund aiming to track the FTSE100 and whose tracking technique is largely based on replication of the index, have been unable to do so without breaching the diversification limits.

Regulators have generally shown themselves unwilling to be flexible in amending the diversification requirements to accommodate managers in these circumstances. A variety of alternative solutions have therefore been found, including:

- The establishment of 'capped indices' which measure the performance of a given index whilst adjusting out the 'excess' weight of any stock accounting for more than a stated percentage of the relevant market. Managers may therefore establish

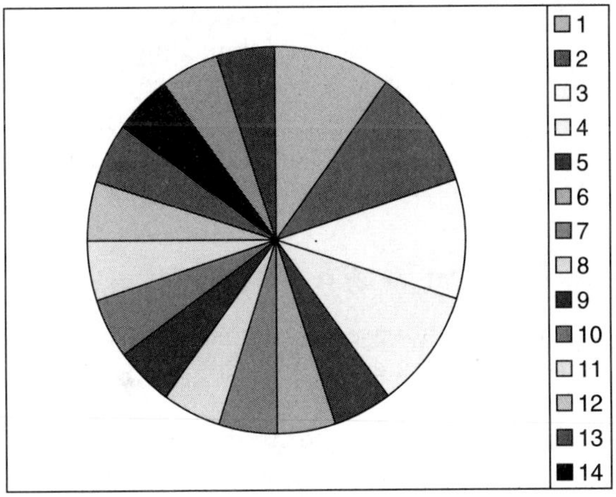

Figure 3.1 Illustrating the maximum concentrations of the assets of Fund ABC to any one securities issuer. Segments 1–4 show that the fund may have a *maximum* exposure of 10 per cent of its NAV in the securities of any one issuer: but it may only do this for four tranches of its assets. The rest of the portfolio (segments 6–16) must be spread in such a way that there is no exposure in excess of 5 per cent to the securities of any one issuer. From this it can also be seen that a fund subject to these requirements should not have exposure to fewer than 16 different securities issuers.

funds which have as their objective the tracking of these capped indices, instead of the standard index.

- Alternative methods of replicating the relevant performance, perhaps by buying substitute stocks which have been shown to be historically good performance proxies for the 'overweight' stock.
- Acceptance and disclosure of a degree of potential tracking error.

Concentration and management influence – 'influential holdings'

Many regulators restrict the concentration of a regulated fund's holding in certain types of investment, by reference this time not to the NAV of the fund itself, but rather to the total amount of that security in issue; typically this will relate to the maximum holding permitted in the shares of any one company.

Thus, a securities fund may not be permitted to hold more than (say) 10 per cent of:

- the issued voting shares of a company;
- the issued non-voting shares of a company;
- the convertible or non-convertible shares of a company; or
- the units of another unit trust or other collective investment scheme.

The rationale here may appear to be more for the protection of investee companies than it is for the benefit of investors (e.g. by preventing fund managers from exercising too great a share of voting rights). However, this is not the main or only reason for the regime; again the principle is mainly the preservation of sufficient liquidity to meet investors' needs. It can be difficult to sell a holding which accounts for a sizeable proportion of that issue, since there may be a limited number of buyers for the stock in the market and any major selling activity could at best seriously depress the price. This can be particularly tricky for index-tracking or quasi-tracker funds, which can, if they end up holding substantial proportions of a given company, get caught in a vicious cycle of falling prices and consequent forced selling activity.

Efficient Portfolio Management (EPM) techniques

Generally speaking, securities funds are unable to make use of derivatives to any great degree. However regulators are increasingly amending their regulations to allow managers to employ "EPM" techniques.

In general, EPM techniques can be used by most retail types of fund (but not by feeder funds). They enable the fund manager to use a range of strategies and techniques that otherwise they would not be able to – but only in certain circumstances. The kind of techniques we are talking about include such things as:

- the use of derivatives, including writing covered options;
- short-selling; and
- borrowing.

Where EPM regulations apply, they allow the above strategies to be used provided the transactions are:

- economically appropriate;
- fully covered (i.e. by way of cash or any other asset which is sufficient to meet any obligation to pay or deliver, that could arise under the transaction); and
- entered into for one of three specific aims. The aims are:
  - the reduction of risk;
  - the reduction of cost; and
  - the generation of additional capital or income for the scheme with no, or an acceptably low level of, risk.

3.13 Typical restrictions on money market funds

These are funds investing in cash and near-cash instruments. Generally, this is taken to include such assets as certificates of deposit (CDs), Treasury notes and bills, commercial paper (CP), and sometimes also bills of exchange and debentures.

Generally, the regulations are such that any CDs, CP, bills of exchange, debentures and so forth must be repayable within 12 months. Similarly, they generally require that any term deposits held are fixed for no more than within 6 months; however, the definitions do vary from jurisdiction to jurisdiction so sponsors should check these with care.

3.14 Restrictions on feeder funds

A feeder fund, as we saw in Section 2.6 of Chapter 2, is essentially a single fund which invests in one other fund. It might be established so as to accommodate (say) a pension scheme which was to invest in a specified underlying collective investment scheme or investment trust.

In most countries, feeder funds are not permitted to invest into geared futures and options funds, property funds, warrant funds, other feeder funds or funds-of-funds.

3.15 Restrictions on funds-of-funds

A fund-of-funds is a collective investment scheme established with the aim of investing solely or predominantly in other funds. So as to prevent investors from paying double layers of charges for an extra layer of administration which in fact provides little in the way of additional diversification, regulators normally require that a regulated fund-of-funds must invest in at least five other funds.

The permitted categories of fund in which a fund-of-funds may invest are generally:

- Securities funds
- Money market funds
- Futures and options funds
- Geared futures and options funds
- Property funds
- Warrant funds.

Additionally, a fund-of-funds may generally invest to a limited degree (which will vary from jurisdiction to jurisdiction) in:

- Transferable securities
- Forward transactions in money or gold
- Cash or near cash
- Gold.

Generally speaking, a fund-of-funds may not invest in:

- A feeder fund
- Another fund-of-funds
- Any part of an umbrella fund which invests in either of the above.

In addition, where investment in another fund-of-funds *is* permitted, regulators normally apply specific rules to avoid the possibility of any 'circular' self-investment. An extreme example of what is meant by this is set out in Figure 3.2.

3.16 Restrictions on futures and options funds (FOFs)

Regulated FOFs are generally permitted to invest in futures and options provided they are also simultaneously invested in other investments which ensure that the risk of loss cannot rise above a certain level (i.e. they are 'covered'). For example, if the manager of an FOF wanted it to be the writer of call options on a particular share, it

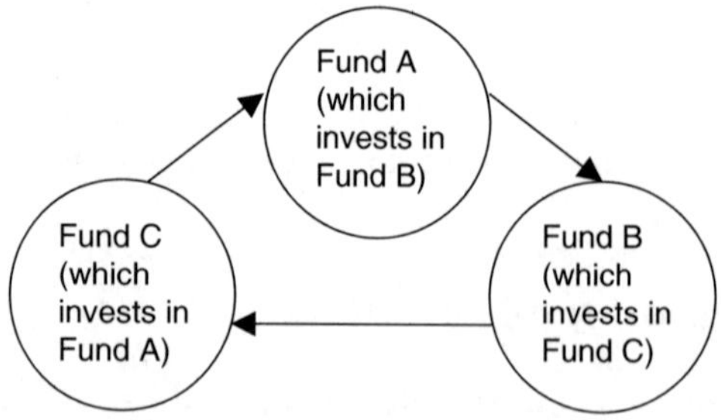

Figure 3.2 Circular investment.

would already have to have a holding of that share – in order to limit the potential loss if the share price were to rise. (If it did not hold that share then its potential losses would be – in theory at least – unlimited.) The 'cover' must be in holdings which are of the right kind and sufficient value to match the exposure relating to the derivative.

To a limited extent, and under some regulatory regimes, a FOF may *hold* options where the potential maximum loss only extends as far as the premium paid. This means that an FOF could hold call or put options in which it had no exposure to the physical stock, but could not write uncovered calls or puts.

3.17 Restrictions on geared futures and options funds (GFOFs)

Regulated GFOFs operate under broadly similar investment restrictions to those applicable to FOFs, excepting that up to 20 per cent of their NAV may generally be used as the initial outlay for uncovered trading in derivatives.

This means that there is greater exposure to the risk of loss, but also that the opportunity for profit is greater. Thus, a GFOF is generally regarded as a higher risk investment than an FOF, especially when markets are volatile.

The manager will generally be required to exercise 'reasonable prudence' in terms of achieving an appropriate measure of diversification, but regulators rarely specify precisely how a regulated FOF or GFOF portfolio should be constructed. This is partly because certain derivatives incorporate a good inherent spread of risk; for example, it is possible to buy instruments which give upside or downside exposure to the performance of an entire index, and more specialized and focused instruments are being developed all the time.

The rationale, is as ever, to protect investors – in this instance from being exposed to a level of risk which is inappropriate for a regulated (i.e. retail) fund.

3.18 Restrictions on property funds

Most regulators provide for the existence of true property funds (i.e. funds which invest in bricks and mortar, as opposed to funds which invest in the shares of property companies). However, property has some inherent liquidity limitations in the context of open-ended schemes. For example:

- property can take a great deal of time to sell, particularly in time of depressed market conditions;
- property is generally not divisible (or it is not usually commercially viable to do so). So, for example, the manager of a residential property fund could not generally sell part of a house in order to raise the cash to meet a small redemption.

For this reason, the regulatory focus is on maintaining liquidity. Generally, retail open-ended property funds will only be permitted to invest between 20 and 80 per cent of their NAV in property. The remaining 80–20 per cent of their NAV will be invested in other property-related assets (e.g. shares in property companies, or shares/units in other property-related collective investment schemes). This ensures that a proportion of the fund's value is invested in assets which are at least reasonably liquid, and which can be sold to fund redemption payments when required.

3.19 Umbrella funds

An umbrella fund is, as we saw in Chapter 2, a single legal entity comprising any number of separate sub-funds (or classes). It is generally established so as to be easy and cheap for the investor to switch between sub-funds, and economies of scale mean that it is usually also cheaper for the manager to administer than a similar number of separate funds.

The rules and specific limits applied to separate parts of an umbrella fund are the same as those applied to corresponding single schemes.

3.20 Investment trusts

The investment restrictions imposed on closed-ended investment funds (which we will refer to by their UK terminology, 'investment trusts'), are far less restrictive than for unit trusts or OEICs. Remember, investment trusts are *closed-ended* vehicles. This means that shares in them change hands on the secondary market: investor sales or purchases do not create any excess of, or need for, liquidity in the underlying investment portfolio. Investors buy and sell to and from each other (usually through a broker) and it is the fact that the fund is listed which provides liquidity in its shares. The only effect of net buyers is to push up the market value of shares, and vice versa. Because of this, the regulatory regime in terms of how and in what investment trusts can invest is quite different from that for open-ended regulated schemes.

In some countries, there are no investment restrictions at all: in others there are certain restrictions, but as investment trusts are not themselves 'authorized' by the financial services regulator in the same way that open-ended funds are, they are often enforced by the tax authorities – the enforcement tools being the removal of certain tax concessions if the fund manager fails to observe the relevant restrictions. For example, in the United Kingdom and under the provisions of the Income and

Corporation Taxes Act 1988, an investment trust must keep to the limits prescribed below in order to be eligible for exemption from tax on the capital gains it makes on its investments:

- A maximum of 15 per cent of its assets (calculated by reference to its NAV) in any one company. This is the equivalent of the 'diversification' provisions for open-ended schemes, and you can see that it is considerably less stringent.
- A maximum of 20 per cent (calculated by reference to the investee company's share capital) taken up of the capital of any one company. This is the equivalent of the 'influential holdings' constraint discussed for regulated open-ended securities funds above, and again is generally considerably less stringent.
- A maximum of 25 per cent of its assets in unquoted shares, property and commodities. Again this is more relaxed than the equivalent 'approved securities' regime for open-ended vehicles.

Another distinction is that investment trusts can generally *borrow* to a much greater extent than open-ended schemes. Any restrictions on their power to borrow for investment purposes is generally controlled by the company's constitutional and offering documents – there are rarely any regulatory limitations. This means that they have the ability to 'gear' portfolios.

This ability to gear means that investment trusts have both the potential for greater profits than their open-ended peers – and the potential for greater losses. For this reason, investment trusts with borrowing powers should be seen as potentially higher risk than unit trusts and OEICs.

The following examples should illustrate this: consider two investment trusts, one (Fund A) with the ability to gear and one (Fund B) without (Table 6).

In certain countries, specific regimes have been developed for specialist kinds of investment trust; in some cases this is so as to facilitate funds aimed at specific types of investors (those who are highly sophisticated, very wealthy or interested in a particular industry). In others, it is motivated by the government's economic objectives: it may, for example, encourage people to invest in particular areas by giving tax breaks to the fund vehicles aimed at them.

Examples would be the UK 'venture capital trust' (VCT). This type of investment trust provides investors with 20 per cent income tax relief on their investments, and the possibility of capital gains tax (CGT) deferral. To qualify, the VCT itself must be listed; but the underlying investments must be largely in unlisted investments. The vehicle acts as a means of encouraging capital into the type of venture which might otherwise struggle to raise capital. In this capacity, we can see that VCTs are performing exactly the function we described in Section 1.8 of Chapter 1 – that is, acting as a node between the investing public, and those segments of the market which are hungry for its investable capital.

At the same time, the VCT is supporting the government's economic aim of encouraging support in certain areas: but in order to ensure that this aim is achieved, it imposes certain conditions on the VCT which must be satisfied if it is to qualify for the 20 per cent income tax relief described above. For example:

- at least 70 per cent by value of the investments must be in qualifying unlisted trading companies, including companies listed on the 'junior' market (the Alternative

	Fund A (can gear)	Fund B (cannot gear)
Scenario 1 – rising markets		
Initial value of portfolio invested in the markets ('A')	£1,000,000	£1,000,000
On day 1 Fund A borrows 50% against its portfolio from the bank at (say) 6% interest:	+ cash added to portfolio £500,000 – overdraft £500,000	
Total cash invested ('B')	£1,500,000	£1,000,000
Total balance sheet at end of Day 1 is still as per 'A'	£1,000,000 (initial portfolio) + £500,000 (new investments) – £500,000 (overdraft) £1,000,000 net total	£1,000,000
Markets rise 50% over the year. Total value of invested portfolio grows to 150% of 'B'	£1,500,000 × 150% = £2,250,000	£1,500,000
Less interest over the year:	6% on £500,000 = £30,000 Net portfolio £2,220,000	£1,500,000
Net balance sheet at end of year	£2,220,000 – £500,000 (overdraft) £1,720,000 net total	£1,500,000 net total
Total annual growth as a percentage of initial capital 'A'	(£1,720,000 – £1,000,000) as % of £1,000,000 = **growth of 72%**	(£1,500,000 – £1,000,000) as % of £1,000,000 = **growth of 50%**

Table 6 Effect of gearing in different market conditions

	Fund A (can gear)	**Fund B** (cannot gear)
Scenario 2 – Falling markets		
Initial value of portfolio invested in the markets ('A')	£1,000,000	£1,000,000
On Day 1 Fund A borrows 50% against its portfolio from the bank at (say) 6% interest:	+ cash added to portfolio £500,000 − overdraft £500,000	
Total cash invested ('B')	£1,500,000	£1,000,000
Total balance sheet at end of Day 1 is still as per 'A'	£1,000,000 (initial portfolio) + £500,000 (new investments) − <u>£500,000 (overdraft)</u> £1,000,000 net total	£1,000,000
Markets fall 50% over the year. Total value of invested portfolio falls to 50% of 'B':	£1,500,000 × 50 % = £750,000	£1,000,000 × 50 % = £500,000
Less interest over the year :	6% on £500,000 = £30,000 Net portfolio £720,000	£500,000
Net balance sheet at end of year	£720,000 − <u>£500,000 (overdraft)</u> − £220,000 net total	£500,000 net total
Total annual decrease as a percentage of initial capital 'A'	(£1,000,000 − £220,000) as % of £1,000,000 = **loss of 78%**	(£1,500,000 − £1,000,000) as % of £1,000,000 = **loss of 50%**

Table 6 Continued

Investment Market). In theory, this means that up to 30 per cent of the VCT may still be invested in shares listed on the main market;
- no more than 15 per cent of the fund to be in any single company or group;
- at least 30 per cent of the investments by value must be invested in new ordinary shares in qualifying companies, with no preferential rights. This is intended to ensure a bias toward new, riskier ventures;
- the balance of the investments in qualifying companies can be in other types of share. Alternatively, they may be in debt instruments such as debentures, or some other fixed or variable interest stock, which must be of at least 5 years term;
- a VCT may not invest more than £1 million in total each year in any single qualifying trading company which had gross assets of under £10 million immediately before such investment;

The United Kingdom's tax authority, the Inland Revenue, may give provisional approval to VCTs for the applicable tax concessions provided it is satisfied that the conditions specified above will be met within a set time limit. As will be evident from the list of criteria above, not all the investment restrictions for VCTs are imposed with the aim of increasing investor protection. Some are actually about encouraging investors to support a riskier than usual type of venture – and the tax incentives are effectively the reward for taking on these risks.

There are various other examples of such incentives, in other markets and aimed at other types of venture.

It should be borne in mind that the restrictions we have looked at above are imposed by regulators and, in some cases (as in the case of UK investment trusts and VCTs), national tax authorities. Where a fund vehicle is to apply for listing on a stock exchange, further requirements may also apply.

3.21 'Offshore funds'

As with onshore regimes, most offshore jurisdictions have a regime of investment restrictions – for open-ended schemes, at least. In general, these follow the principles we have looked at in Sections 3.11–3.19 above. Further, funds may be established which are completely unauthorized; in this case they do not need to comply with any particular requirements but cannot be freely promoted.

However, the offshore world also often allows for an intermediate regime where investment restrictions are considerably lighter and more flexible, and where this increased flexibility (and consequent potential risk) is tempered by increased disclosure and/or controls over the way in which the fund may be distributed.

So, for example, a jurisdiction such as the Isle of Man will operate several 'tiers' of regulation, each with differing levels of restrictions. For example, the Isle of Man regulatory regime provides for a category of fund which is, in investor protection terms, intended to mirror the UK Financial Services Authority's 'Authorized Scheme' requirements – indeed the Isle of Man equivalent is also referred to as the Authorized Scheme Regime. A second category of fund is operated under a lighter layer of regulation – the Isle of Man 'International Schemes' regime, with its several sub-sets; and a third category allows schemes to be set up which are effectively unregulated (the Isle of Man

Exempt Scheme regime). A fund in this last category is effectively unrestricted in how its investments are placed, but operates under considerable restrictions as to how and to whom may be sold.

As to closed-ended vehicles, it is not common to see offshore governments placing particular restrictions on how these vehicles invest their money. Since such schemes are generally established in international financial centres so as to pay little or no tax, there is little point in attempting to use them to encourage investment in one area or another through tax incentives.

3.22 Hedge funds

There is no single statutory definition of a hedge fund. The term first slipped into common usage in the 1950s to signify a type of fund which operated outside the regulated sector, and therefore was not constrained by the investment restrictions usually imposed on retail funds. Indeed, the US President's *Working Group on Financial Markets* (1999) defined a hedge find as 'any pooled investment vehicle that is privately organized, administered by professional investment managers, and not widely available to the public'. It is generally taken today to cover any lightly regulated, or unregulated, fund vehicle which has a large amount of freedom to invest – both under applicable regulations and under its specific mandate – and which is targeted at relatively sophisticated investors. However, investor appetite – and of course the appetite of managers to find a target audience for their funds! – means that there is increasing pressure for such funds to be made available to investors of a more retail nature.

Hedge funds have been in existence in one form or another since the 1940s, and many commentators regard the first 'true' hedge fund – one engaging the use of both short selling and leverage – as having been established by A.W. Jones in 1949. The market did not, however, begin to expand rapidly until in the 1980s, partly as a result of increasing investor awareness, and partly because of technological advances that supported the use of relatively complex strategies by smaller, more entrepreneurial sponsors as well as the large investment houses.

Because the term "hedge fund" could be seen as defining what the fund is *not* (i.e. it is not regulated in such a way that it can be distributed to the retail investing public) instead of what it *is*, there is a huge range and much blurring at the boundaries: is a fund a 'hedge fund' simply because it gears, for example? Some would say yes, others no.

Nonetheless, hedge funds do generally have some common characteristics. This text is not intended to be a primer on hedge funds *per se*; but it may be worth setting out some of the differing strategies that are employed, so as to illustrate how wide the term is. They include, but are not limited to:

- ***Long/Short equity***: Those funds which can sell stock which they do not hold.
- ***Convertible arbitrage***: Those funds which aim to exploit pricing differentials by (for example) going long of a convertible security, whilst at the same time shorting the ordinary shares/common stock.
- ***Event arbitrage***: Those funds which aim to make (usually short-term) profits from specific corporate events, such as takeovers and mergers.

- *Emerging markets*: Those funds which aim to capitalize on the inefficiencies of relatively immature markets, or on arbitraging situations arising from lack of liquidity in these markets.
- *Global macro*: Those funds which aim to profit from major economic trends.
- *Short biased*; Those funds which predominantly hold short positions in equities and/or equity derivatives.
- *Dividend arbitrage*: Those funds which aim to exploit opportunities for profit arising from an investee company's dividend payment pattern;
- *Statistical arbitrage*: Those funds which trade on the assumption that prices will tend towards a statistical norm, and which use mathematical models to identify opportunities.
- *Fixed income arbitrage*: Those funds which aim to arbitrage temporary interest rate differentials.
- *Managed futures*: Those funds which primarily deal in listed commodity and financial futures markets.
- *Equity market neutral*: Those funds which aim to exploit inefficiencies in the equity markets whilst maintaining minimal market risk.
- *Distressed debt*: Those funds which seek to profit from arbitrage opportunities in, or re-ratings of, distressed debt.

Separately from these 'true' hedge funds, we should also consider funds-of-hedge-funds. These vehicles are funds which invest in a range of underlying hedge funds, aiming to combine their different styles and biases to achieve an optimal risk/reward profile.

Many of the strategies used by hedge funds are not new – they are simply newly commoditized, by packaging them into a fund. That is, the types of strategies historically used by large institutions to protect and gear, or otherwise optimize their investment and currency positions have been applied to a vehicle which allows access to a wider pool of investors.

Hedge funds are usually structured in an offshore environment. In part, this is because of the tax-friendly regimes to be found in such locations. More important, however, is the fact that these jurisdictions usually have regulatory regimes which can accommodate the types of strategies that hedge fund managers typically employ, and which cannot always be employed in an onshore environment.

Of course, a hedge fund can be established and operated in some onshore environments, and simply remain outside the regulatory framework – the United Kingdom would be a good example, although the only open-ended structure available to the fund manager would be a unit trust or partnership, since 'true' OEICs may only be used to establish authorized schemes. This may change, however: consultations have been underway in many jurisdictions with a view to the establishment of regulated regimes for certain types of hedge funds, so as to enable them to be more widely promoted provided they can adhere to certain requirements. These discussions have been taking place at both national and international levels: for example:

- The IOSCO (International Organisation for Governmental Securities Commissions) report on regulatory and investor protection issues arising from retail investor participation in (Funds of) Hedge Funds.
- The work being carried out by the European Committee on Economic and Monetary Affairs on the 'Future of Hedge Funds and Derivatives' and the recommendations

in connection with a regime for 'Sophisticated Alternative Investment Vehicles' or SAIVs.

- Certain countries have already made moves to allow for the regulation of hedge funds, and their marketing to the retail public, or are at least consulting on the possibility – for example:
  - Hong Kong
  - Singapore
  - UK
  - Guernsey
  - United States.

In any event, a manager may prefer not to operate his scheme as a wholly unregulated vehicle. In this regard, the benefits of international fund centres come into play: the multiple fund classification regimes of jurisdictions like the Isle of Man, Jersey, Guernsey and Bermuda provide a means for the manager to select the structure, and level of regulatory oversight, which a manager believes is appropriate to his investor base and strategies.

Indeed many of these countries established new fund classifications precisely in order to attract hedge fund business: a good example would be the introduction by the Isle of Man Financial Supervision Commission of the Professional Investor Fund, and, more recently, the Experienced Investor Fund. These new categories were introduced following industry representations, to meet the perceived needs of scheme operators catering to a more sophisticated investor base, and one where the target audience was deemed sufficiently well informed to understand the implications of the differing regimes.

Onshore regimes can provide friendly environments, however: both Dublin and Luxembourg have tax and regulatory regimes which can accommodate many types of hedge fund; and their fund industries have benefited accordingly.

Part 2

Practical Aspects of Fund Management

4 Overview of the operation of a fund

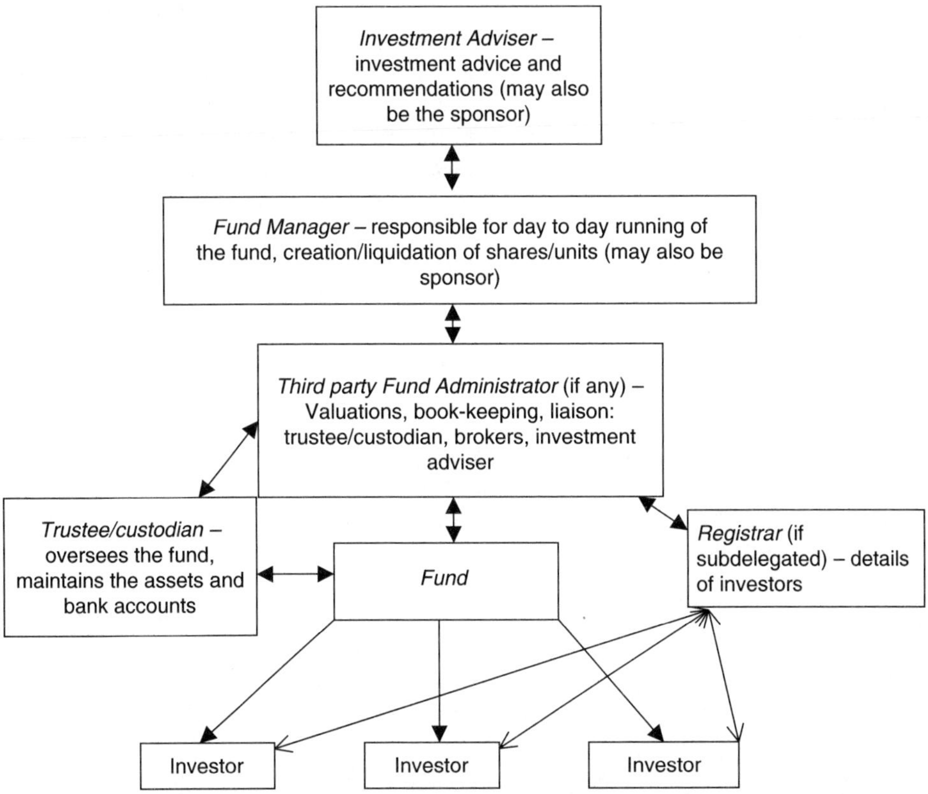

Figure 4.1 The parties to a fund.

The parties to a fund, their roles and obligations are given in figure 4.1.

4.1 The fund sponsor

The sponsor of a fund is the party 'behind' its establishment: the motivator for its being set up (most likely because it sees an opportunity to make a profit from doing so). The sponsor may be the same party as the manager, or as the investment adviser; on the other hand, increasingly, it may not. In any event it is likely that it is the sponsor's 'badging', brand and reputation which motivates the investor to buy.

Consider the following examples:

- An investment house which undertakes its own fund administration and provides in-house investment management, has a small but well-regarded range of open-ended investment companies (OEICs) on offer. It decides to expand this range by adding a further fund offering, doing so under its own branding. The investment house is both sponsor and fund manager.

- The same investment house now wants to expand its domestic fund range, and to begin offering offshore fund products – using its in-house expertise. It establishes an offshore infrastructure, with management and administration of the offshore fund range being provided by a third-party fund services provider (see below). Whilst this means that the fund's 'housekeeping' is kept offshore, the investment house will be keen to ensure its in-house investment views are reflected in the funds' investments, since that is in essence what the investors are buying. The investment house is the sponsor, but the management will be conducted by a 'managed manager' in an appropriate offshore location. The third-party fund services provider will most likely sub-contract the purchase of investment advice back to the sponsor firm (or one of its subsidiaries); we will look at the process for doing this in more detail below. Thus, in this example the sponsor is also the investment adviser and may also own the managed manager.
- A well-known food retailer decides that it can capitalize on the brand loyalty it has established in a particular market, by offering financial services products as well as the consumer goods for which it is already known. It establishes a range of unit trusts, outsourcing both the fund administration and the investment selection to a firm of reputable fund managers. Here the retailer is the fund sponsor: its contribution to the project is not its fund management or administration skill, but rather brand awareness and trust it has built amongst its customers.
- A bank, with a range of traditional banking products, but no in-house investment expertise, establishes that its customers have an unsatisfied appetite for packaged investment products. It has the choice of distributing other institutions' packaged products, and perhaps earning introductory commissions on these; instead, however, it decides to establish its own branded range, again administered and managed by a third-party firm. Here the bank 'brings to the party' not only the brand loyalty it has built, but also its powerful existing financial services distribution infrastructure – whether this be by way of a branch network, introductions from independent financial planners or internet capabilities.

The fund sponsor will usually hold a number of voting shares or units in the fund itself, giving it a certain amount of control – although to preserve investors' rights certain major decisions must be voted on by them, in exercise of their own shares' rights. The shares owned by the sponsor (known as founder or management shares) will not however, entitle the sponsor to distributions or dividends; nor will they enable the sponsor to participate in the fund's investment performance. For this reason they are termed 'non-participating shares'.

4.2 The fund manager

The 'fund manager' is a concept which exists in relation to unit trusts and (generally) to OEICS in most 'offshore' jurisdictions. In some 'onshore' territories, the regulatory requirement for a fund manager has been replaced by other functionaries: for example, in the United Kingdom an OEIC must have an 'Authorized Corporate Director' (ACD) – see below. Further, in several jurisdictions, certain types of fund can be self-managing – they have no external management, and the responsibility for the fund's management rests with its directors.

The fund manager is (in the case of an OEIC) appointed by the directors of the fund, and it can be removed by them.

Its function is, broadly, to manage the fund in accordance with its Memorandum and Articles (M&As) and offering documents, and in accordance with any applicable regulations. In effect, the manager takes care of every aspect of a fund's 'housekeeping'; but it is more than a mere administrator in fulfilling this role. The manager can certainly be seen as a co-fiduciary (along with any trustee/custodian), which is why trustees take particular care when a fund is established with no separate manager. We will look at this issue separately in a later chapter.

These responsibilities can be summarized as follows:

- to make the necessary investment decisions for the fund's portfolio – assisted by the Investment Manager or Adviser, if there is one;
- to buy shares/units from investors in the fund, and to sell shares/units to them – essentially, to act as a market maker in shares/units in the fund;
- to maintain the books and accounts of the fund;
- to maintain the statutory and administrative records and documentation for the fund;
- to prepare and distribute interim and annual Reports and Accounts to investors;
- to carry out regular valuations of the fund and the pricing of its units/shares;
- to calculate and pay distributions/dividends to unitholders/shareholders;
- to market the funds;
- to liase with and instruct the trustee/custodian(s) and stockbrokers in respect of the underlying portfolio transactions;
- to liase with and instruct the trustee/custodian in connection with the creation/ redemption of units/shares so as that the cost/proceeds can be received from or paid to the investor, and so that the trustee can amend the register where applicable;
- to calculate and administer the payment of commissions to brokers and other intermediaries introducing investors to the fund;
- to ensure the investment manager/adviser is apprised of the anticipated creation/ liquidation of units/shares, and can take account of this in repositioning the portfolio;
- to arrange annual and other meetings, if required;
- to issue share certificates, maintenance of share register (in the case of a unit trust this function is usually the responsibility of the trustee, but the trustee may in any event delegate it to the manager). Where the responsibility is of the manager's, this function may be sub-delegated to a separate Registrar (see Section 4.8);
- to ensure that the fund is operated in compliance with the trust deed, if the fund is constituted as a unit trust; the partnership agreement, if it is a partnership; or the M&As if it is a company;
- to ensure that the fund is operated in compliance with all applicable legislation;
- to provide a point of contact, and to deal with investor enquiries, complaints and so on;
- to liase with any other relevant parties on the affairs of the fund – for example, legal advisers, auditors, etc.

In many cases, the manager will delegate out a large proportion of these activities – although in so doing it cannot generally avoid responsibility for them. That is, in most cases the manager remains responsible for the actions of any sub-delegees. If those delegees fail to carry out their tasks adequately, and cause loss to the fund's investors, then it is the fund manager against whom the investor will have a claim; and if this is successful, the fund manager may have to try and recoup its loss from the party to whom it had delegated the task.

The fund manager earns fees for fulfilling these responsibilities by way of some or all of the following:

- *Initial fees on investors' subscriptions*. These are usually expressed as a percentage of an investor's subscription amount (e.g. 5 per cent of the value of the shares/units acquired).
- This fee may be expressed as a percentage of the gross value of the shares/units being acquired (i.e. 5 per cent of the entire value of the investor's subscription), or it may be expressed as a percentage of the net (i.e. the manager's initial charge will be 5 per cent of the net value of the investor's holding, after the initial charge has been deducted; that is, 5 per cent of roughly 95 per cent of his investment). This clearly has both financial and presentational implications for the manager. Five per cent of a big figure is clearly more appealing to a manager than 5 per cent of a smaller one, but investors are increasingly alive to the costs of investment. In addition many agencies now publish comparisons of fund charges on a like for like basis. We will look at the basis of these two different methods of calculation in Chapter 5.
- *Annual management charge*, again generally expressed as a percentage of the net asset value (NAV) of the fund. The sponsor should establish not only the means of expressing this charge, but also the frequency with which it will be levied. It is common for annual management fees to be accrued on a daily/monthly basis (depending on the frequency of dealing/valuation points of the fund), but to be levied on a less frequent basis and the periodicity may be important to the manager from a cash flow perspective.
- Depending on how the fund is structured, a manager who has delegated away or outsourced certain activities (e.g. administration, investment advice) may levy a high fee and pay the delegees from his annual management charge. Alternatively he may levy a slightly lower annual management fee and allow the delegees to invoice the fund directly. The decision as to which to do may be based on a variety of factors including:
  - any value added tax (VAT) or tax implications arising out of the way the fee income flows; and
  - any implications as to ease of administration of the agreements and of flexibility in making changes. Where a delegee contracts direct with the fund, and a change to that delegee is regarded as a material change, it may – if agreements are not carefully drafted – be necessary to seek investor consent before substituting a new service provider. Where the manager is the primary service provider, he may find it easier to fire one delegee and appoint another.
- *Performance-based fees* over and above the annual management fees set out above. Performance fees are most commonly encountered in the hedge fund industry,

reflecting the skills-based approach of that industry. Some comments on the calculation of performance fees are set out in a later chapter.

- *Exit fees* levied when investors redeem their holdings, usually expressed as a percentage of the value of the redeemed shares/units. Exit fees are often calculated on a stepped basis (e.g. 5 per cent for investors redeeming before the first anniversary of their subscription; 4 per cent for investors redeeming before the second anniversary; and so forth). Not all administrators can calculate exit fees on this basis, since many do not have systems that can automatically discriminate between holdings of different ages and apply differential fees accordingly. Consequently it is critical that sponsors wishing to apply exit fees discuss this with their prospective administrators early on. Nonetheless and despite their added administrative complexities, exit fees can be a very useful tool for encouraging investors to give their holdings sufficient time before switching to another fund.
- *Roundings* falling out of the calculations of NAVs per share/unit. Funds are often dealt in fractions of a share/unit, and in addition they may specify the number of significant figures to which the price of a unit/share will be calculated (e.g. fractions of a cent/penny/etc). Roundings are almost invariably calculated in favour of the manager.
- *Brokerage* on underlying investments (e.g. trail commission on the funds in which a fund-of-funds invests). Local regulatory requirements may affect whether income can be earned in this way, and in any event there should be appropriate disclosures of any conflicts of interest arising: for example, 'Investors should be aware that the manager may earn, and shall be entitled to retain for its own benefit, initial and recurring commissions earned on the investments into which the fund invests; for example, on unit trusts and other forms of collective investment scheme.'

4.3 Managed managers

A managed manager is a fund manager like any other; and it has the same responsibilities as an ordinary fund manager (i.e., those set out in Section 4.2). It merits specific mention, however, because it is common for international/offshore funds.

The fund manager is, as well as being the body responsible for much of a fund's 'housekeeping', also frequently used as the fee-earning vehicle by way of which the sponsor earns his return for operating the fund. However, a sponsor based in (for example) Paris or London is unlikely to want to staff and resource his own management company in the offshore jurisdiction from which he operates his fund. For this reason, he may well wish to consider requiring that the administrator to whom he has outsourced the administration of his fund, also manages and administers his fund management company. Third-Party Fund Administrators (see Section 4.7) generally provide this service as an integral part of their offering – taking responsibility for the managed manager's licensing and operation, and ensuring that it complies with any applicable regulations and legislation.

A managed manager will therefore typically be ultimately owned by the sponsor; and will likely have a board comprising individuals who are part of the sponsor's group, and individuals who are part of the third-party fund administrator's group. In many cases it will require a license, although for certain types of fund, and where the managed manager is itself administered by a licensed third-party administrator this requirement may be waived.

4.4 The Authorized Corporate Director

In certain countries, and in connection with OEICs only, the role of the manager is occupied by a separate corporate body which is also required to be on the board of the OEIC itself. This body is known as the Authorized Corporate Director (ACD). The ACD is, for example, a requirement for the UK version of OEICs (known in the United Kingdom as 'Investment Companies with Variable Capital' (ICVCs)); the ACD therefore takes the role which would be occupied by the fund manager in the context of a UK unit trust.

The ACD can usually be any company, so long as it has applied for and received the appropriate authorizations from the relevant regulator; in practice, however, it will almost invariably be a company within the fund manager's group. In the case of an 'in-house' fund, it would usually be the group's existing fund management entity.

The ACD is, broadly, responsible for a similar range of functions to those we looked at for the fund manager in Section 4.2 that is:

- the OEIC's compliance with investor protection requirements as set out in the applicable regulations;
- day-to-day management issues such as valuation, pricing and dealing;
- the preparation of accounts; and
- the management of investments.

It is however also a director of the fund itself. This may leave it exposed to a somewhat wider range of risks, in that as well as being potentially liable to investors for the exercise of its functions as (in effect) the manager of the fund, it may also be sued in its capacity as a director of the fund company. It would be quite possible for the fund company itself, for example, to sue one of its directors on the grounds that the director had failed to carry out his/its fiduciary duty. We will look at issues relating to liability (and insurance for such liabilities, where applicable) in a later chapter.

Again an ACD may delegate certain functions; for example, it will be responsible for the scheme's investment management, but may typically delegate this function to a third party. Where an outside investment manager is appointed, this may be done by way of a tripartite agreement – that is, one executed between ACD, ICVC and investment manager; alternatively the appointment may be by way of agreement direct between ICVC and Investment Manager. In any event care must be taken to ensure that the agreement is consistent with any requirements under the relevant regulator's rulebook.

4.5 The investment adviser or manager

The fund manager is, as we have seen, responsible for a very wide range of matters – from the administrative 'housekeeping' of the fund through to the management of its investment portfolio. In essence, it is regarded as being responsible for the overall operation of all of the fund's affairs, and should be regarded as a co-fiduciary along with the trustee (if there is one). Whilst a fund manager may delegate many specific tasks to a third party, it cannot – as we have noted – usually delegate away liability for their proper conduct. That is, a manager will generally remain responsible for the activities of the delegees. This can lead to some ambiguities where a fund manager appoints an investment manager, as we shall see below: the situation is more clear curt where the appointee is an investment adviser only.

Where a fund's sponsor is not an investment house (and therefore establishes a managed manager or some similar arrangement), it will not generally have an in-house team to provide the asset allocation and underlying investment selections for the fund.

In this case it may appoint an external investment adviser, to evaluate investment opportunities, determine the most appropriate strategy and make specific recommendations as to what assets should be bought or sold. An investment adviser will not be empowered to make decisions on behalf of the fund. It should only make recommendations to the fund's manager, and should not execute them without the manager's prior approval. Indeed the fund manager may place the transactions itself based on the recommendations of the adviser (assuming it decides to accept them).

In practice, of course, it is rare for a fund manager to reject an adviser's recommendation since this is what the adviser has been appointed for: but it does happen that advisers inadvertently recommend transactions which would (for example) breach prescribed investment limits, such as those which we looked at in the previous chapter. Where a fund manager puts such recommendations into effect, it is the fund manager itself that will be liable to investors for any loss suffered as a result; and whilst the manager may then have an actionable claim against the adviser, this is no protection against the reputational damage and regulatory sanctions to which it may in the meantime itself be subject.

In many cases the fund manager appoints an external investment manager instead of an investment adviser. Here the external investment manager generally has the ability to execute transactions without prior approval from the manager. There is, in some jurisdictions, some ambiguity as to whether this removes the fund manager's liability for breaches of investment restrictions or limits: in many cases the answer will be 'no', and the fund manager should therefore ensure that there is some mechanism that will allow it to oversee investment transactions before they are actually placed, and to object to them if it believes they will result in a breach. For some types of fund and in some jurisdictions, however, the fund manager's role and liabilities may be restricted so as to remove responsibility for investment management; and its liability may be further limited where the external investment manager/adviser contracts directly with the fund vehicle, rather than by way of a delegation of duties by the fund manager.

Any contract between a fund manager and third-party investment manager/adviser should be drafted in such a way that the investment manager/adviser is obliged, in providing its management/advisory services, to take account of the investment restrictions and parameters laid down in the fund's constitutional and offering documents; and also that it must operate within any regulatory investment constraints applicable to the fund.

The investment manager/adviser will provide periodic reports to the fund manager, and also investment reports in a prescribed format for the fund's annual and interim report and accounts to investors.

The investment manager/adviser is usually paid a percentage of the NAV of the fund. This percentage is often subject to a flat minimum fee per annum, to protect the investment manager/adviser from suffering if the fund falls to a small size. A typical annual fee for a fund-of-funds or equity-based fund might be 1 per cent per annum. For bond funds the fees will be lower, and for money markets lower still. Depending on the fund's overall fee structure, this fee may be paid direct from the fund but more often it is paid by the fund manager, out of its annual management charge.

In certain cases (predominantly the hedge fund industry), investment managers/advisers may be rewarded on the basis of performance-related or 'incentive' fees. These performance fees are usually levied in addition to a set percentage of the NAV, and may typically be set anywhere between 5 and 50 per cent of the increase in NAV (generally with 'high watermark' adjustments to ensure that investors only pay for net new highs). We will look at the mechanism for this in more detail in a later chapter.

Remember that in some cases the investment manager will also be the fund manager, and his charge for making investment decisions may be bundled with the overall fund management fees.

4.6 The directors of the fund company (OEICs and investment trusts, not unit trusts)

Where a fund is established as a corporate entity, its board of directors will generally have similar responsibilities under law to those of any other type of company. The situation may be slightly different from those jurisdictions where open-ended companies are not established under 'traditional' company law. However, in most jurisdictions, including the offshore locations favoured for the establishment of international funds, directors of a fund company will find that they are subject to the same duties as those in any other jurisdiction. In general, these are likely to mean:

- a duty to act in good faith in the best interests of the company, its shareholders and its present and future creditors;
- a duty to exercise proper skill and care in carrying out these obligations; and
- a requirement to comply with statutory and regulatory obligations.

In the context of a fund company, these responsibilities will include oversight of the proper running of the fund company's affairs, and for the accuracy of the prospectus/offering documents. Where an offering document is inaccurate or misleading the directors may be personally liable for any consequent loss suffered by an investor.

Whilst the directors may be of the view that they have delegated many aspects of the fund company's operations to its manager/administrator, they will nevertheless remain responsible for this and should ensure that they exercise adequate oversight over these activities. Where errors, breaches or losses occur investors may pursue the manager for redress: but it is also quite possible that they may, through the fund company, pursue the directors for any failure to ensure that the fund is properly managed and administered.

Sponsors appointed to the board of a fund company which is managed by a third-party administrator, for example, should ensure that the fund's compliance record, and the incidence of errors, losses and breaches is reviewed at board meetings and that these deliberations are appropriately minuted. This should enable them to adequately fulfil (and demonstrate that they have fulfilled) their obligations to their shareholders.

For UK ICVCs (the form which OEICs take in the United Kingdom), external directors may be appointed in addition to the Authorized Corporate Director (see Section 4.4). It is unlikely that many individuals would wish to be appointed in such a role, because not many people would wish to assume the considerable liabilities and duties arising from such an appointment; corporate directors are the norm. The appointment of additional directors will be subject to approval by the UK regulator, the Financial Services Authority, as the role is a 'controlled function'.

4.7 Fund administrators

Whilst some fund managers carry on all of the administrative, or 'housekeeping', activities needed to keep a fund operating effectively and in compliance with the law, others outsource the majority of this work to specialist administrators. A fund administrator might be part of the same group as the manager; where it is not, it is generally known as a Third-Party Fund Administrator (TPA).

Whilst a manager may delegate many tasks to an administrator, it generally remains responsible and liable for the proper performance of those functions. In addition, of course, the TPA is the entity with which investors will generally deal, and its performance will therefore have a great influence on investors' perceptions of the sponsor's fund offering.

Given the level of operational, regulatory and reputational risk which is therefore concentrated in the hands of the TPA, it is therefore critically important that sponsors choose their TPA with care. Where, and to the extent possible, the manager should also seek appropriate indemnifications against failings in the TPA's activity.

In general, a manager will outsource some or all of the following activities to the administrator:

- maintenance of the fund's records and books of accounts, including statutory accounts;
- liason with investors, including dealing with queries and investigating complaints;
- alerting the fund manager to any matters which give cause for concern, or which may need to be investigated further. These matters would include any unresolved complaints or breaches of any regulations;
- liaison with the trustee/custodian in connection with investor subscriptions/redemptions, so that cash flows arising from subscriptions and redemptions can be accommodated;

- liaison with the trustee/custodian in connection with underlying investment activities, so as to ensure that transactions will be settled successfully;
- provision of fund valuations and share/unit pricing in accordance with applicable regulations and the terms of the fund's constitution/offering documents;
- various support services in connection with the publication of agreed information (e.g. communication of up-to-date fund prices to publications such as the Financial Times, Bloomberg, etc.);
- communication of daily prices to its dealing department;
- cash management;
- assistance in the preparation of income projections;
- preparation of regular asset reconciliations between trustee/custodian records and the books of the fund, extending to both cash and investments.

We have noted that the choice of an appropriate administrator may be critical to the success of a fund. This is true not only of the day-to-day operations, but also where future development (e.g. of new sub-classes) may be envisaged. Funds which have multiple share classes will need to be administered by an organization with appropriate systems, and an administrator whose system can cope with (for example) simple unit trusts (where there is a simple proportionate allocation of value to undivided units) will not necessarily be able to deal with the complexities of multiple unit or share classes with different features.

In addition, an administrator which has the capability to deal with dual priced funds, or for single-priced funds as operated in some offshore jurisdictions, will not necessarily be able to deal with single pricing under the regulations required in certain other locations.

It is therefore important that sponsors establish the limitations of an administrator's systems at the outset, since moving administrators is not an easy, cheap or pleasant task: but the limitations of an administrator's systems can materially fetter future developments and the manager's ability to add new classes, amend charging structures or target new markets.

The above paragraphs deal with the facilities which administrators can provide in general. However, this function is often broken down into three key components:

- *Transfer agent (open-ended schemes).* This role may typically comprise all three of registrar, transfer and paying agent. It typically covers all activities relating to investor subscriptions and redemptions, and the compilation and maintenance of the share/unit register. A transfer agent should provide:
  - the processing of all subscriptions and redemptions;
  - the book-keeping associated with these transactions;
  - settlement of the above transactions;
  - maintenance of the shareholder register;
  - liason with investors, that is, transmitting communications;
  - liason with the trustee/custodian in connection with net cash inflows/outflows;
  - liason with the fund administrator (if different), liason with the manager and if applicable investment manager/adviser, so as to enable them to consider the impact of net inflows/outflows on portfolio positioning. In some cases, regulatory provisions, or those in the fund's constitutional and offering documents, will

provide that the manager may decline or defer very large redemptions for a period, where to process the transaction in one immediate step would adversely impact on the fund – and therefore be detrimental to the interests of the remaining investors. In this case a decision by the manager/directors of the fund may be necessary as to how to proceed and the transfer agent should ensure that information is passed to the manager promptly so as to enable it to consider matters.
  - usually, shareholder servicing in a wider context: for example, dealing with investor queries, supporting marketing activity and so on;
  - investor due diligence (it is essential that a prospective sponsor discusses the transfer agent's processes and requirements for investor due diligence). We will look at this issue in more detail in a later section;
  - transfer agents may well also be able to support a fund manager/sponsor's marketing initiatives by providing information on the breakdown of investors by geographic region, intermediary, intermediary type or distribution channel.
- *Fund valuation and accounting*, dealing with the generation of portfolio valuations and NAVs per share/unit and attending to matters relating to the fund's assets, liabilities and transactions.
- *Corporate secretarial*, including ensuring that statutory and compliance returns are dealt with on a timely basis.

4.8 Registrar

Under the heading of transfer agency above we noted that the administrator may take on the role of *registrar*. Not every fund has a separate registrar: in many cases, this role is fulfilled by one of the other functionaries. Where this function is delegated to a registrar, the appointment will be made by the party with primary responsibility for it (and this will depend on the way in which the fund is established):

- where a fund is established as a unit trust, the primary responsibility for registrar functions usually rests with the trustee; and
- where it is established as an OEIC or an investment trust, with the manager.

The registrar will take on the function of maintaining shareholder/unitholder records, including details of the investor's address, the number of shares/units held and the date on which they were acquired. The registrar's books of record are the primary evidence of who owns what units/shares, at any given record date (and so they are important for establishing entitlement to dividends/distributions and other corporate actions).

4.9 The trustee (unit trusts)

The trustee of a fund established as a unit trust, by acting to protect the interests of investors in that fund, occupies a similar role to the trustee of any conventional trust. However, its role is generally codified in regulations which prescribe the manner in which its duties must be performed.

In many jurisdictions, the regulatory regime is such that the trustee of a regulated scheme may only be a bank. In others, the regime permits for other entities to act in this capacity, but where a scheme is intended to be publicly promoted the requirements will in any event limit this role to entities with substantial capital resources and tried and tested asset administration and custodial systems.

One of the main functions performed by the trustee is the holding of the fund's assets. Assets will be segregated from the trustee's own assets, so as to ensure that they will not be at risk should the trustee become insolvent. That said, managers should still exercise caution when selecting a trustee since the trustee's insolvency (or any equivalent state of financial instability) would nonetheless be likely to cause any assets held by it to be frozen for a period at least. Managers who have suffered from events such as these have had to deal with increased market risk (as they are unable to trade their portfolios), investor anxiety and generally a degree of administrative chaos. Thus, even where regulations do not limit the choice to first-tier banks, a sponsor/manager well advised to select a trustee with an eye to financial soundness and robust regulatory supervision.

Sponsors may wish to review the credit ratings of prospective trustees (issued by bodies such as Fitch IBCA, Standard & Poors, and/or Moodys): where no credit rating is held (as is sometimes the case with smaller banks, their subsidiaries and other types of trustee) it would be wise to ascertain the strength of the organization's capital base and to enquire into the nature of any exposures to which it may be vulnerable. Reasonable questions would include: *does your organization make commercial loans? Does it have high levels of long-term debt to questionable borrowers? Does the organization have large proprietary trading positions which could undermine its financial strength? What are the regulatory requirements with regard to the organization's solvency, and how are these monitored and enforced?* No matter what the financial strength of the trustee, sponsors – especially those establishing potentially substantial funds – should ensure that it has appropriate professional indemnity and other insurances in place, and that these extend to the trustee activities being proposed.

Broadly, the trustee's responsibilities include the following:

- to provide independent oversight of the affairs of the fund; with an eye to protecting the interests of the beneficiaries (i.e. the investors);
- to safeguard the assets of the fund. This function goes further than safekeeping and will require that the trustee is active in ensuring that appropriate action is taken in connection with any corporate actions, and that all income is collected and applied on a timely basis;
- to maintain the bank accounts of the fund, either itself (where the trustee is a bank) or otherwise by placing funds on appropriately designated deposit with other banks;
- to settle the investment trades placed by the fund manager or investment manager, that is, by delivering assets/cash and by ensuring that appropriate cash/assets are received in return;
- to ensure that such trades do not place the fund in breach of its investment mandate and limits;
- to ensure that the assets of the fund are appropriately registered, either in the name of the trustee itself or its nominee/sub-delegee;

- to ensure that the fund is, on an ongoing basis, managed in accordance with the terms of the trust deed (to which the trustee will be a party). We will look at the typical contents of a trust deed in Chapter 6;
- to ensure that the fund is managed in accordance with applicable legislation and regulations, and with its stated investment objectives and restrictions as laid down in the offering documents;
- to maintain the register of unitholders (although this activity may be delegated to a third-party such as a registrar, see Section 4.7);
- to create/cancel units in the fund in order to meet subscription/redemption requests;
- generally, to approve any promotional literature or advertising material for compliance with regulatory requirements and to ensure that it is fair, not misleading and does not underplay any relevant risks;
- there will generally be a regulatory requirement for the trustee to make a statement in the annual Report and Accounts of the fund, commenting as to its compliance (or otherwise) with the trust deed, offering document and any applicable regulations;
- in many cases, to actively review the operational procedures of the fund's manager.

This last item generally entails physical visits by the trustee to the offices of the manager, and bears some resemblance both to an audit visit, and to the supervisory visits carried out by many regulators. That is, the trustee should be ensuring that the manager is operating the fund in accordance with applicable regulations and the terms of the fund itself, so as to protect the interests of the investors; it will generally look to test this by reviewing files and procedures, and by interviewing relevant staff. Where trustees find something amiss they can and do take action, in extreme cases by removing of the manager. However, in the majority of such cases the process is positive for both sides, with the trustee making recommendations as to how controls and procedures can be improved and the manager benefiting from this additional risk management oversight.

Trustee fees are generally paid direct from the assets of the fund (as opposed to by the manager). They are generally expressed as a combination of some or all of:

- a percentage of the fund's NAV;
- a fee per transaction settled or corporate action/dividend dealt with; and
- a minimum sum to protect the trustee should the value of the fund shrink below a certain level.

Many trustees have international networks: that is, they are able to hold overseas assets through their agents in the relevant countries where those assets are domiciled. Sometimes these agents are part of the same financial group as the fund's primary trustee; this is often the case where the trustee is part of an international banking group. In other cases, where the trustee does not have such a wide geographic branch network, it may sub-delegate work to a number of third-party sub-custodians who are not a part of its corporate group.

In either case, local fund regulations may well require that the primary trustee/custodian remains fully responsible for the entire trustee/custody function, and for the actions of those to whom it delegates work. It is important to establish this at the outset so as to clarify the extent of the primary trustee's liability if things should go wrong, the degree of supervision it will be exercising over its delegees and the basis on which they are selected.

Since the trustee is responsible, *inter alia*, for settlement of the fund's trades, sponsors should establish at the outset that it uses robust and up-to-date systems to communicate with its network of agents: for example, Society for Worldwide International Fund Transfers (SWIFT) payments and the like.

Trustees are far from passive agents and the service they provide goes considerably beyond that of simple safe-custody of assets. They provide a valuable function in ensuring that their clients (i.e. fund managers) are promptly apprised of investor communications put out by securities issuers in connection with corporate actions (rights issues, stock splits, bonus and scrip issues, etc.). A well-established and resourced trustee will take information and data feeds not only from the issuers themselves, but also from a wide range of sources such as Telecurs, Datastream, Reuters, Bloomberg and Valorinform. The appropriate feeds will depend on the markets in which assets are expected to be held, and a trustee should ideally use at least two so that information from one can be verified against that of another.

In addition, trustees should employ validation methods (such as investigation of price movements in excess of a certain percentage, stale prices) to minimize the incidence of errors. We will look at these issues further in Chapter 5 when we consider pricing issues.

Provision of proxy voting services should be available in the markets in which the sponsor anticipates holding assets on which the fund will have voting rights. The trustee should also undertake to pass on details of Annual General Meetings and Extraordinary General Meetings, which should ideally be translated into the sponsor's home language or a common business language.

In many cases, trustees will also process matters such as tax reclaims for fund clients, and it can be useful for a sponsor to ensure that the prospective trustee has the right expertise in connection with any relevant double taxation treaties, and so forth.

Sponsors should also discuss the nature of a trustee's reporting and the degree to which this can be tailored to meet their specific needs. Ideally, a trustee will have the ability to adapt reports, and in some cases value can be added by the provision of reports on investment value-at-risk, simulating the impact of different market scenarios on the fund's portfolio. The trustee's reports should, as a matter of course, report on any deviations from prescribed asset allocation limits. If possible they should also indicate deviations from any additional, less formal, overlaid guidelines – so as to provide the manager with an early warning signal that (for example) market movements are likely to require remedial action if the portfolio is not to drift into breach.

Standard reporting will include:

- multi-currency portfolio valuations, with the flexibility to select the basis of currency and asset valuations (since one fund may, for example, value its assets on the basis of the previous day's close of business mid-price as published by one source, whilst another may value on some completely different basis);
- transaction statements, both at summary level and in more detailed format;
- statistical analyses of transactions;

- income statements, with projections by currency if applicable;
- compliance with applicable regulations and the fund's mandate. This is generally done on an 'exceptions' basis – that is, there will be no report if there has been no breach.

In addition, a fund trustee's reports to fund managers may also include:

- graphical representations of the asset allocations within the fund;
- risk reporting functionality, addressing such issues as tracking error and Value at Risk calculations;
- specific reporting in connection with derivative positions (position values, exposures, extent of cover);
- tax reporting, including the value to date of any reclaims by country, and/or overall fiscal impact reports;
- securities lending activity, if applicable. This may include reports on loans outstanding and completed, exposures to particular counterparties and so on.

Some trustees support securities lending on behalf of their fund clients. In an ideal world they will be able to do this:

- on an undisclosed basis, so that the fund's positions are kept confidential. This can be especially important to hedge fund managers, who may be keen to ensure that their positions do not become public knowledge;
- it may also be worth asking whether the trustee stocklends for its own account. If not, this will give comfort to a fund manager that the trustee will not be subject to conflicts of interests and will seek out the best prevailing rates for its clients;
- where a trustee does stocklend, managers/sponsors should enquire into the basis on which the trustee selects its counterparties (if this is not already prescribed for it under local regulations) so as to ensure that they are of appropriate credit quality.

Trustees who act as banker to a fund should ideally offer systems that allow any uninvested cash to earn an optimal rate of interest (consistent with the fund's liquidity needs). For some funds, it may be beneficial for the trustee to make use of fiduciary deposits: where these are held in appropriate jurisdictions this may allow for some element of tax deferral, or for the avoidance of withholding taxes: it may also assist in ensuring that the fund's credit risk is spread across a number of institutions. Again it is worth spending time discussing the possible arrangements with a prospective custodian at the outset.

4.10 The custodian (OEICs, investment trusts, not unit trusts)

In general, the responsibilities of a fund custodian are not dissimilar to those of the trustee of a unit trust. Indeed, despite the fact that there is no trust deed, and the fund is a corporate vehicle, the regulations in many jurisdictions specifically provide that the custodian of a regulated fund must exercise a similar level of oversight as if it were the trustee of a unit trust, and a custodian may well find that it is regarded as acting in as full a fiduciary capacity as if it were a trustee. This can be particularly important where things go awry, since the level of liability which a fiduciary has towards its client fund's investors is materially higher than that of an entity providing no more than a glorified safekeeping and asset administration service.

Where this is the case the custodian's responsibilities, and the functionality which a sponsor may wish it to provide, will be largely as for a trustee (as in Section 4.7).

In other cases – for example, where the regulations are not so strict or in the case of lightly regulated or unregulated funds – the fund custodian's role may genuinely be restricted to just that: pure custody of the assets. The element of oversight of the manager's activities, and the degree of proactiveness with which the custodian will monitor affairs in the investors' interests, will be much less.

In the context of a UK ICVC, an entity known as the 'Depository' stands in place for the trustee of a unit trust, or (for OEICs in other jurisdictions) the custodian.

The Depository's role comprises both custodianship of the ICVC's assets, and a supervisory role in connection with its operations. Although the scheme is not established by way of a trust, these supervisory duties are enforced by statutory provisions so that the Depository does in fact act as a fiduciary. In many cases UK ICVC Depositories will be aexisting UK unit trust trustee, which has applied to the UK regulator (the Financial Services Authority), for permission to extend the range of its permitted activities to include acting as depository of an ICVC.

4.11 The regulator

Whilst it may seem odd to discuss the role of the regulator as a functionary of a fund, this can have a marked impact on the marketability and flexibility of any fund vehicle. Without going into detail as to specific regimes (which we will look at later), sponsors should consider the regulatory regime in any jurisdiction in which their fund is to be domiciled, operated or otherwise administered, with an eye to:

- the level of protection which results from the regulatory regime. This may include any applicable compensation schemes or ombudsman arrangements, and can, by providing a measure of comfort to investors, enhance the fund's marketing appeal;
- the level of supervisory oversight exercised over the fund's functionaries, which may similarly be of comfort to investors and sponsor alike;
- the level of flexibility provided, and whether the sponsor is likely to be able to operate the fund in the way he hopes, promote it to his intended target audience or make use of certain investment strategies;
- the cost of the regulatory regime (including any applicable authorization fees); and
- the level of investor due diligence required within that regime and the costs and practicalities of satisfying these requirements.

Funds may be subject to multiple regulatory regimes: for example, a fund may be incorporated in the BVI but managed and administered in the Isle of Man, and promoted to the public in South Africa. In this case, the requirements of all three regulators would need to be taken into account.

4.12 Distributors

The way in which an open-ended fund is sold will depend on the manager's policy and on the regulatory status of the fund itself. Options include:

- Distributing the fund through independent intermediaries; that is, professional agents who may be remunerated by way of initial and recurring (or 'trail') commissions on sales. Such intermediaries may include independent financial advisers (IFAs) and stockbrokers;
- establishing a network of tied agents, who will sell only the products of a single fund management group and who may be paid either on a salary or a commission/incentive basis;
- selling direct to the public by way of advertising in the press, on billboards and so forth. This option is, in many markets, only open to the more highly regulated categories of fund; and
- increasingly, distribution through institutional agents such as fund supermarkets, linked investment service providers, insurance companies offering fund-linked policies and investment management houses with fund-of-funds or portfolio-of-funds offerings.

Closed-ended funds (e.g. for example, investment trusts) are usually 'quoted' – that is, they will be listed on a recognized stock exchange. Certain exchanges have developed regimes particularly suited to the listing of funds, as a means of improving their competitiveness: in any event sponsors should consider the options carefully since some markets impose particular constraints, some enjoy a greater degree of recognition than others, and the costs of listing and subsequent reporting requirements can vary considerably. We looked at the types of issues which investors should consider in Section 1.9. of Chapter 1.

4.13 Auditors

For a very few categories of fund, there may still be no audit requirement; this might be the case where, for example, the fund is completely unregulated *and* it is constituted in such a way that no statutory audit requirement is imposed because of its legal structure (e.g. it is a unit trust).

However, even where there is no statutory or regulatory requirement for an audit, investor appetite is likely to mean that all but the most closely held funds are in fact subject to some form of audit; and that audited accounts are sent to investors. We will concentrate in this section on the usual requirements for the audit of a regulated fund.

In most jurisdictions, the regulator will require that audited accounts are submitted to it for any locally regulated fund: indeed some regulators also ask fund managers and administrators to submit the accounts for those unregulated funds to which they provide services as well and despite the fact that there may be no statutory necessity to comply, most do so.

It is usual for a regulator to place constraints on the type of audit firm which may audit a locally regulated fund. Requirements may include:

- a local presence. This can create difficulties where a fund manager wishes to use its group auditor to audit a particular fund in a location where that firm has no presence on the ground. In some cases it has meant that dual audits, or some other form of signoff arrangements with a local firm, have been necessary;
- demonstrable track record and expertise in the audit of funds of the nature in question. In some cases regulators have insisted that where a local firm does not have the necessary expertise, the audit is supervised and signed off by a partner from one of the firm's other offices; and
- the auditor holding specified levels of Professional Indemnity insurance.

Regulators also generally require that the audit engagement letter sets out additional reporting responsibilities, over and above those comprised in the financial audit of a non-financial organization (e.g. that the auditor will review the fund's compliance with a specified range of regulatory requirements). These may include:

- a requirement that the regulator is copied on the auditor's 'Management Letter', the letter in which it advises the fund's manager of any control weaknesses and other failings it has unearthed;
- a requirement that the auditor includes a statement in the fund's Annual Report and Accounts commenting on the fund's compliance with certain regulatory requirements; and increasingly,
- a statutory 'whistleblowing' obligation which requires that the auditor takes active steps to alert the regulator to any regulatory breaches which come to its attention in the course of its audit work. This is usually coupled with a statutory indemnity, which protects the auditor from suit by the fund or its manager for breach of confidentiality, provided any such report has been made in good faith.

The auditor will, in the case of a unit trust, usually be appointed by the manager of the fund; in the case of an investment trust (a closed-ended company) or an OEIC, it will be appointed/reappointed each year, by the shareholders at the fund vehicle's annual general meeting.

Auditors may also provide additional services, such as assistance in the preparation of accounts, reviews of procedures and controls, comments on IT systems upgrades, general business intelligence and taxation advice. This is, however, less common than it used to be since increasingly regulators focus on issues of corporate governance and conflicts of interest, and have expressed reservations as to the ability of auditors to provide a thorough and impartial audit when they are also heavily reliant on their client for consultancy fees.

Audit fees are usually paid direct from the assets of the fund.

Of course, audits serve to protect the fund's sponsors, directors and management as well as its investors: and so, the above considerations aside, a sponsor will be well advised to select an auditor which has the requisite skills and experience to understand the business and to give added value through risk management advice, where appropriate. This is particularly important in the case of complicated fund structures, or where complex underlying investments or strategies are to be employed. Audit fees paid to a firm which does not understand the various exposures and risks are audit fees wasted.

4.14 Legal adviser

The role of the legal adviser should begin well before the fund itself is established; and a sponsor who is considering establishing an offshore fund or one which is intended to have international appeal should consider his choice of adviser carefully. Legal advisers vary greatly in their levels of expertise, and a firm which is experienced in its local funds market may not be placed to advise a sponsor whose offering involves multiple jurisdictions, or who requires advice as to which location to select.

The legal adviser will advise the fund, via its sponsor, board or manager (as appropriate) when required – for example, on regulatory or contractual matters. A good legal adviser who is experienced in the fund industry will also be able to advise on and assist with:

- appropriate structuring, including the wording of any guarantee mechanisms to be incorporated;
- taxation matters arising from the location of the fund, its target investor base and its underlying assets;
- preparation of any necessary applications for authorization of the fund itself, any service providers for whom applications must also be made, and any 'key person' applications which must be sought (e.g. the board of the fund, who are likely to be subject to some 'fit and proper' requirements);
- submission of the applications to the relevant regulator, and liaison with them in connection with any queries which arise;
- drafting (and sometimes negotiation) of material contracts between the fund and the various service providers;
- fund launch procedures and any listing requirements;
- permissible distribution methods in light of the regulatory requirements; and
- the implications of any changes to the applicable regulatory and taxation regimes.

4.15 Brokers

The term 'brokers' is also often used of the type of intermediaries who may introduce new investors to a fund (see Section 4.12). This section, however, refers to the traditional usage.

A fund's investment transactions (i.e. the buying and selling of the underlying assets of the fund) are usually carried out by the fund through intermediaries such as stockbrokers, bond brokers and the like. Information is exchanged between manager, broker and custodian to ensure that investment purchases and sales are effected and settled on time and securely, with each side delivering the assets and receiving the consideration expected.

The costs of brokerage can be considerable. Some brokers offer fund managers additional benefits to encourage them to place their business with them; and in practice this may benefit manager and investor alike. However, regulators are increasingly conscious of conflicts of interest, especially in the cases of:

- Bundling, where a broker agrees to provide other services in addition to pure brokerage, the costs of which will be wrapped into a single commission charge. Such services might include access to the broker's in-house research.
- Softing, whereby a broker agrees to pay for services from some third-party provider to the fund manager, so long as the fund manager puts a certain volume of business through it. The services might include software and support, or data feeds.

Before entering into discussions on these should additional services, a fund manager ascertain any regulatory implications, and to consider the reasonable expectations of his investor base – will they benefit from the additional services, to a degree which is appropriate in light of any perceived dealing bias? Will one group of investors benefit to the detriment of another? The manager should also consider the types of disclosures which should be made to investors if he proceeds down this route.

In some cases, the trustee can also act as trade broker for certain assets. This can have cost benefits, especially if the organization charges reduced or nil trade settlement fees where it acts in this dual capacity: however the manager will wish to ensure that the fund will benefit from best execution and that fees are in fact transparent and competitive.

4.16 Insurers

Fund sponsors are well advised to check that their service providers have appropriate Professional Indemnity (PI) cover. This is insurance which pays out when a service provider's client suffers loss because of its breach of professional duty, and it is an important protection where claims could be sizeable and the service provider cannot itself meet such a claim. PI policies often also include cover for additional risks such as breach of confidentiality, loss of documents and breach of copyright. Ideally, a sponsor should enquire as to the exact nature and scope of any cover, but service providers can be coy about providing too much detail in case they are seen as the 'deep pockets' to fund any claim, regardless of ultimate liability.

Sponsors who intend to go on the board of their fund company, or of any dedicated manager, should also consider taking out Directors' and Officers' insurance. We have already touched on the liabilities which can attach to directors of fund vehicles, and it is entirely possible that if things go wrong investors may look to sue not only the service provider who is at fault, but also, through the fund company, its directors if they feel that the board has failed to supervise these service providers adequately. We will look at issues relating to insurance in a later chapter.

4.17 Putting it all together

The prospective fund sponsor should find no shortage of assistance and guidance in putting together a team of fund servicing agents: nor indeed in obtaining advice as to how best, and where, to structure the fund itself. An approach to a good custodian or third-party administrator will usually result in recommendations on all these issues, and the sponsor may well be offered model documentation and assistance in the licensing process into the bargain. Whilst it may be tempting to accept the additional support that service providers offer, sponsors should remember that the make-up of their team, and the way in which their fund is structured, could be critical to the long-term flexibility and success; in some cases it may be worth declining any free offers of support and paying for independent advice from an adviser who is paid to come up with an optimum solution.

The key is to get good, unbiased advice and a sponsor is well advised to talk to at least three or four service providers before making a decision. Free advice is not necessarily as good as advice which has been paid for: and a service provider who professes to be able to provide a one-stop-shop may in practice be selling the sponsor what it *thinks* it can best provide, as opposed to the structure and arrangements which will benefit the fund most.

New fund sponsors should take comfort from, and not be intimidated by, providers who ask a great number of relatively searching questions: as with so many things, the devil can be in the detail and slapdash structuring at the outset can severely limit a sponsor's flexibility in the future. Further, you should not underestimate the time, costs and disruption of changing a service provider once a scheme is established.

It is not uncommon for a single service provider to provide combined services – for example, many trustee/custodians also have in-group third-party fund management administration units. This can be beneficial in terms of cost and cohesiveness of services, and can minimize the potential for communications mishaps between administrator and trustee/custodian; however, it is not permissible for all classes of fund. In many jurisdictions, regulators will insist that for the most highly regulated class of funds, the manager and trustee/custodian must not only be separate entities, but also completely independent – that is, not part of the same corporate grouping. This is intended to ensure that the trustee/custodian can exercise its fiduciary duties in overseeing the manager's activities in a truly independent fashion, and will carry out its obligations to report to the regulator on areas of concern; something that could be in question if the two entities share a common parentage, or have common directors.

In some cases, third-party service providers can also take advantage of their international reach, and of developments in regulation on outsourcing, which allow them to break components of the work they undertake into different disciplines and to service them in different areas. For example, a manager/administrator may contract with a fund sponsor to provide services through its Caribbean office. However its staffing and systems arrangements may be such that NAVs are best generated by its team in Luxembourg, whilst its transfer agency services are carried on through an Isle of Man-based team. Depending on regulatory approvals and servicing standards, this may be entirely acceptable to the fund sponsor – indeed communications are such nowadays that to all intents and purposes the sponsor and investors might be largely unaware that the Caribbean office had sub-delegated out many of its activities (and contractually the Caribbean office would in any event normally remain responsible for the activities of its delegees). However, the sponsor should ensure that it understands any implications in terms of:

- the acceptability of such arrangements to any relevant regulators;
- any systems constraints that will arise because of time differences and the geographic remoteness of the various teams;
- that responsibility does, indeed, remain with the primary service provider with whom the fund is contracting;
- that the service provider's PI insurance is such that no material gap in cover will arise because of these arrangements;
- that any data protection/investor confidentiality obligations are borne in mind (e.g. will it be necessary for the fund's offering documents to disclose the fact that investor information will be transferred to a jurisdiction which may have different data protection legislation to that in the one from which the fund is operated – or indeed no statutory data protection at all? If so, how acceptable will such disclosures be to investors?);
- will the transfer of such activities mean that subscriptions are being processed in, and are subject to, a regulatory regime where investor due diligence requirements are different from those in the fund's home jurisdiction, and does this have servicing and cost implications?
- are the business continuity arrangements in the various delegee entities adequate, and what arrangements are in place in the event of a disaster in any of the remote delegee jurisdictions?
- will the servicing in fact be seamless, and can the fund sponsor obtain timely and accurate information as easily as if all processing was being done locally?

4.18 Tax considerations and the allocation of responsibilities

It can be important from a tax perspective to ensure that mind, management and control of a fund is demonstrably 'offshore' – especially where the sponsor is a fund management business located in an onshore location, which has outsourced the management and administration to an offshore provider.

This might arise where the onshore manager has investment management and administrative infrastructure in its home location, and already runs a stable of domestic funds. It may decide that for tax reasons, a parallel stable of offshore funds would also be commercially viable to market in its home market. It may however be unwilling to invest in infrastructure – premises, staff and systems – in its chosen offshore location, either as a long-term strategy or at least until the viability of the offshore range is established. In such cases, as we have already seen, it may establish an offshore 'managed manager' (which it will probably own) and outsource the bulk of the work to an offshore third-party administrator.

The onshore sponsor will have an onshore investment management team with the skills to make the appropriate decisions (and indeed to execute transactions too, because of its proximity to the broking community). It therefore makes sense for the offshore managed manager to appoint the onshore, in-house team as investment adviser or manager to the fund; depending on applicable tax rules, it may in fact be preferable to appoint the onshore entity as adviser only, and not investment manager, because of the importance of demonstrating that the mind, management and control of the fund is indeed offshore: and that material decisions are not being made onshore. Thus:

- the contract with the investment adviser will clearly establish that it is to offer only *advice* to the manager;
- the manager must consider and approve all transactions before they are executed;
- usually, the execution of these investment deals will also be conducted by the manager on behalf of the fund; and
- care must be taken if the adviser is to be permitted to place deals, since the integrity of the structuring will be undermined if sloppy processes lead to the adviser automatically placing deals, to which the manager has given only cursory (if any) thought before approval – or worse, documents its ratification of recommendations after the event or not at all.

Sponsors should ensure that their offshore service providers understand the importance of such issues, and can demonstrate that they have appropriate procedures in place. Indeed it would not be unreasonable, after the fund is established, to seek verification that these procedures are being adhered to and that appropriate documentation is being maintained, by inspecting the files periodically.

5 Valuations and pricing

In this chapter we will consider the mechanisms used to determine prices for both open- and closed-ended funds, and the adjustments that may be made to them so as to ensure the fair treatment of investors.

Open-ended funds are priced using a formula based on the net asset value (NAV) of their portfolios: supply and demand for shares/units in an open-ended fund should make little or no significant impact on their price. The price of shares in a closed-ended vehicle, on the other hand, is based on supply and demand with only a relatively elastic relationship to the NAV of the underlying portfolio (this value being filtered, as it were, through the refractive lense of the market's perception and consequent demand for shares). It is because of this that insider dealing laws generally extend to disclosures of information about, and dealings in, closed-ended vehicles but not to open-ended vehicles. Whilst information could be price-sensitive in connection with shares in a closed-ended vehicle, by affecting demand for shares, in theory no increase or decrease in demand for shares/units in open-ended vehicles will affect their NAV and so most countries' insider trading laws do not include such vehicles in the range of securities to which they apply.

5.1 Open-ended schemes – first principles of pricing

We have already seen that open-ended funds are valued on the basis of the NAV of the fund as a whole. Broadly, this means that the fund as a whole is valued on the basis of:

- everything it owns or which is due to it (its assets)
- less everything it owes (its liabilities)
- = the NAV of the fund.

The NAV so created is translated into a price per unit or share, which will – subject to certain adjustments which we will look at later – be the basis of the price at which investors deal.

Taking our calculations to the next logical stage, that of generating dealing price per share/unit, we can say (very broadly, and again subject to some adjustments which we will look at later) that:

$$\text{NAV per share/unit} = \frac{\text{Total NAV of the fund}}{\text{Total number of shares/units in issue}}$$

5.2 Why are valuations carried out?

The valuation process is carried out at regular intervals for a fund so as to ascertain its NAV. The NAV is required so that the manager can:

- set the unit/share price at which investors may deal in the fund; and
- measure the fund's performance over various periods.

5.3 What are the various elements of a valuation?

Any fund valuation must include all of the following elements:

- *Value of investments (including all unrealized gains/losses).* At the valuation point, the current value of each holding of investment must be determined, with reference to current market prices. This is usually done on one of the following basis, although there are many variations:
  - *Offer price:* the price at which the underlying holding could be bought in the market;
  - *Bid price:* the price at which the underlying asset could be sold in the market; and
  - *Mid-price:* a figure mid-way between bid and offer prices.

In many jurisdictions and for certain categories of fund, there are regulations which prescribe how the underlying asset may be priced. In certain markets, some categories of fund must have 'dual prices' calculated – that is, an offer price for units/shares in the fund must be calculated using the offer price of the underlying assets, and a separate bid price must also be calculated using the bid price of those assets. In effect, two valuations are carried out at each valuation point. Whilst regulations of this nature are becoming less widespread, many countries (especially those of which the regulatory regime has historically been influenced by that of the United Kingdom, and indeed the United Kingdom itself) still retain the option of dual pricing on this basis. In international fund centres the regime is generally more flexible, and typically a single mid-price might be adopted. We will look at the mechanics of producing a set of dual prices, and contrast this with the production of a single priced NAV, below.

Clearly for a valuation to be meaningful, all of the fund's assets must be valued – from the more common security types such as equities and bonds, through to more complex investment positions involving derivatives, swaps and the like. It is important that the entity carrying out the valuation has the systems and skills to value complex assets, liabilities and exposures accurately and on a timely basis.

Certain investments can be difficult to value for other reasons: for example, because they are thinly or rarely traded, highly illiquid or because only estimated values are available. It is unlikely that highly regulated funds will be able to make significant investments in such assets because of these difficulties (as we have already seen in Section 3.12, Chapter 3). However, many more lightly regulated or unregulated funds employ such assets and it is important that the valuation policy (and any flexibility which might be accorded to the manager or fund's board of directors in valuing these securities) is clearly articulated in the fund's offering documents. Fund managers should ensure that they have a process in place which clearly documents the way in which valuation decisions have been taken, and the rationale for that decision, since discrepancies or variations in policy could leave them or (depending on the decision-making process permitted) the fund's directors liable for damages to investors who lose out because of an unreasonable or indefensible valuation. We will look at the issue of liability for incorrect valuations again shortly.

- *Cash*. All cash with bankers or brokers must be included. In addition, if the fund has made any loans these must be taken into consideration. Again where cash is held in foreign currencies, the basis of valuing such currency deposits must be clearly understood. Similarly, where deposits are structured in any way (e.g. those fixed deposits which bear an 'interest rate' which varies with the performance of certain markets), the means of identifying a reasonable valuation should be understood.
- *Subscriptions monies receivable*. As with any balance sheet, debtor balances should be included – and this will include subscription money in the course of clearing for which units/shares have been allocated (i.e. effectively money owed by incoming investors to the fund). Fund managers aim to keep the amount outstanding to a minimum, so as to reduce the risk of default on the part of an investor (e.g. where a prospective investor has stopped his cheque because of a fall in the fund's value). Generally, managers will not permit uncleared funds to be treated as received and issue shares/units on the basis of them, but for favoured customers this may arise.
- *Redemption monies payable*. Similarly, sums due to exiting investors should be deducted, where the relevant shares/units have been redeemed. This will apply to money still sitting in the fund's bank account which cannot yet be paid away, since although the deal has been agreed and effected, no form of renunciation or equivalent has yet been received; or where there is some other technical reason the redemption monies cannot be paid out.
- *Accrued income*. This will include income earned by the fund but not yet received into its bank account. It will be made up of such items as:
  - dividends declared but not yet received;
  - bond interest accrued but not yet received; and
  - accrued bank interest.
- *Accrued expenses*. The valuation will be reduced by any expenses which have been accrued but not yet paid out. This might include such items as:
  - annual management fee (which may be accrued on (say) a daily basis but debited only quarterly);
  - investment advisory fees, if these are not paid by the manager out of its fee;
  - trustee/custodian fee;
  - auditors' fees;
  - legal fees; and
  - printing and publishing fees in connection with the fund's marketing literature, annual report and accounts, and publication of its NAVs in relevant periodicals.

5.4 Recap: the basis of NAV-based pricing

Before examining the nature of the adjustments which we will need to make, first refer back to Section 2.1 of Chapter 2, where we made sure that we understood the basic principles of an NAV-based price calculation using the example of the SJT Fund. You may wish to revise this, before we proceed to the next level of complexity.

We will now look at two potential pricing models: the first in respect of a *dual priced fund* (a model which is becoming less common but which is still an option in many markets, including the United Kingdom, Isle of Man, Channel Islands and Bermuda). The second model we will look at will be that for a *single priced fund*.

5.5 Typical dual pricing models

The example which follows is typical in those jurisdictions whose regulations are based on the United Kingdom's formerly mandatory model for United Kingdom Authorized Unit Trusts. This regime has since been overhauled in the UK itself, with single pricing now optional for all authorised funds and likely to become mandatory in the near future: but its legacy lives on in a variety of jurisdictions.

Using the example of a unit trust as a model, the formula is generally as follows. The manager will in effect generate two unit prices for his fund. The bid price of the fund (that is, the price at which the manager will buy back units from investors) will be calculated using the format set out in the column on the left-hand side of the page, and the offer price (that is, the price at which investors can buy units from the manager) using the column on the right.

CURRENCY
(say) £ Sterling

Price calculated in pence per unit

<u>Bid Basis</u>	<u>Offer Basis</u>
Total Investments at Bid Value	Total Investments at Offer Value
divide by units in issue	**divide** by units in issue
= Total of investments at bid value per share	= Investments at offer value per share
less Brokerage per units in issue	**plus** Brokerage and (if applicable) Stamp duty
= Net figure per units in issue	= Net figure
plus Accrued income per units in issue **plus** Cash per units in issue	**plus** Income **plus** Cash
= Cancellation price per unit	= Creation price per unit
	plus Manager's initial charge per unit
= Unrounded bid price	= Unrounded offer price
less Rounding	**plus** Rounding
= Bid price	= Offer price

To follow the above, you will need to bear in mind the following points:

1. Whatever the base currency of the valuation, it is important to ascertain whether the price is quoted in (for Sterling-based funds) pounds or pence, and the same for other currencies. For example a United States Dollar-based fund may quote its prices in cents not dollars, and the manager calculating the NAV per unit will need to base his calculations on this basis.
2. In many jurisdictions, including the United Kingdom at the time of the formulation of this model, the convention is that the manager should calculate every line of the valuation in terms of its value per unit/share (instead of generating a total NAV for the fund and then dividing it by the number of shares in issue). So, for example, at the line which deals with accrued income, if the fund's total accrued income was £3 000 000 and the number of units in issue was 2 000 we would arrive at a figure of £1 500 of accrued income per unit. However, if the format required that we work in pence per unit and not pounds, we would then multiply this by 100 to get a figure of 150 000p per unit. It is this figure of 150 000 which would go in on that line. If this appears complex, do not panic: we will look at a practical example in a moment!
3. Stamp duty is a tax payable in the United Kingdom on the purchase of certain investments only (e.g. UK equities). For this reason it will not be applicable to all types of investment; it is not, for example, applicable to United Kingdom funds investing in UK government stocks ('gilts').
4. Further, where stamp duty does apply, because it is a purchase tax it only affects the **offer** price being calculated.
5. The initial charge is a levy paid by investors buying into the fund, not on those exiting it. Thus it is only applicable when calculating the offer price. Of course, if a fund manager applied exit charges instead of initial charges, then a different calculation would have to be applied.
6. For regulated funds, the regulator will generally prescribe the manner and number of decimal places to which roundings must be effected. It is clearly more accurate to use a higher number of decimal places for the first few lines of the calculation, rounding down to a lower number of decimal places only at the final stages of establishing the bid/offer price.
   - It is common for regulators to require the manager to work to four decimal places in the initial stages (see example below).
   - The final Bid and Offer prices are generally rounded to two decimal places, down and up respectively. The fact that the bid price is rounded down and the offer price is rounded up has the effect of slightly widening the bid–offer spread (see Section 5.7 below), and these roundings go to the benefit of the manager.
   - The final stage of the process is to calculate the actual rounding amount.

5.6 Simple practical example of a dual pricing valuation

Taking the following set of data, we will use the above model to generate bid and offer prices for a dual priced fund:

Bid value of investments	£33.5 million (this is the **total value** of the portfolio, and of course the fund may contain many lines of stock)
Offer value of investments	£34.2 million
Brokerage charge	0.25% (i.e., the manager estimates that a stockbroker would charge him an average of ¼ of a per cent in commission if he were either buying or selling the stock)
Stamp duty	0.5% (i.e. we are assuming that UK stamp duty is levied at ½ per cent on purchases, and that all the holdings in the portfolio are of a type that will attract it)
Accrued income	£1 140 000 in total
Initial charge	6.5% (i.e. the manager levies 6.5% of the price at which units are 'created')
Units in issue	18 million

The calculation would look like this:

	Pence	
	Bid	**Offer**
Investments	186.1111	190.0000
Brokerage	(0.4653)	0.4750
Stamp duty		0.9500
	185.6458	191.4250
Accrued Income	6.3333	6.3333
Cancellation/Creation prices	191.9791	197.7583
Initial Charge *(i.e. 197.7583 × 6.5%)*		12.8543
Unrounded bid/offer prices	191.9791	210.6126
Rounding	(0.0091)	0.0074
Bid/Offer prices	**191.97**	**210.62**

5.7 Dual priced funds and 'spreads'

The 'spread' of a fund's price is the difference between its bid and offer prices, usually expressed as a percentage of the bid price.

Bid–offer spreads vary from fund to fund but there are industry norms. Many equity-based funds will operate on a bid/offer spread of around 5–6 per cent, although the figure can be as high as 10 per cent or more for funds investing in exotica, reflecting the high market spreads which apply to such investments. Similarly, the spread on a fund invested in very liquid investments, with low dealing costs on its underlying assets (e.g. a gilt fund, or money market fund investing in such assets as treasury bills) may have a much lower bid–offer spread.

From our calculations above, we can see that the elements that have made up our spread are (in this case):

- the spread on the bid/offer price of the underlying investment portfolio;
- any brokerage on the holdings;
- stamp duty, if applicable;
- the manager's initial charge; and
- roundings.

In the above example, the spread would be:

$$(210.62 - 191.97)/191.97 \times 100$$

$$= 9.71\%$$

5.8 Calculating yields

This is a subject we will come back to in Chapter 9 when we look at income distributions. However, it is convenient to touch on it here, since we have just created a live example of a fund.

Investors who are seeking high levels of income (or a high total return) will generally wish to compare the income yield of one fund with another, or with that of bank deposits or the market as a whole. The 'yield' of a fund is the level of income it distributes, expressed as a percentage of the **offer** price. Using the example above, and assuming that the accrued income of 6.333 pence per unit is the sum total of what the fund will distribute in that year, the yield would be:

$$6.333/210.62 \times 100$$

$$= 3.00\%$$

This is the **Current yield.** It is based upon the income generated by the portfolio during the last 12 months. It is generally used for bond and income funds.

In some cases, it is more meaningful to consider a fund's **Historic Yield,** which is based upon previous distribution payments. This means that the calculation is weakened by the fact that it compares a historic distribution (which may not be repeated this year) against a current price: but its strength is that it is based on actual figures, not a projection which may or may not be achieved. It is generally preferred for equity and growth funds.

5.9 Adjustments to the spread on dual priced funds: pricing on a 'Bid' or an 'Offer' basis

As you can see from the model above, the formula for calculating a retail dual priced fund's prices will take into account the manager's initial charge, the market bid and offer prices of the underlying securities, and the dealing costs of those securities – including stamp duty if this is applicable.

Having calculated these prices, the manager is then generally at liberty to set his actual bid and offer prices anywhere between the highest possible buying price (i.e. the 'creation price' calculated in the course of the above valuation, plus the initial charge), and the cancellation price.

Keeping the spread to the maximum permissible – that is, using the bid and offer prices generated above – is in theory profitable for the manager since any difference between the two prices, less his dealing costs, will be for him to retain. However, keeping the 'spread' wide is bad news from a marketing perspective. This is because the wider the spread, the more a fund will have to perform before investors have even made up their entry costs, let alone begun to make money. Investors are increasingly aware of these issues and many will compare the bid–offer spreads of similar funds before investing, so as to determine which is the more cost-effective.

Consequently, managers frequently choose to set the actual bid and offer prices somewhere within the maximum spread. This keeps the fund competitive from a cost perspective, and helps its performance figures on an offer-to-bid price basis. Thus, most of the time the manager will set a bid, or 'selling' price – the price at which he will buy units back from investors – at a slightly higher level than the cancellation price: he may not set it any lower. The opposite is true for the buy price – he may set it at a price slightly below the sum of the creation price plus the initial charge.

So, using our model above, on the particular day in question the manager knows that:

- he can set the bid price as low as (but no lower than) the rounded cancellation price of 191.97 pence per unit; and
- he can set the offer price as high as (but no higher than) the creation price plus the initial charge; 210.6126 pence per unit.

In general, the manager will set the bid price so as to be greater than the cancellation price and the offer price to be lower than the (and therefore the bid–offer spread to be narrower than the maximum permissible of 191.97–210.62 in the example above). He may, for example, set the dealing prices at 193–208.62 pence; that is, a significantly lower spread, albeit one which he should have ensured is likely to cover any dealing costs.

However, whilst managers *may* (and usually do) set their bid and offer prices somewhere in between the maximum and minimum levels calculated by reference to the model at Sections 5.5 and 5.6, their pricing model can 'swing' between the maximum and minimum prescribed. This may happen if:

- a manager experiences a prolonged period when more unitholders are selling than buying (i.e. net redemptions); or
- the converse; or
- in connection with 'large deals'.

The definition of a large deal may be prescribed by the regulator (e.g. any deal over £15 000) or may be specified in the fund's offering documents.

In such cases, the manager may (e.g. where he is experiencing net subscriptions) move his pricing basis to an 'offer basis', that is, the offer price will be set at the maximum permissible under the model we have used above. Similarly, if he experiences net redemptions he may price on a 'bid basis', that is, set the bid price at the cancellation price during a given dealing period.

It is worth noting that a manager who is advised that there is (for example) net demand for new shares would not only consider moving his pricing policy to an offer basis: he should also advise the investment adviser/manager, so that it can consider what investment transactions should be undertaken to place the new cash coming into the portfolio.

5.10 Typical offshore pricing models

Single pricing has been common for many years in mainland Europe and many of the offshore centres. Some locations which have traditionally used dual pricing models have in recent years introduced single pricing regimes in tandem, or indeed are moving to replacing their dual pricing regimes with mandatory single pricing. The rationale is that many in the industry believe that single pricing improves transparency by providing investors with a simpler pricing structure. This is not a universal view by any means, and there are also many who believe that investors have no more difficulty in understanding a fund with a buy price and a sell price, than they do with a fund which has a single price, which is then adjusted by a percentage on purchase or sale.

For the purposes of this section, we will concentrate on the typical offshore single pricing model – that is, taking into account the level of flexibility typically permitted in such jurisdictions.

In essence, the manager of a single priced fund will calculate a single share price calculated on (say) the mid-market prices of the underlying assets, or whatever other pricing basis is specified in the fund's constitutional and offering documents. Having used this as the basis for generating an NAV for the fund as a whole, he will then use this to generate an NAV per share and add any appropriate buying/selling charges for the shares to arrive at the subscription or redemption price. Commonly, managers will sell at NAV plus 3 per cent commission. Less commonly, they may also (or instead) apply an exit or redemption charge, for example, redeeming shares at the NAV less (say) 1 per cent.

The model we will look at below is one that might be used by an offshore fund in a jurisdiction allowing for a certain amount of flexibility in terms of the means of pricing. Essentially, in these circumstances the regulatory approach is generally that the manager's approach must be:

- reasonable;
- consistently applied; and
- disclosed in the offering documents.

The format is also generally simpler, in that a total NAV is generally calculated for the fund as a whole, with the end result *then* being divided by the number of shares in issue: but again this is not mandatory and fund managers can generally adopt the format they wish provided they are consistent and are complying with the fund's constitutional and offering documents.

We will start, again, win a dual – priced model.

CURRENCY

Bid Basis	**Offer Basis**
Investments at Bid/Mid-value (depending on provisions in offering docs)	Investments at Offer/Mid-value
less dealing Costs/Investment Charge	**plus** dealing Costs/Investment Charge
= Net figure	= Net figure
plus Other Assets **less** Other Liabilities **plus** Accrued Income **less** Management shares (Founders, nominal shares) **less** Dividend payable	**plus** Other Assets **less** Other Liabilities **plus** Accrued Income **less** Management shares (Founders, nominal shares) **less** Dividend payable
= NAV of Fund (Bid) divide by Shares In Issue	= NAV of Fund (Offer) divide by Shares In Issue
= NAV per share (Bid)	= NAV per share (Offer) **plus** Initial Charge
= Unrounded bid price **less** Rounding	= Unrounded offer price **plus** Rounding
= Bid price	= Offer price

Again, to follow the above you may need to bear in mind the following points:

1. The format above could be easily adapted to single pricing. Essentially, mid-prices would be used for the investment portfolio and the dealing costs would not be added/deducted from the value of the portfolio to widen the spread. Instead, they would be reflected in the addition of a greater initial charge and possibly the deduction of an exit/redemption charge for sales, once the single price had been calculated. The application of a dilution levy also addresses these dealing costs (see Section 5.12). The rest of the valuation would look much the same, but we would have a single column of figures instead of two columns generating two prices.
2. The convention for international funds is to work with the entire value of the fund (not 'per unit') until its entire NAV has been calculated. Until the 'divide by shares in issue line', you would therefore state the figures in whole numbers of currency.
3. The fund's constitutional and offering documents will dictate whether bid and offer prices should be used for the underlying investments, or mid-prices on both 'sides'. In some cases, regulations will prescribe which may be chosen, but generally there

is more flexibility offshore. In any event the manager must be consistent. Since different funds will use different conventions, third-party administrators who provide valuation services to many funds must have systems which can accommodate different pricing bases.

4. Management shares are non-participating shares, which is to say that they do not share in the assets or returns from the investment portfolio. They are held by the manager/sponsor and give it control over certain matters by way of voting rights.
5. In the case of international funds, the initial charge is often expressed as a percentage of the offer price, *not* the NAV per share. This results in a slightly higher 'take' for the manager (recall that we looked at this earlier). This is because an initial charge of (say) 5 per cent of the 'gross' bid price (i.e. bid NAV plus initial charge) is greater than 5 per cent of the NAV before it has been grossed up by the initial charge. So to calculate the Initial Charge value, the formula might be:

$$\text{NAV per share (Offer)} \times \text{Initial Charge per cent}/(100 - \text{Initial Charge}) \times 100$$

6. The convention on roundings may differ: in the following example, we will assume workings to six decimal places, then bid and offer prices to two places. Sponsors may wish to ascertain from their prospective third-party administrators what their systems will accommodate.

5.11 Simple practical example of an offshore fund

Taking the following set of data, we will use the above model to generate bid and offer prices for a single priced fund:

Investment portfolio at bid value:	US$38 million
Investment portfolio at offer value:	US$39 million
Investment charge (i.e. stock-brokerage and associated costs):	± 1%
Management shares:	US$3500
Dividends accrued but not yet received:	US$380 000
Accrued expenses not yet paid:	US$150 000
Dividend declared but not yet paid by the fund to investors:	US$1 750 000
Cash in bank:	US$800 000
Other Debtors/Receivables:	US$1 800 000
Shares in issue:	20 million
Initial charge:	**5% of offer price**
Roundings:	to nearest cent, in Manager's favour.

Our valuations team should come up with a valuation looking something like this:

	Currency	
	US Dollars	
	Bid	**Offer**
Portfolio	38 000 000	39 000 000
Investment charge	(380 000)	390 000
	37 620 000	39,390,000
Management shares	(3 500)	(3 500)
Dividends receivable	380 000	380 000
Accrued expenses	(150 000)	(150 000)
Dividend payable	(1 750 000)	(1 750 000)
Cash	800 000	800 000
Other debtors	1 800 000	1 800 000
NAV of Fund	38 696 500	40 466 500
NAV per share	1.934825	2.023325
Initial charge		0.106491
Unrounded bid/offer prices	1.934825	2.129816
Rounding	(0.004825)	0.000184
Bid/Offer prices	US$ 1.93	US$ 2.13

5.12 Adjustments to single prices: dilution levy (also known as 'Dealing Charge')

The 'dilution levy' can be seen as the single pricing equivalent of the dual priced swing to a bid or offer basis which we looked at in Section 5.7 above: that is, it is the means by which the manager can adjust pricing to take account of the dealing costs on the underlying portfolio, where there are large net investments/redemptions, so that existing investors do not bear the costs of accommodating these new or exiting investors.

The dilution levy might be better known as an 'anti-dilution levy'; it represents an amount that the operator (manager) of an OEIC *may* decide to charge on the purchase or disposal of shares, etc. and is designed to ensure that existing investors do not bear the costs associated with placing/disinvesting money as a result of inflows/outflows resulting from other investors subscribing for or redeeming shares.

The manager will assess the costs of, or a representation/approximation of the costs of, investing newly subscribed money or disinvesting because of redemptions and will estimate what, if any, levy is applicable. He is not obliged to apply a dilution levy, but his policy must be stated in the fund's offering documents. The manager must then be consistent in the application of the charge; that is, he may decide that he is going to apply a dilution levy to all deals, or only to those which are over a certain value (e.g. 3 per cent of the value of the fund) or where the fund is experiencing large levels of subscriptions or redemptions relative to its size. However a levy, if one is to be applied, must be applied to all deals falling within the stated relevant criteria on each dealing day.

The amount is added to the purchase costs, or deducted from the proceeds of sale, of the open-ended investment company (OEIC) shares or unit trust units and is paid into the fund to reimburse it for expected dealing costs. The levy does not go to the operator (i.e. manager or – in the United Kingdom – Authorized Corporate Director) but into the fund, and it is shown on the contract note separately. Typical levies are of the order of 0.2 per cent (i.e. they are quite small).

They are unusual outside the United Kingdom and countries whose regime has been influenced by the United Kingdom; some managers, particularly those who have operated single pricing in overseas markets for some time, do not believe that the dilution phenomenon is significant. Many other regions ignore the issue and it is seen merely as a factor in the fund's overall performance.

5.13 Valuation checks

Managers or the administrators to whom they delegate the task of calculating NAVs need to have in place robust systems for double-checking and validating the prices they have generated. Sponsors should enquire into these processes as incorrect valuations (whilst they may be for the manager/administrator to remedy) still reflect poorly on the sponsor and fund.

The valuations department should, at the least:

- Check the percentage price movement of the fund between the last valuation point and the current one, against the percentage movement in a relevant index over the same period. Divergences may not automatically indicate an error (e.g. they may result from high levels of liquidity in the portfolio or a high tracking error), but they should put the team on enquiry. The divergence may be due to a simple outperformance or underperformance, but on the other hand it could indicate that (for example) a whole line of stock has been missed off. For example, a fund investing predominantly into United Kingdom large capitalization listed equities might be benchmarked for its movements against the FTSE 100 Index. The valuations supervisor should investigate any meaningful divergence, for example, if the FTSE were to have fallen by 2 per cent but the fund had risen by 3 per cent in the same period.
- Research any individual security price movements which are outside given tolerances (e.g., 5 per cent in either direction in any one day). Different tolerances may be appropriate for different types of assets. Again there may be a good reason for any marked movement – such as a stock having gone 'ex-dividend', a bond's credit rating being downgraded or a company becoming a takeover target. In any event, the cause should be investigated in case the movement has arisen from a simple error.
- Reconcile each cash account and agree the balances with the trustee/custodian/bank.
- Ensure forex calculations have been correctly carried out.
- Reconcile portfolio holdings to trustee/custodian records, and to broker records if applicable.
- Carry out reconciliations to ensure all investment trades are reflected in the portfolio and cash records.

- Similarly, ensure creations/liquidations are correctly reflected in both the cash balances held and the number of shares in issue.
- Ensure all dividend and interest accruals are correctly accounted for (i.e. shown as debtors on the balance sheet).
- Ensure all fee and expenses accruals are correctly accounted for.
- Ensure any dividend or distribution declared by the fund itself has been correctly accounted for (i.e. the declared distribution should be shown as a liability on the balance sheet).
- Ensure any taxation accruals have been correctly accounted for.

The following should *not* affect the price per share/unit of an open-ended fund significantly:

- Net creation or liquidation of units, since this is compensated for by the inflow or outflow of cash from the fund (see Section 2.1 of Chapter 2 under the example of the ABC Fund).
- The purchase/sale of investments, which again will be compensated for by cash movements. These should only affect the valuation if their volume is such that the dealing costs impact on the fund, in which case mechanisms such as the dealing charge (recap Section 5.12 above) may be brought into play.
- Investments within the portfolio going 'ex dividend', since the fall in the price of the investment should be approximately compensated for by an equivalent increase in debtors (the dividend due).
- Receipts of income or payment of expenses, since these cash movements will generally be compensated for by movements in accrued debtors or creditors.

The manager is responsible for rectifying errors in valuations which result in a mis-pricing of the fund. This will entail:

- re-working the valuation(s);
- re-calculating the dealing prices;
- establishing whether any investors, or indeed the fund itself, have suffered loss as a result; and
- paying compensation where applicable.

5.14 Consequences of over- and under-pricing

Where the manager has mis-priced the fund and the mis-pricing has resulted in too high a NAV per share/unit:

- Buyers of shares/units will have paid more than they ought, and should be reimbursed.
- Sellers of shares/units will have received too much in redemption proceeds. The manager may attempt to recover the amount overpaid, but this could cause more reputational damage than it is worth and in any event the manager may be unable to reclaim the money. In any case, he will have to reimburse the fund for any shortfall – either from a recovery from the exiting investors, or out of his own pocket.

Where a valuation error has resulted in shares/units being under-priced:

- Buyers of shares will have paid too little. The manager may ask them to remit a further amount of money (alternatively if the sums are too small or the reputational risk outweighs the benefit of doing this, he may compensate the fund from his own pocket).
- Sellers of shares have been underpaid and the outstanding proceeds should be sent to them.

Errors are administratively burdensome – especially when they are not discovered for some considerable time and a number of dealing days have elapsed on which wrong pricings have resulted. In addition, they create reputational problems for administrator, manager and sponsor alike, and may result in regulatory action or even a suspension of authorization.

In certain jurisdictions, the regulator imposes a materiality test to determine whether compensation need be paid. Typically, this might be such that for regulated schemes, where the error is (say) 0.5 per cent or more, all parties who have lost out must be compensated. Where errors are for less than the prescribed amount, the manager may be permitted to waive compensation provided the trustee agreed that no one will lose a material amount, and provided also that the manager can satisfy the trustee that his procedures are normally sufficiently robust and that the error was an isolated incident.

The importance of accurate valuation and pricing cannot be too highly stressed. Major errors in the valuation process can have catastrophic consequences – and not just for the fund, since it will not be liable for the errors of the parties servicing it. Rather, if the manager or administrator mis-prices a fund, it is that party which may have to pay compensation.

5.15 Forward and historic pricing

As we have already seen, pricing bases can differ depending on applicable regulations; for international funds, these regulations may be quite flexible and the manager may have a choice as to his methodology (which should however be disclosed, and implemented consistently). Funds may also be priced on either a 'forward' or a 'historic' basis.

Forward pricing means that whenever a deal instruction is taken from an investor or prospective investor, the price at which it will be dealt will be determined at the *next* valuation point. In theory this is unappealing to some investors, because the investor is dealing 'blind' – that is, he does not know the actual price at which his deal will be placed, until after the event. Many publications, such as the Managed Funds pages of the *Financial Times*, carry an indication of the basis used for each fund and the actual valuation point. Thus, for example, a fund shown as dealing 'forward' with a 12-noon valuation point would be dealt as follows:

- an investor telephoning at 10 a.m. will receive the price calculated that day;
- an investor telephoning at 2.30 p.m. will receive the price calculated at 12 o'clock the **next** day.

Historic pricing means that the managers will normally deal at prices determined at the last valuation point. The principal perceived benefit is that investors know what price they are dealing at. In many jurisdictions, however, the regulations are such that managers who normally deal on an historic basis are required to – or may choose to – deal on a forward basis in specified circumstances. The circumstances in which a manager must deal forward are generally:

- where he believes that the fund value has moved (up or down) by more than a specified amount – commonly set at 2 per cent by regulation; and
- where the investor specifically requests that his transaction be dealt at a forward price.

The managers *may* (not must) choose to deal on a forward basis on 'large deals'. The manager may define what this level is to be by way of the scheme particulars/prospectus – for example, by specifying a figure of £15 000.

5.16 Valuation patterns for funds with income and accumulation units/shares

Certain funds offer two classes of unit/share for investments in the same fund portfolio (Figure 5.1). **Income units/shares** are intended to provide investors with regular income distributions, whilst **accumulation (capital) or 'rollup' units/shares** retain the income, rolling it up into the capital value of the shares.

Since one class of unit/share is distributing its income and the other is not, the prices of the two classes will diverge over time.

Holders of distribution units/shares will see the value of their shares/units rise less strongly (or fall more quickly!) than holders of rollup units/shares. However, they should not be disappointed, since they have been compensated for this apparent underperformance by way of regular income receipts.

Whilst the operation of two share classes of this type does create an administration burden, since the shares have different prices (and will also have to have separate

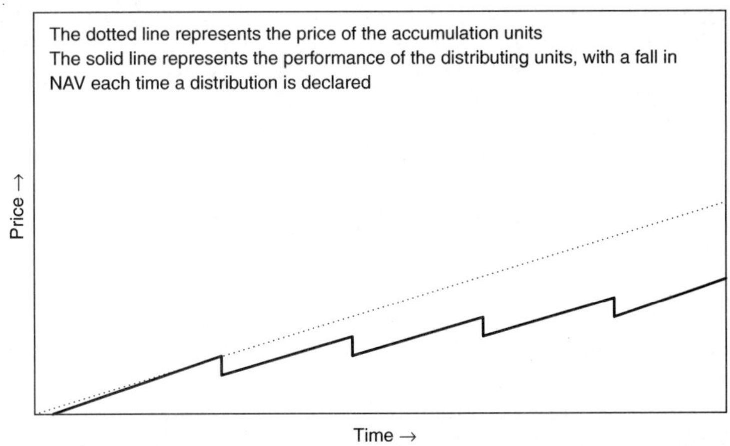

Figure 5.1 Accumulations units versus income units.

registers maintained), it does improve the marketability of the fund by increasing its appeal to a wider investor base.

5.17 Pricing of closed-ended funds (e.g. investment trusts)

You should recall from Chapter 1 that there are a number of key distinctions between closed- and open-ended vehicles. In particular, closed-ended funds:

- have a fixed number of shares in issue;
- generally have their shares listed on a stock-market and are bought and sold by investors through a broker or by some other private matching arrangement;
- are priced in accordance with **supply and demand**;
- this price could therefore at any point be at a premium (greater than) or a discount to (less than) their NAV. It could also be more volatile than would be the case for an open-ended fund.
- there are also fewer investment restrictions on a closed-ended fund than there are on a regulated open-ended fund restrictions; in particular, closed-ended funds may be 'geared' (i.e. they may borrow so as to increase their exposure to the markets), and they may be heavily exposed to unquoted stocks, etc.

5.18 Publication of pricing data

It is generally in the interests of fund managers to ensure that their fund prices are publicly available. Not only does this raise the profile of the fund; investors also like the comfort of the transparency and visibility afforded by an easy source of pricing information. It is generally the fund manager's job to ensure that correct pricing data is communicated to the organizations who publish it, although this may be delegated to a third-party administrator.

Organizations publishing such information include the *Financial Times Fund Services* pages, Bloomberg, Micropal Standard and Poors, and others. The information may include:

- the fund's name;
- its valuation point (i.e. the time of day at which the valuation is generated – for example, 12 noon);
- whether the valuation is 'forward' or 'historic';
- for regulated funds, the manager's address and phone number;
- the initial charge, if any, expressed as a percentage;
- any additional notes;
- the latest selling price;
- the latest buying price;
- the change since the previous valuation point (+ or −); and
- the fund's gross yield.

For unregulated funds, which may suffer from limitations on how they can be promoted, some publications limit their information to:

- the fund's name only, but not its contact address;
- its latest selling price;
- its latest buying price;
- movement (+ or −);
- yield.

For quoted investment trusts (i.e. closed-ended companies), publications tend to list:

- the fund's name;
- any applicable notes (e.g. whether it has been suspended);
- its latest close of business prices;
- its price high/low for the year;
- its current yield;
- its NAV per share; and
- the discount or premium at which it is trading.

Many such organizations charge to publish fund prices, and the costs of this are often borne by the fund itself.

6 Documentation

6.1 Introduction

A large number of documents are involved in the *establishment* of a fund, and thereafter in its *ongoing operation*. Some deal with the *constitution* of the fund (i.e. how it is set up and brought into being), and set out how it may operate. Others deal with *communications between those involved in running the fund and its investors.*

Constitutional documents include such items as:

- the trust deed (if the fund is established as a unit trust); and
- the Memorandum and Articles (M&As) of Association (if it is a company).

Operating documents which will be required from the outset include:

- operating agreements, for example, between the trustee and the manager (for a unit trust), or the fund and the manager (for a company); and between the company and custodian (for a company). In addition agreements may be needed with any investment manager, investment adviser, and/or third-party administrator. Collectively these are often known as the 'material agreements';
- regulatory authorizations and license;
- Scheme Particulars/Prospectus (collectively known as the 'offering documents').

On an ongoing basis, the following will also be required so as to facilitate dealings with investors or prospective investors:

- in some jurisdictions, a 'key features' document (essentially a shortened form of the offering documents);
- an application and investor registration form;
- contract notes;
- in some jurisdictions, cancellation forms;
- for some funds, share/unit certificates;
- form of renunciation;
- Report and Accounts;
- dividend vouchers and warrants;
- statements of investor's account;

- fund updates and market information;
- in some cases, literature relating to associated offerings such as management services, nominee holding facilities, related funds offerings and the like.

We will look at the main ones in more detail.

6.2 Trust Deed (unit trusts only)

A unit trust is set up or constituted by a trust deed, which is generally an arrangement between the Trustee and the Manager of a Fund (but see Section 6.3 below). Many of the detailed rules as to what items *must*, and what other items *may (and may not)* be in the trust deed are, for regulated funds, prescribed by way of regulations. There is generally little variation in the prescriptions from one jurisdiction to another, and typical requirements are as follows.

Matters which must be included in the Trust Deed

- *The fund's name.* This should be consistent with the fund's regulatory status (see below), and with any restrictions on its economic or geographic focus. As an extreme example, it would be inconsistent, and therefore unacceptable, to name a fund 'The Allegra UK Bond Fund', when the investment objectives restrict the fund to investing directly in Japanese Smaller Companies.
- *The regulatory category to which the fund belongs.* In the United Kingdom, this would mean the scheme's categorization according to the Collective Investment Scheme (CIS) Regulations, which you should remember is used for the basis of a regime of investment restrictions. The CIS Regulations cover the following different categories of scheme:
  - Securities funds
  - Money market funds
  - Futures and options funds
  - Geared futures and options funds
  - Property fund
  - Warrant fund
  - Feeder fund
  - Funds of funds.
- *The applicable governing law.* A statement that the deed is made under the law of a particular country, for example, England and Wales, Cayman, the Isle of Man. This is important since it is the governing law which will be used for purposes of interpretation, should there be any disputes over how a particular matter is to be dealt with. The deed may also deal with the *jurisdiction* which will be used in the event that a dispute goes to court. This may be different from the governing law (although this would be very rare): it may also be stated to be *exclusive*, in which case all parties submit to the jurisdiction of the courts in the named jurisdiction alone, or *non-exclusive*, in which case and subject to agreement matters may be heard in the courts of other countries.

- A statement that the deed is binding. The deed should generally contain a statement to the effect that it is binding on each unitholder as if he had been party to it (despite the fact that individual unitholders will not actually sign the deed itself), and that the deed requires both manager and trustee to act in accordance with its terms.
- *The base currency of the fund.* It is important that investors appreciate the currency in which returns are to be generated, since positive returns in (say) US dollars may be turned into an effective loss for an investor whose spending needs are in (say) sterling if the dollar falls against the pound. The investment objective of an international fund should therefore also include reference to the currency in terms of which that objective is to be met. Further, there should be a statement in connection with currency *risk*. In addition to any investment risks a fund may run, it will also be exposed to currency risk if its base currency is different from the currency in which its investments are denominated – unless the exposure is 'hedged' (i.e. unless transactions are undertaken to neutralize the effect of any adverse currency fluctuations).
- *Declaration of trust.* The trust deed should include a statement that, subject to any applicable regulations, the property of the fund is held by the trustee on trust for its investors, in proportion to the number of units held by each investor.
- *Limitation of unitholder's liability to pay.* The deed should include a statement to the effect that a unitholder is not liable to make any further payment to the fund, after he has paid the purchase price for the units, and that no further liability can be imposed upon him in respect of the units he holds.

Matters which may be included in the trust deed

- *The duration of the scheme.* If it is intended that the trust will terminate after a set period, this should be stated.
- *The manager's initial charge, if any.* The deed may include a statement authorizing the Manager to make an initial charge, and specifying a *maximum figure*, either as a fixed sum or as a percentage of the creation price. From time to time, the manager may vary the initial charge he levies provided it does not rise above this maximum: for example, he may charge less than the maximum for competitive and marketing reasons. Any move to increase the initial charge above this stated maximum would require a variation to the trust deed, which may require investor consents and in some cases regulatory approval.
- *The manager's charge on redemption ('exit charge'), if any.* This allows the manager to deduct a charge on investors' redemption of units, which may be used instead of/in conjunction with an initial charge. Exit charges cannot be imposed on redemption of units which were sold to investors before the charge was introduced, since this would be a variation to the terms on which they agreed to invest: they can therefore only be introduced so as to be effective for new investors, on their eventual disinvestment.
- *The manager's periodic charge ('annual management fee').* The deed will, again, generally refer to the *maximum* charge that may be levied, expressed as a percentage of the fund's net asset value (NAV). It should also refer to the accrual periods, and how the charge is to be paid out of the property of the fund (i.e. whether the charge be deducted from the capital of the fund, or from its income).

- *The managers' charge on switching*. Where the fund is an umbrella fund, the deed may contain a clause dealing with whether the manager is permitted to levy a charge on switches between different sub-funds, and if so what the maximum level of this charge will be. Again this will normally be expressed as a percentage of the NAV of the holding being switched.
- *The level of trustees' fees*. The deed will normally authorize the maximum level of trustees' fees, and set out the manner in which these will be accrued and paid.
- *The fund's investment objective and policy*. The deed should generally deal with any restrictions on the fund's investment and borrowing powers. Whilst regulatory restrictions may apply, and will be over-riding, a fund's deed may further restrict its investment parameters (e.g. by focusing on a particular geographic region or asset class). Where the deed does this, a breach of these terms will normally be regarded as seriously as a breach of the regulatory limitations.
- *The fund's investment powers in connection with 'eligible markets'*. In jurisdictions where an 'eligible markets' regime is operated (see Chapter 3), the deed may state that the fund has the power to invest in any eligible securities market, subject to restrictions from regulation or the trust deed.
- *Whether the trustee may issue different types of unit in the fund*. The trust deed will set out whether different types of unit will be available – for example, income and accumulation units. Income unitholders will be entitled to regular distributions of the fund's distributable income. Accumulation unitholders, on the other hand, will find that the income earned on their units will instead be 'rolled up' in the NAV of the unit.
- *The means of determining the fund's NAV*. The deed will normally prescribe the manner in which the NAV will be calculated; that is, the time of day and frequency at which the valuation point will be set, the basis of valuing underlying assets, and so forth. The deed will also indicate whether and to what extent the manager has any discretion where the value of an underlying asset is difficult to establish.
- *Dealing days*. The deed should set out the days on which investors may subscribe for or redeem funds, that is, daily, weekly etc., and should address national and bank holidays (e.g. if the fund deals on a Monday weekly, and a particular national holiday falls on a Monday, will the fund then deal on the following Tuesday – or will all subscription/redemption requests be held over until the following Monday?).
- *The issue and redemption of units*. The trust deed may deal with provisions governing the issue and redemption of units by the trustee.
- *Suspension of dealings in units*. The deed may set out the conditions in which the fund's manager may suspend dealings in units. This might be permitted, for example, in highly volatile markets, where the market on which assets are dealt are themselves suspended, or where it becomes impossible to obtain a realistic underlying valuation.
- *Distributions*. The deed may deal with the fund's distribution policy, the frequency of any distributions and the procedures to be undergone each time.
- *Annual accounts*. The deed will normally set out the fund's annual financial year-end and accounting date, and address the production of its annual accounts.
- *Audit provisions*. The deed should set out procedures for the appointment, re-election and replacement of the fund's auditors.

- *Winding up*. The deed will normally set out the order of events on the wind-up of the trust, and how its assets will be distributed.
- *Limitations on unitholders*. The deed may provide that the fund is open only to certain types of investor. For example, it is common for non-US funds to exclude US persons from eligibility, so as to avoid contravention of the Securities and Exchange Commission regulations. International funds may also exclude residents of the country where they are constituted, so as to retain certain tax exemptions. Other funds may be open only to sophisticated or high-net worth investors for regulatory reasons, and still others are aimed at very specific categories of investor (e.g. pension funds or charitable organizations).
- *Certification*. The deed may deal with the issue of certificates (or otherwise): it is becoming less common for funds, especially those with an institutional investor base, to issue certificates but some funds offer the choice of certificated and non-certificated units.
- *Other*. The deed will deal with any other enabling provisions or restrictions to which the scheme is to be subject – for example, if the fund were a fund-of-funds it might deal with whether the funds could invest in other funds offered by the same management group.
- *Duties of the trustee*. The deed should set out the trustee's duties and obligations (see Chapter 4).
- *Change to the trustee*. The deed should set out the provisions for any change in trustee. Any such change will normally necessitate a supplementary trust deed, which will require the unitholders' approval by way of extraordinary resolution.
- *Provisions for other changes*. Again, and depending on the nature and materiality of the change, a supplementary trust deed and investor approval may be required. The cases when this might *not* be necessary would include:
  - changes necessitated by an alteration in applicable legislation or regulations;
  - a change to the fund's name;
  - a change to the fund's financial year-end/annual accounting period;
  - voluntary changes to the manager or trustee, where either wishes to retire and be replaced.

6.3 Declaration of trust

In some circumstances the manager may *not* be a party to the trust deed along with the manager. This is usually because of some specific tax planning requirements: for example, in certain countries the fund may be regarded as locally resident for tax purposes if a management company which is itself resident there is a party to the deed. In these cases, the trust may be best established by way of a 'declaration of trust', effected by the trustee alone and to which the manager is not party.

Trustees are generally unenthusiastic about declarations of trust, but some will accommodate them where there is a persuasive commercial argument for doing so. In these cases, they will normally require certain undertakings from the manager or sponsor. This is because a manager who is a party to the trust deed is, in effect, a co-fiduciary in respect of the various operational and other requirements set out in that deed. In the event of some problem which results in investors' claiming for compensation, the manager is liable along with the trustee for any default. Where a trustee is the only signatory to the deed, its liability is correspondingly increased since the manager is not party to the trust deed (which is an enforceable agreement).

The trustee's solution, where it is the sole party to a declaration of trust, is generally:

- to seek certain undertakings from the manager;
- to charge significantly higher fees than might otherwise be the case, in compensation for the increased exposure arising from being the sole fiduciary.

In addition, and so as to limit its obligations – and therefore the fiduciary risk arising out of these obligations – the trustee will generally require the following:

- that the declaration of trust relieves the trustee of certain discretions which a manager would normally, in a two-party deed, otherwise have had. (For example, the trustee will likely require that the appointment of a named manager is one of its express obligations in the deed);
- that the deed provides that the trust will terminate if the manager resigns or is removed and no acceptable substitute can be appointed in its place.

In addition the trustee will require that the manager and/or distributor separately undertake:

- to verify the contents of the offering documentation, indemnifying the trustee in respect of any claims or losses arising from inaccuracies;
- to carry out appropriate anti-money laundering and 'due diligence' checks on prospective investors; and
- to observe all applicable regulations and legislation in terms of distribution in the target market.

Trustees will normally also want to ensure that there are no representations or warranties in any distribution agreement which are binding on them in connection with matters of law which are outside their control (hence, for example, the requirement that the manager/distributor carries out any anti-money laundering verification on investors). Finally, the trustee will normally require that by way of the investment management agreement, the manager assumes responsibility for a range of functions which would normally be visited on it by way of a two-party trust deed. Further, the manager will be required, by way of this agreement, to assume an element of fiduciary responsibility by undertaking to carry out its appointed functions in the best interests of the fund's unitholders.

6.4 Memorandum and Articles of Association (OEICs, not unit trusts)

For those funds constituted as companies (i.e. open-ended investment companies (OEICs) and closed-ended vehicles such as investment trusts), the memorandum and articles (M&As) take the place of the trust deed since they, along with the company's certificate of incorporation, evidence its constitution.

The memorandum of a company is the document which governs how it deals with the outside world: its articles of association, in contrast, govern its internal arrangements – for example, the rights of its shareholders, and the means by which directors may be appointed and retired.

Generally speaking, the matters which will be dealt with in a fund company's M&As are similar to those which we looked at in Section 6.2 above. However, the statement declaring the trust deed to be binding on holders as if they had each been a party to the deed will be missing, and the declaration of trust will not be included. This aside, the M&As will generally deal with all of the following:

- the company's identity (i.e. its name and place of registration and operation);
- information relating to its share capital (i.e. the type of shares to be issued, information relating to share premium and reserve accounts, and details of the voting and other rights attaching to the various share classes);
- details of how shareholders' meetings will be convened, including the means of notification, and amount of notice to be given;
- the duties and powers of the fund company's directors;
- details of certain material contracts (e.g. the management and custodian agreements);
- provisions relating to dealings in shares (e.g. for an OEIC, how shares may be issued and redeemed, including dealing days, suspension of dealing etc.);
- provisions relating to the calculation of the fund's NAV (i.e. the means of valuing underlying assets, and the amount of discretion which the fund's board may have where underlying asset values are difficult to determine);
- details of the fund's investment objectives, and its policy (including any investment restrictions over and above those laid down by regulations);
- details of the fund's annual financial year-end and accounting date, and the production of its annual accounts;
- procedures for the appointment, re-election and replacement of the fund's auditors; and
- winding-up provisions, including distribution of the fund's assets.

In certain jurisdictions, notably the United Kingdom, specific legislation has been introduced to facilitate the establishment of OEICs, which are consequently not operated in that country under the 'traditional' company law. A UK OEIC is termed an 'investment company with variable capital' or ICVC, and its operation is governed by an 'instrument of incorporation' as opposed to M&As. UK ICVCs generally adopt, as a template, a model document put forward by the Institute of Fund Managers (IFM), formerly known as the Association of Unit Trusts and Fund Managers. However, even where the model is used, it is important to ensure that professional advice is taken so that the individual provisions reflect the needs of the specific ICVC – for example:

- the method of calculating the vehicle's NAV;
- its investment objectives and parameters/restrictions; and
- the various share classes, and rights attaching to them.

The UK regulator, the Financial Services Authority, is well acquainted with the IFM Model and so new applicants need generally only highlight any variations from the model, when they submit an application.

6.5 Partnership agreement (funds established as partnerships)

Where a fund is constituted as a partnership, it is the partnership agreement which takes the place of the trust deed/M&As. Similar issues will be dealt with as in these other documents, excepting that the partnership agreement will reflect the differing nature of the arrangement.

The general partner will be appointed in much the same role as the manager of a unit trust or OEIC: whilst the investors as limited partners will have limited liability in connection with the activities of the fund, the general partner is usually required by regulations to have unlimited liability, and will generally also require authorization from the relevant regulator in the same way as the manager of a corporate or trust-based scheme.

6.6 The management agreement

Having looked at the various constitutional documents set out above, we will now move on to some of the various 'material contracts' which will exist between the fund's various service providers. The first we will look at is its management agreement.

Where a fund is established as an OEIC or investment trust, this will generally be executed between the fund itself and its manager. Where it is established as a unit trust it will (since the fund has no legal personality in its own right) be executed by the fund's manager and its trustee. The purpose of the agreement is to set out the manager's powers and duties. These are fairly wide-ranging, covering at least the following matters:

- The manager's obligations in terms of servicing the fund, that is:
  - management of the assets of the fund;
  - calculation of the fund's NAV (including the frequency and basis of the calculations);
  - arranging settlement of investor subscriptions and redemptions;
  - liaison with the fund's trustee/custodian so as to ensure smooth settlement of transactions;
  - where the manager is also the fund's registrar, the obligation to register share/unitholdings. Where the manager sub-delegates this task, the agreement will deal with the manager's obligations and liability in this respect;
  - payment of dividends/distributions, including provisions as to timings;
  - production of reports and accounts, and their distribution to share/unitholders;
  - maintenance of the fund's books of account and records; and
  - where the fund is a unit trust, appointment of the auditor.
- Provisions relating to the manager's resignation (i.e. how much notice must be given and what remuneration will be due in these circumstances).

- Provisions relating to the manager's remuneration:
  - initial charges, if any;
  - exit fees, if any;
  - annual management charges;
  - performance fees, if applicable.
- Provisions relating to other charges and expenses which the fund will pay.

6.7 Other agreements

The other material agreements relating to a fund's operation will include:

- the custodian agreement (if the fund is constituted as a company);
- the investment management/advisory agreement, if one has been appointed;
- the administration agreement, if the manager is not to carry out administration in its own right;
- the registrar's agreement, if this is being sub-delegated by the trustee/manager (as appropriate).

6.8 The offering documents and scheme particulars

Aside from the above, before it can be promoted to its target audience a fund will need to have an offering document.

In the case of a fund constituted as a company this will be the prospectus; in the case of one established as a unit trust or partnership, the information document used will more generally be known as the 'scheme particulars', although scheme particulars may also be prepared in connection with a fund company. In any case the term 'offering documents' may also be used, although technically scheme particulars do not of themselves (and unless any statement is made to the contrary in them) constitute an offer for sale to potential investors; but they may well include an application form by way of which prospective investors can apply for units.

The purpose of the offering documentation is to give a prospective investor all the information which he might reasonably wish to have, so as to be able to make an informed decision as to whether the fund meets his needs.

The manager will be responsible for preparing the offering document, and for maintaining it in an up-to-date condition on an ongoing basis. In the case of a corporate vehicle, the Prospectus document is legally binding on the directors of the fund company itself; shares in the scheme are offered for sale on the basis of the information contained in it.

The prospectus/scheme particulars will contain broadly the same information as a scheme's trust deed/M&As. The difference is that the former documents are the fund's constitutional documents, whilst the latter are mainly for the information of potential investors.

The contents of a fund's prospectus or scheme particulars should include:

- The basic details of the scheme (i.e. its name, the country in which it is registered or domiciled, the legal form by which it is constituted, and its regulatory status).

- Provisions relating to the timing, frequency and notice period for shareholder meetings and other shareholder information (e.g. report and accounts, other periodic reports).
- Details of the key service providers and other parties: manager, administrator, investment adviser/manager, trustee/custodian, directors, auditors, legal adviser etc.
- Details of the fund's investment objective, its investment policy and any restrictions to its investment mandate and (if applicable) any eligible markets provisions.
- Details of any risks involved, with specific warnings for certain types of situation (e.g. highly leveraged portfolios, uncovered derivatives positions and the like).
- The characteristics of the different classes of unit/share in issue (e.g. accumulation/distribution units).
- The manager's initial, periodic and exit charges (as applicable).
- Details of the other charges and expenses which may be borne by the fund.
- Details of the fund's distribution/dividend policy, including the periodicity of distributions if applicable.
- Details as to the issue and redemption of shares/units (i.e. where and how investors may apply, and what the relevant dealing dates and times will be).
- The basis on which shares/units will be valued and priced.
- The procedure for settlement of investor purchases/redemptions, including relevant time scales for receipt of proceeds.
- Any minimum investment levels.
- Where applicable, details of any statutory compensation schemes which may offer investors protection or (in some cases) a statement to the effect that the fund is *not* subject to the protection of such a scheme.
- Where applicable, reference to any statutory ombudsman or other arbitration service to which investors may refer in the event of an unresolved complaint.
- Details of any ancillary services offered by the fund manager – for example, regular savings plans, nominee holding facilities, share exchange schemes, foreign exchange facilities, switching facilities between sister funds and the like.

The document should give investors, prospective investors and their advisers sufficient information to be able to assess the suitability – initial or ongoing – of a scheme to their particular situation – including the risks involved.

Offering documents clearly have to cover a wide range of material: nonetheless, it should all be relevant to the fund to which the document relates.

The offering documents should generally be made available to all prospective investors, without charge. In the case of regulated funds, the manager will not generally be permitted to sell units/shares until the document has been prepared and forwarded to the regulator for approval. Where an investor contacts the manager direct, for example, by telephone or e-mail, the manager should offer to send him a copy of the latest Scheme Particulars/Prospectus. The provisions may be more relaxed where the manager is approached via an intermediary, who should in theory already have taken cognisance of the investor's situation. However, the documents should in any case be available on request and reference should be made to this availability in all advertisements and other literature.

We noted above that the manager will be responsible for the accuracy of the document. This means that it must ensure that, to the best of its knowledge, there are no false or misleading statements included and no omissions of requisite information. Where a manager becomes aware that offering documents are incorrect, it will need to:

- inform investors of the correct state of affairs; and
- issue an amended document as quickly as is possible (withdrawing copies of the faulty document).

Revisions will be needed whenever there are significant changes to the fund or its service providers, and as a consequence most managers review their documentation at least annually.

For UK ICVCs, as with any form of company, the offering document takes the form of a prospectus. An ICVC's prospectus must be made available to prospective investors before they invest, as would be the case for the Scheme Particulars of a unit trust.

6.9 Key features document

In many jurisdictions, managers are permitted to issue a 'key features document', essentially a summary of the most salient features of the scheme. Key features documents are often used as marketing tools to alert potential investors to the availability and nature of a range of funds, but in most jurisdictions the regulations will require that they are then offered the prospectus/scheme particulars if they express an interest in investing.

The intention behind key features documents is to produce material which is more user-friendly than a full-blown prospectus, and which will deal with the issues which are (or should be!) uppermost in investors minds. They are often laid out using a 'frequently asked questions' format – for example:

- How do I invest?
- What documents will I receive?
- What are the key risks of investing in a fund of this nature?

and so on. The point of such documents is really to solve the problem of scheme particulars being so detailed as to put investors off reading them at all: in an attempt to ensure that all possibly salient information is available, regulators and fund managers can end up making their literature impenetrable to all but the most determined of investors. The regulations governing the contents of key features documents vary from jurisdiction to jurisdiction, but normally include the following:

- details of the fund's investment objectives, policy and restrictions;
- minimum investment requirements;
- any relevant risk factors;
- details of the fund's dividend policy;
- details of how to buy/sell shares/units;
- details of the fees and other expenses to paid by the fund;
- details of any charges to be paid by the investor (e.g. initial management charge, annual management fees and exit fees); and
- details of where the investor can get more information.

6.10 The fund's license/authorization

If a fund is to be regulated, it will (as we have seen) need to apply to the relevant regulator(s) for appropriate approvals. It is quite possible that a fund may require authorization in more than one jurisdiction – for example, that in which it is domiciled; that in which it is managed/operated; and that into which it is to be sold. It will usually be the fund manager's job to ensure that the appropriate approvals are applied for and maintained, with the assistance of the fund's legal adviser where necessary.

Of course, as we have already seen, a fund may not be required to apply for authorization; it may simply operate as an unregulated pooling vehicle, intended to satisfy the needs of a small number of investors or indeed a single institutional investor. There is, in most jurisdictions, a requirement that there is no public offering in connection with such a fund. An example would be a UK unregulated unit trust, or an 'Exempt International Scheme' operated from the Isle of Man.

In addition, and whether or not the fund itself is authorized, separate authorizations may be required by those of the fund's service providers who are carrying on regulated/licensable activities. That is, as we saw in Chapter 3, generally:

- the fund manager;
- the investment manager/adviser; and
- the trustee/custodian.

In certain cases a fund manager may be exempted from the need to apply for a license. This may be the case where the manager operates only a single scheme which is not to be offered to the public, or, in some cases, where the manager is a 'managed manager' whose activities are outsourced to a third-party administrator which is itself appropriately authorized. An example of the former would be the manager of a single Isle of Man Exempt International Scheme. An example of the latter would be the manager of one or more Isle of Man Exempt International Schemes, where the manager is itself serviced by a Third-Party Fund Administrator holding a Category 4 license under the Investment Business Act 1991–3 of the Isle of Man.

Where a license is held it must normally be displayed in the holder's place of business, and reference to it must generally be made on the holder's advertising literature and letterheadings.

6.11 Application/registration details form

We are now moving on to look at those forms required for communications and dealings with investors.

The application and registration forms are dealt with together, since in many cases they are combined in the one document (though some providers prefer to keep them separate).

The application form should, if properly designed, when completed by the applicant capture all the information which will be required by the fund's manager or registrar, in order for them to register the holding. It should also, ideally, elicit the information required for investor due diligence purposes (for compliance with anti-money laundering

XYZ FUND LIMITED

The XYZ FUND APPLICATION FORM

I/we acknowledge receipt of the Scheme Particulars of the above fund. I/we confirm that I/we have read the Scheme Particulars and carefully considered the risks outlined therein.

Subscriber's Name :	
Please attach evidence, e.g. certified copy of passport, National Identity card or Drivers' Licence	
Address :	
Please attach evidence, e.g. recent original or certified copy of a bank statement, mortgage statement or utility bill addressed to your home address	
Telephone Number :	
Facsimile :	
Amount Remitted US$:	
Source of funds. *We may require further substantiation.*	
To :	ABC Bank, Anytown, Anywhere Swift: XXXX *[NB this will be the name of the correspondent bank with whom the fund company's accounts in the relevant currency are held]*
For the account :	**XYZ Fund Management Services Limited** **as Manager of the XYZ Fund Limited**
For further credit :	**XYZ Fund Subscriptions - Clients account.** **Account Number: 1234567**
Introduced By: **(Please insert details of any intermediary)**	
Settlement Date :	

Date:____________________ Signature:______________________________

Please return this form to: **XYZ Fund Limited**
Attn: Subscriptions Desk
XYZ Fund Management Services Limited
Address......

Tel. (+12) 3456 7890
Fax. (+12) 3456 7899

Figure 6.1

legislation). Managers of funds operated from jurisdictions subject to the EU Savings Directive (including non-EU countries such as the Isle of Man, BUI and Cayman) may also currently be re-assessing their forms, so as to ensure that they elicit sufficient information to satisfy the relevant residence tests for the purpose of the Directive. In many cases this may require some work, since the due diligence which is satisfactory for anti-money laundering purposes may not be to that used for EU Savings Directive purposes; alignment of the two will be desirable where it is possible, so as to keep administration to a minimum and reduce the hurdles to investment.

An example of the contents of an application form (which has not been adapted for EU Savings Directive purposes) is given in Figure 6.1.

Where a prospective investor applies to subscribe by contacting the manager direct, by letter, telephone, fax or e-mail, and if for some reason no further subscription form is needed, a registration form will still need to be sent to him by following post so that the registrar has details of the account name, the holder's address, and any designation details.

6.12 Contract note

Promptly following the sale or repurchase of shares/units in a fund, the manager should issue the investor with a contract note setting out the details of the transaction. In many jurisdictions the regulator will lay down minimum turnaround times for this.

Contract notes are nowadays of increasing importance as more and more funds move to non-certificated status (see Section 6.14 below). In effect, the contract note is now perceived as the main document acknowledging the investor's subscription or redemption; although in practice his position is protected by the trustee and/or registrar, whose records provide the definitive evidence of who holds what.

6.13 Cancellation forms

In certain jurisdictions, including the United Kingdom and many countries operating similar investor protection regimes, private investors are permitted by law to change their minds about investments they have made, provided they do so within a short period of submitting their application. These rights are called 'cancellation' rights.

Where such regimes are in operation, managers are normally required to send out notices advising new investors of these rights, immediately on investment and along with their contract notes. Investors wishing to take advantage of the facility then complete the form and return it to the manager, within a set period (usually limited to 14 days or so).

The cancellation regime is not intended to protect investors from poor investment timing and/or falls in the markets; only from being sold products which they then realize, on reflection, are not appropriate to their needs or risk profile. For this reason an investor exercising his rights will receive back the sum he originally invested (i.e. with initial charges reimbursed), less any shortfall arising from falls in the NAV of the shares/units.

6.14 Unit/share certificates

Few jurisdictions now impose a legal requirement for funds to issue certificates, although many managers and trustees still do so. The practice can be extremely unwieldy, especially where a fund has institutional investors who hold units *en bloc* but who periodically need to liquidate a small proportion of their holding.

This is because the registrar will, on a partial sale, require the return of the certificate so that a new one for the reduced holding can be issued in its place. However, the receipt of the original certificate, and the issue and return of its replacement, all takes time – during which period further investment activity may have taken place which also necessitates the return of the certificate. In these cases, certificates may serve only to complicate matters, rather than to improve them.

It is in any event the entry on the share/unit register which provides definitive evidence of a holder's title – the certificate is only *prima facie* evidence of title. Where possible, then, trustees and managers are taking the opportunity to 'dematerialize' – to move to non-certificated status. In some cases, this means that a fund has two sets of shares or units in circulation: one set being certificated, and one uncertificated.

Where issued, a certificate should show the following information:

- the full name of the fund in which shares/units are held;
- date of acquisition (and entry into the register);
- the names and addresses of the fund's manager and trustee;
- generally, a reference number identifying the investor (which may provide a link to a number of other certificated holdings in the same fund, or indeed in other funds operated by the same manager);
- the number of units/share represented by the certificate;
- where applicable, the type of units/shares held (i.e. income or accumulation units);
- the investor's full name; and
- some form of authentication of the certificate. This is usually effected by way of the signature of an appropriate functionary of the trustee.

It is rare for a fund to issue bearer certificates, especially since bearer instruments as a whole are unpopular with regulators keen to clamp down on opportunities for money laundering. However, some examples do exist, mostly in connection with Caribbean or continental European funds. These are, in many cases, likely to be 'immobilized' in the near future, as a result of regulations being introduced in many jurisdictions. Immobilization is generally effected by changes to the applicable company law, such that holders will have to register their holdings if they are to exercise any of the rights arising from their holding. Nonetheless, it is worth touching on their operation briefly, for completeness.

As we have noted, *registered* fund certificates contain the details of the registered holder of a particular holding, as reflected in the fund registrar's books. They must consequently be replaced whenever the shares are sold/transferred.

Bearer certificates, on the other hand, do not contain the details of the holder; they simply contain the name of the fund, details of the relevant unit/share class and the number of these units/shares represented by the certificate. Ownership of the holding can therefore be effected simply by passing the certificate to the new owner. Whenever holdings in respect of which a register is maintained change hands, the share register must be amended to reflect the new situation. When bearer certificates change hands there is no entry made in a register of ownership.

Where a fund issuing bearer certificates is also a distributing fund, there is clearly a potential difficulty since the manager does not know who holds units/shares as at any particular record date. Each bearer certificate therefore carries a number of 'coupons', which are attached to it in perforated strips, each with a reference number and date on it.

The investor tears off the relevant coupon on the appropriate date and sends it in to the fund manager with a request to pay him the relevant dividend/distribution. The last coupon on the strip is called a 'talon', and when this is returned the manager will send the investor not only his dividend but also a new strip of coupons. It is clearly very important, when buying bearer shares/units, to ensure that you receive the full set of coupons and talon to which you are entitled and that none are missing.

Because evidence of ownership passes with the certificates, the trustee/custodian will keep any unissued certificates in secure storage.

6.15 Form of renunciation

Before an investor is sent the proceeds of his redemption or sale of shares/units, the manager of an open-ended scheme will require that he completes a form of renunciation. This is a statement that he renounces any interest in, or rights arising from, the holding that he is selling.

Since where a fund is certificated, the manager will also require the return of the investor's certificate before he will cancel the investor's holding, many managers opt to print the renunciation form on the back of the unit/share certificate itself – so that the return of the one necessitates the return of the other.

6.16 Report and accounts/financial statements

In most jurisdictions, it is a regulatory requirement that both an annual, and a semi-annual, set of report and accounts should be produced for any regulated funds. These must then be made available to investors.

Responsibility for the preparation of the report and accounts falls to the manager. The annual report will then be audited, and (in the case of a corporate fund) presented for shareholder approval at the annual general meeting.

The Prospectus/Scheme Particulars will state the time tolerances within which the fund's report and accounts must be sent to holders; in some cases this will be prescribed by regulations. In some cases, and where a fund is subject to dual regulation, the various applicable laws may set out different requirements as to the latest date by when the report and accounts must be sent out: in this case it will be the shortest time-frame which must be adhered to.

Regulations will generally also prescribe the contents and (sometimes) also the format of the financial statements. This will almost invariably require:

- a statement from the trustee/custodian, as to whether the manager has adhered to applicable regulations and to the fund's constitutional documents; and

- a statement from the auditors, who will usually, in addition to commenting on whether the accounts have been properly prepared, also to comment on adherence to specific regulations.

The annual report and accounts is the main tool by which the manager communicates with investors, once the initial application process is over. It enables existing and potential investors, and their advisors, to be updated on the fund's financial position and investment performance, and on any other material changes that may have taken place.

Where funds are marketed internationally, it may be necessary for the manager to produce versions of the report and accounts in different languages. Alternatively, and if it does not make for too unwieldy a document, a single, multi-language document may be produced.

The annual report will invariably be more detailed than any interims which may be produced. It will include the following:

- *Auditor's report*. This forms an integral part of the annual report and, as noted above, may include not only the normal statements as to whether the accounts have in the auditor's opinion been properly prepared and give a true and fair view of the fund's financial position – but also, in many cases, some additional statements in connection with adherence to applicable legislation and regulations (typically those dealing with the treatment of client money and assets). In this regard, the auditor may be seen as exercising some extra supervisory oversight over the fund manager, in the interests of protecting the investors' security.
- *Trustee/custodian's report*. An additional feature is normally the trustee/custodian's report, wherein the trustee/custodian will be required to state whether, in its opinion, the manager has managed the fund during the period in question, in compliance with applicable legislation, regulations, and the fund's constitutional documents. Where a trustee/custodian is unable to confirm this, it will then be required to state what steps it has taken to rectify any shortcomings. In cases of serious breach, the trustee/custodian may have to take action to secure the investors' interests and in any event will report the matter to the relevant regulator.
- *Director's report (OEICs and investment trusts only)*. The directors of the fund company will comment on significant events which have taken place during the reporting period. They may also comment on the outlook for the period ahead.
- *Financial statements*. Preparation of the financial statements is the responsibility of the manager (although this may be delegated to the administrator). In many countries there will be legislation governing the standards which must be applied – e.g. for a UK authorized fund, accounts must be compiled in compliance with applicable 'Statements of Recommended Practice' (or SORPs), the provisions in the trust deed/M&As, and with 'generally accepted accounting principles'. In many offshore jurisdictions, regulators – recognizing the international nature of their funds' client bases – have instead stated that fund accounts may be produced in accordance with any internationally accepted standards, or with the standards of any individual country. The financial statements are usually split into three sections:
  - The balance sheet (also known as the 'statement of net assets', or 'statement of assets and liabilities'). This will set out the fund's total assets, liabilities, capital

and reserves as at the specified accounting date and is a snapshot of its financial status at that point.

- The revenue account (also known as the 'income and distribution statement'). This should set out the fund's income from assets (e.g. bank and bond interest, dividends and distributions received), and how that income has been allocated in paying dividends, tax and expenses.
- The capital account. This accounts for movements in the value of the fund's property, any changes to the assets comprising that property, and items which have been charged to capital. The following subsets of the account are likely to be shown:
  - Current investment portfolio, setting out the investment assets of the fund and detailing the value of all the investments held at the accounting date, together with the nominal amounts held for each line of stock;
  - A statement reconciling movements in the investment portfolio over the period.

- *Investment manager/adviser's report.* This will be prepared by the investment manager/adviser, as appropriate, and should include:
  - Relevant performance figures – for example, the highest and lowest NAVs of the fund's unit/share price over the past 10 years, and its NAV per unit/share for the past 3 years;
  - Comparisons of the above against a relevant benchmark – that is, a comparable market index or fund peer group;
  - Commentary on relevant events in the markets over the reporting period;
  - Generally, a commentary on the investment outlook for the period ahead.
- *Details of significant parties.* The annual report and accounts should detail the names and addresses of the fund's manager, investment manager/adviser, trustee/custodian, registrar, auditor and legal adviser. This enables investors to be updated if any of these parties have changed or moved (since the last time they may have been notified of them may have been when they received the offering documents).
- *Scheme objectives.* The report and accounts should restate the fund's investment objectives.
- *Significant changes.* The report and accounts should set out any other significant changes (which can generally be taken to mean any items which would have been noted in the latest Scheme Particulars or offering documents), which have happened since the issue of the last report.
- *AGMs.* Where the scheme is established as a company, the report and accounts should contain notice of the next AGM.
- *Notes.* The financial statements will generally be supported by notes, giving background information explaining the figures.

The annual report will be used by a variety of parties:

- existing investors, who will use it to stay informed of matters relevant to their investment;
- prospective investors, who will find it of value in deciding whether to proceed with an investment;
- financial advisers, so that they can advise potential and new investors;
- regulators, seeking to maintain an overview of the fund's financial status; and

- statistical analysts and the like, who may use the report to support their analyses of (for example) a fund's total expense ratio as compared to its peers.

The annual report is a substantial document, which can be fairly daunting to the retail investor. However, some managers now produce a second, much shorter document containing only the most salient information in a simple format (bearing a similar relationship to the full report and accounts, as the 'Key Features' document we looked at in Section 6.9 does to the scheme particulars or prospectus). This document may be useful to prospective investors, and typically includes:

- information relating to the fund's record of investment performance;
- a re-statement of its investment objectives, mandate and risk factors;
- a brief commentary on its recent investment highlights;
- a comparison of its performance against a relevant benchmark;
- a statement in connection with its management charges;
- details of any additional relevant services such as a share exchange scheme, or a nominee holding facility;
- information relating to (say) the 10 largest current holdings and the general geographic/industrial spread of the portfolio; and
- a statement that more information is available by way of the full report and accounts.

6.17 Income distribution voucher/warrant

When a fund makes a distribution (unit trusts) or pays a dividend (OEICs, investment trusts) the payment to investors should be accompanied by a voucher. This should set out how the amount paid has been calculated (i.e. the number of units/shares held on the XD date and the sum paid per unit/share), and any tax deductions which have been made. At one time it would have been common for the dividend cheque/warrant itself to be attached to the voucher. Nowadays dividends and distributions are often paid direct into the investor's bank account (often using account details elicited on the original application form) – but the voucher will still be needed by the investor, for the completion of his tax returns.

6.18 Grant of probate

A grant of probate will generally be issued to the executors of a deceased investor's estate. It gives them powers to issue instructions in connection with his assets, including to the manager of a fund in connection with how the fund holding should be dealt with.

Obtaining the grant of probate can be time-consuming and (if the help of a lawyer is required) quite costly, especially where an investor had not made a will in the country of domicile of the fundholding. This can cause difficulties for the beneficiaries of a deceased investor's estate, since the manager will be forced to freeze the holding pending completion of the necessary formalities. There are a number of ways in which these problems can be mitigated, including – potentially – holding the shares in joint names with a provision that of the joint holders, either one may sign. In this case the manager will, on notification of the death of one joint holder, generally simply request sight of the death certificate and then amend the share register accordingly. He will then generally carry on accepting the instructions of the remaining shareholder, in the same way that he would have done beforehand. (This does not mean, however, that there may not be tax and other implications arising from the death of one holder: simply that the necessity to freeze the account, and attendant delays, may be avoided.) Care should be taken, however: the term 'joint account' does not mean the same thing in all countries or to all service providers and in some cases what looks like a joint account is in fact an account in the name of one individual, who has given a delegated power of attorney to another. When the primary signatory dies, his authority to accept the secondary signature may die with him. Managers wishing to allow for joint signatories should ensure that the terms of any such arrangements are explicitly covered in the application form, so as to avoid any confusion.

6.19 Power of attorney

A power of attorney (PoA) is a document by way of which one party authorises another to give instructions with regard to certain assets as if they were the beneficial owner of those assets.

Managers should take care, when in receipt of instructions issued under an power of attorney, to ensure that:

- the PoA is still in force (i.e. that it has not been revoked since it was granted);
- that the instructions are within its scope and that it has been properly drawn up. For example, a PoA may grant powers to an individual to deal with the grantor's local investment assets, but it may not extend to his overseas assets; and
- that the person purporting to act as attorney is indeed who he says he is.

7 The dealing desk

7.1 Communications with existing and prospective investors

Dealing, along with valuations and the pricing of shares/units, forms a substantial part of the fund administration function. For open-ended schemes, units/shares are created by the trustee/fund on the instruction of the manager, who must then pay the trustee/fund for them. Once they have been created, the manager issues them to investors who have applied to buy at a price determined by the manager (the 'buy' or 'offer' price, which will be set using the process we looked at in Chapter 5).

- 'Dealing', in the context of this chapter, means the manager's handling of sales and repurchases of shares/units by investors; and not trading the underlying assets of the fund's portfolio;
- 'Valuation' means calculating the net asset value (NAV) of the fund; and
- 'Pricing' means setting a dealing price (or, for dual priced funds, prices) for the fund's shares or units.

The dealing desk is therefore the division within the manager's organization which handles sales (subscriptions) and re-purchases (redemptions) of shares/units in a fund and a 'deal' is the process of taking and placing an order for the sale or repurchase of shares. The dealing department may, once an investor has been acquired, be his main point of contact with the fund and its operator, aside from periodic written reports.

It is therefore important that this department is staffed by well-trained and courteous individuals, since a happy experience with it may encourage an investor who is selling his holding in one fund to switch to another with the same manager; and conversely, a poor experience may prompt him to switch his investments to another manager who is more competent or helpful. Sponsors considering the services of a third-party administrator may therefore wish to interview the administrator's dealing staff, as well as its senior management, since these individuals may affect investors' perceptions of their offering.

7.2 Placing investor deals

The different terms involved in the buying and selling of shares or units are:

- Creation: the manager buys shares from the fund;
- Liquidation: the manager sells shares back to the fund;
- Sale: the manager sells shares to the investor (subscription); and
- Repurchase: the manager buys shares back from the investor (redemption).

Sales (i.e. sales by the manager to the investor: also known as 'subscriptions'). Depending on a fund's regulatory status (which affects whether and where it can be promoted direct to investors), sales deals may be placed over the telephone, by post sometimes using application forms which have been printed in a shortened format), and sometimes by electronic means (e.g. by e-mail or over the internet). Where they are placed by telephone, dealing lines may be recorded. Remember, there may be a requirement for the investor to be offered the scheme particulars/prospectus.

A deal might be placed either direct by the investor himself, or by an agent such as his financial adviser.

The dealer taking the call or receiving the application form may, depending on the manager/administrator's systems, write the details onto a dealing slip or ticket, or enter them straight into a computer dealing system. It is his job to collect the information needed to complete the deal, some of which will come from the investor and some from other sources – that is, information about the fund itself in which the investor wishes to deal, most likely generated by his colleagues in another department.

To place the deal, the dealer will need to know:

- the name of the fund in which the investor wishes to deal;
- the type of transaction; that is, is the client buying, selling or switching?;
- the price of the shares/units in which he wishes to deal (which will have been generated by the valuations and pricing department);
- the basis on which the fund prices – that is, whether the fund generally deals on a historic or a forward pricing basis, and whether there is any variation in the case of this deal:
  - Historic: the dealing price is based upon the NAV per share/unit which was calculated at the last valuation point;
  - Forward: the dealing price is based upon the NAV to be calculated at the next valuation point;
- the number of units/shares *or* the value (e.g. $5000) being dealt;
- the identity of the client (name, address, and if he is already known to the manager, his account or reference number);
- that appropriate identity and address verification details are already held or are on their way, so as to satisfy any anti-money laundering requirements;
- that the client is eligible to deal, if the fund has any restrictions – for example:
  - Nationality
  - Age
  - Tax status

- the identity of the agent or intermediary introducing the business, if applicable;
- any commission or discount;
- whether the fund is certificated or not;
- the deal reference and time of taking the order.

Repurchases (i.e. purchases by the manager from the investor: also known as 'redemptions'). Much the same information will be required by the dealer, with the focus being altered by the following factors:

- Whereas with a new investment the dealer will be keen to establish who the investor is from an anti-money laundering perspective, the procedures for the proper processing of redemptions may be more focused on preventing fraud.
- Therefore, procedures will include steps to be taken where an investor alleges that he has lost his certificate – for example, completion of a form of indemnity; they should also include signature checks, making reference to the initial application form.
- Care should be taken where an account has joint signatories (is it any one, or both to sign), and where a power of attorney has been granted (is it still valid).
- Many managers decline to pay funds away to a third-party account without an original signature from the investor (as opposed to a faxed instruction).
- Increasingly the focus is also, from an anti-money laundering perspective, on ongoing transaction monitoring and the prevention of terrorist financing. Managers may therefore have procedures in place to identify redemptions which have occurred very soon after the initial investment, and may also run some form of vetting on the recipient of any proceeds of redemptions (e.g. checking against sanctions lists and the like).

Investors can usually give instructions in the same way as for sales, that is, by telephone, post or electronic means, and either directly or via their agent. However, in these circumstances a manager may refuse to pay the proceeds away to anywhere other than the bank account from which the initial investment came, or for which the details were collected on the original application form so as to limit the possibility of making a payment to someone who is not entitled to it.

A redemption request should be accompanied or followed up by a form of renunciation (the document by way of which the investor renounces his title to the shares/units – see Chapter 6). The manager may place his transaction immediately, but should not pay out redemption proceeds until the form, properly completed, has been received. The form is often printed on the back of the original unit/share certificate, if one is issued.

Dealing room procedures should also address the following:

- Procedures to ensure that deals placed by telephone etc. are followed up by confirmation in writing.
- Most managers will decline to accept cash because it is simply too unwieldy and impractical. In any case, if for any reason they do there should be specific checks as to the reason for the cash placement, and whether it carries any indications of money laundering.

- Anti-money laundering procedures which comply with local requirements should be in place and implemented.
- Redemptions should be settled promptly, in accordance with any regulatory requirements or turnaround times set out in the offering documentation.
- Dealers should be made aware of whether sales and redemptions can be settled in currencies other than the base currency of the fund, and if so what procedures for conversions should be followed.
- Procedures should be in place so that large deals receive management authorization. For some funds, deals of over a certain amount may be declined or only accepted in certain circumstances. In any event, large deals should be notified to the fund's investment manager/adviser, so that it can take appropriate action to liquidate underlying assets (to raise the cash to pay the redemption proceeds), or consider how to place incoming cash, so as not to unbalance the portfolio.
- The procedures should set out any minimum investment/disinvestments figure so as to comply with any regulatory requirements (some funds may only be sold to investors placing a certain sum), and to ensure that uneconomic deals are not placed.
- The turnaround times for the issue of contract notes and certificates should be established.
- The dealing room function should carry out periodic reconciliations of the deals placed, against other records (e.g. the fund's unit/share register, its bank accounts).

In addition, dealers should be fully trained in the necessary components of a properly completed application form. In particular, it is important to carry out regular checks to see that subscription forms are properly signed by the applicant or a properly authorized nominee; and dealers need to understand what proper authorization means (so, for example, what constitutes a valid power of attorney). In the case of corporate investors, a copy of the company's authorized signatory lists and in some cases a copy of the relevant resolution may be required. Special care should also be exercised when dealing with intermediaries, such as independent financial advisers. The manager should ensure that the investor has in fact authorized the intermediary or agent to act on his behalf, and should establish the extent of his powers.

Dealers should also appreciate the risk at which they can place the manager if a deal is overlooked or its placement delayed: should an investor place an order to sell in a falling market, for example, and the redemption is held up because of an error or oversight in the dealing room, he may well be entitled to compensation for the consequent difference between the proceeds to which he should have been entitled and those which he actually received. Where a deal is being held because the manager is awaiting cleared funds, or the receipt of further documentation or a written confirmation, this should be explained to the investor at the outset.

Conversely, the manager is also at risk where a subscription deal is placed on the basis of uncleared funds which in the event fails to clear at all (perhaps because the investor's cheque bounces or – as has happened on a number of occasions – because he stops it in light of falling markets). Where a deal has to be unwound because of such circumstances, the manager may find that there is compensation to be paid to the fund as a result of the issue of the new shares/units; or, alternatively, that it is stuck with a holding in the managers' box (see below) which is falling in value, to the manager's detriment. For this reason, dealing rooms should have clearly established procedures regarding deals placed 'on credit' or in advance of cleared funds: the simplest being to decline to deal in such cases!

7.3 Other dealing room activities

A fund dealing room may facilitate transactions other than straightforward sales and re-purchases:

Switching. 'Switching' is the term used where an investor redeems his holding and immediately reinvests the proceeds in another fund with the same management group. The redemption will be effected at the bid price, and the reinvestment at the offer price; however, typically managers will offer a generous discount on the initial charge which would otherwise be applied to the investor's purchase. This is, in effect, a means of encouraging him to retain his investment within the same group rather than moving to another management group altogether.

Withdrawal schemes are a means by which investors can set up regular withdrawals (repurchases) from their fund holdings. For example, an investor might establish an arrangement whereby sufficient shares/units are sold by the manager to pay proceeds of (say) £1000.00 into the investor's bank account each month. Investors need to be aware of the taxation implications of such schemes. In our example, the investor might perceive his monthly receipt as being a regular 'income'; however (and depending on the nature of the fund and his local tax requirements) it may be regarded as made up in whole or in part of capital. Some complexities can arise where the fund is invested predominantly in income-producing assets and the investor lives in a regime which regards capital withdrawals from such funds as a receipt of income.

Initial offer periods. When a fund is first launched, the manager will fix a price at which its units/shares are to be offered to investors. The price is fixed for the period of launch or 'initial offer period', which may be subject to regulatory limits. This initial offer period will be set out in the fund's scheme particulars and/or offer documents. The stated offer price will include the initial charge, if any.

During this period, and whilst new investor subscriptions are being gathered, a manager may choose to create new units/shares on a daily basis; alternatively, he may elect to create all the units/shares at the end of the launch period, subject to the minimum amount of subscription moneys having been received.

The launch of a new fund is generally a time when energy is focused on publicity and promotion, and the manager may offer investors a discount on any initial charge for subscriptions received during this period, so as to improve the chances of meeting any minimum launch sum. Any discount will be met out of the standard initial charge – for example, by reducing it from the standard (say) 5 per cent to (say) 2 per cent.

Unitizations. Certain jurisdictions make specific provision for 'unitizations' in their legislation. A unitization involves the winding-up of one collective investment scheme, and its absorption into another. The assets (investments) of the old scheme are transferred into the new scheme (unit trust or investment trust company). They are more common in the case of closed-ended funds than for open-endeds, and a common example of their use would be in the case of a UK investment trust coming to the end of its defined life. Shareholders in the trust might be offered shares or units in a new fund (either open-ended or closed), which would then and subject to their approval, takes over the assets of the old fund.

Regular Savings Plan/Monthly Investment Plans. These are typical of the more retail-oriented schemes, and provide investors with a means of investing regular amounts (usually monthly) into a fund at a level significantly below the minimum lump sum usually required. Regular investment amounts can be as little as £20.00, although a level fixed as low as this would require that the operator had extremely efficient systems and banking economies to make it profitable. The benefits to investors are generally perceived as being:

- Pound cost (or dollar cost) averaging, which we looked at in Chapter 1. You should recall that investors benefit when the price of the fund falls, since their cash buys more units/shares than when fund prices are high – keeping their average unit/share cost low. In theory, then, regular savings plans have something of a smoothing effect in volatile market conditions.
- Investors can invest regular small amounts as they receive their income, and do not have to postpone the implementation of an investment plan until they have amassed a larger lump sum (something which might, with a financially undisciplined saver, never happen!).
- Flexibility, in that an investor whose circumstances change should simply be able to suspend subscriptions. Whilst there may in the early days be some penalty – a manager might, for example, deduct a penalty where a regular saver cancels his savings within the first three or six months of inception – these are not generally as severe as for other types of product.
- There are generally no extra charges for this service.
- Subject to the investor's subscription being received – invariably by way of standing order or direct debit order – the investment will be made on a fixed date of each month, at the then-applicable offer price.
- Generally, the default arrangements will be that any distributions will be automatically reinvested into the plan.
- Regular savings plans often also allow the investor to switch from one fund to another on attractive terms.

Share exchange schemes. These are arrangements which allow investors to offer their existing portfolio of shares as payment for units/shares in a fund, instead of cash. The investor's shares will, depending on their nature and how well they match the fund's investment objectives, either:

- be sold in the market through a stockbroker, in which case all that is happening is that the manager is arranging the sale on behalf of the investor, and then applying the proceeds of that sale to a purchase of fund units/shares in the usual way; or

- be taken into the portfolio of the fund. This may be done if the investor's shareholding is one which the fund's manager would be happy to hold in the fund portfolio. The manager may be able to buy the shares from the investor at a price which benefits both, since the services of a stockbroker (and his commission) have been avoided and there is no marketmaker to take a bid–offer spread. So, for example, and if regulations permit, the manager may acquire the shares from the investor at the mid-market price – giving the investor better sale proceeds than he would otherwise have received, and at the same time allowing the fund to acquire the portfolio for less than it would normally have paid for it in the market.

Nominee services are commonly provided by fund managers, and allow the investor to have his fund holding registered in the name of a nominee company operated by the fund manager. The fund manager will then be responsible for ensuring that the holdings of its various investors are properly accounted for in the books of its nominee company. So, for example, investor Catherine Turner, investing with ABC Fund Managers Limited, might (instead of having her holding registered in the name 'Catherine Turner'), have it registered in the name of ABC Nominees Limited. ABC Nominees would have many such investors and would be required to reconcile the aggregate holding in its names, as reflected in the registrar's books, with the individual holdings by each investor.

The benefits to the investor are:

- safe custody of all unit/share certificates, avoiding the possibility of loss by the investor and the administrative burden of resolving this;
- confidentiality: since shares are registered in the name of the nominee company, the individuals holders' names do not appear on any share register. This may be important for investors for whom privacy is a concern;
- ease of administration, since the nominee company will collect any dividends/distributions, apply any new holdings arising from distribution reinvestments and deal with any other corporate or similar actions;
- flexibility for joint holders. That is, usually a nominee facility will allow for joint holders to opt for either an 'either one to sign' arrangement, or for the arrangements to be set up such that instructions will be accepted only where all parties have signed.

Nominee arrangements are often offered free of charge to investors with holdings in the manager's stable of funds, as an incentive to invest with that group; they are a relatively simple add-on facility for a manager to offer where it is also the registrar of the fund in question.

Payment of intermediary commissions (also known as brokerage – but not to be confused with the brokerage paid by the fund to stockbrokers, in respect of trading activity on its underlying portfolio). Many funds – particularly those aimed at the retail investor – are structured so as to pay a commission to agents for introducing business. For equity based funds, a commission of up to 3 per cent mighty be paid. This is usually funded from the manager's initial charge, which itself would for a similar fund typically amount to 5 per cent of the sum placed by the investor. An intermediary may choose to waive this commission – perhaps because he is being paid by his client on a fee-for-time-spent basis instead, perhaps because his professional rules prevent him from accepting commissions. Where an introducer waives his commission, the fund manager may (depending on his systems and policy):

- simply treat the waiver as a discount to the investor. So, in our example above, if an intermediary waived his 3 per cent of the 5 per cent, the investor would pay only 2 per cent in initial charges;
- alternatively the 3 per cent may be rebated to the investor, that is, by way of a cheque.

Where there is no intermediary, a manager may retain the entire (say) 5 per cent; alternatively, he may be open to negotiating with larger investors so as to waive a part of that initial fee.

Depending on how flexible the manager and intermediary are, some composite arrangement might also be reached. An example of what might be levied is as follows:

Initial charge on the deal	5 per cent (levied by the manager)
of which:	
Manager retains	(2 per cent)
Intermediary receives	(2 per cent)
Discount to client (agreed by agent)	(1 per cent)

Many managers also pay recurring or 'trail' commission to intermediaries, as an incentive for them to retain business in the funds. This recurring fee is paid from the manager's annual management charge: so, for example, on an annual management charge of 1 per cent, an intermediary might expect to receive trail fees of 0.25 per cent per annum. However, this practice has come under attack in some countries, as consumer groups and regulators have questioned whether the payments are justified where the intermediary gives the investor little or no ongoing financial planning support. Some fund management groups have signalled their intention not to pay recurring commissions unless there is clear evidence that ongoing financial support is being provided to the investor.

7.4 Registration

Units/shares may be registered investments, just like equities, and where this is the case a register of the details of holders must be maintained. For international funds, as we saw in Chapter 4, the manager often acts as registrar; alternatively it may delegate this function to an administration company.

In the case of a unit trust, it is the trustees who are responsible for the registration function; but again the trustee may delegate this to the manager or a third party. The trustees should carry out periodic (usually half-yearly) inspections of the register to ensure compliance with the regulations in the relevant jurisdiction. These include a requirement that the register be kept in legible format at all times, although nowadays this includes maintaining it on computer rather than in paper-based form.

The register should, for each fund, show:

- the name and address of each holder;
- the number of units or shares (including fractions of units/shares where issued) of each type held by each holder;
- the date on which the holder was registered as holding those units/shares; and
- the number of units/shares of each type in issue, and the numbers of the certificates which represent them (if applicable).

The manager and trustee must ensure that the information contained in the register is always complete, accurate and up-to-date. It is the manager's responsibility to obtain registration details for each investor, and to notify the trustee of these, whether for initial registration of the holder or where any alteration is being made to his details.

As we have said earlier, there is nowadays no regulatory obligation to issue certificates, and many management groups do not do so. The process of dispensing with paper certificates is called 'dematerialization'. The entry in the register is the conclusive evidence of title of the holders, not the certificate (which is only '*prima facie* evidence'). Units/shares in funds which do not issue certificates are often referred to as 'non-certificated units' or 'NCUs'.

Where holdings are registered for joint investors, communications from the manager to investors may be sent to the first-named holder on any joint holding only, this being deemed to constitute communication with all the joint holders to that holding.

Where one of the holders dies, the default assumption is normally that the interest is one of 'joint tenancy'; that is, both parties have an interest in the entirety of the holding (rather than one having an interest in one part of the holding, and the other in the remainder). This may not be the case in every jurisdiction, however, and so it is important to establish what the situation will be under the applicable governing law, and/or to deal with the matter explicitly in the offering documentation. Where a joint tenancy is the case, and one of those parties dies, the other joint holders continue to be holders. On sight of the death certificate, the name of the deceased holder is deleted from the register and a new share certificate (if any) issued.

7.5 The manager's box

For open-ended schemes, investors carry out their purchases and sales of units/shares through the manager. Most managers operate a 'box' (also known as a 'book'), through which they buy and sell units in the fund, so as to enable them to net off purchases and sales rather than having to effect (say) the creation of 100 000 units and the liquidation of 90 000 units on the same dealing day.

In operating a box, the manager is in effect dealing for his own account rather than simply as an agent for the fund (Figure 7.1). In this way, he fulfils his role as market maker for the shares/units, and may well make some profit on them along the way.

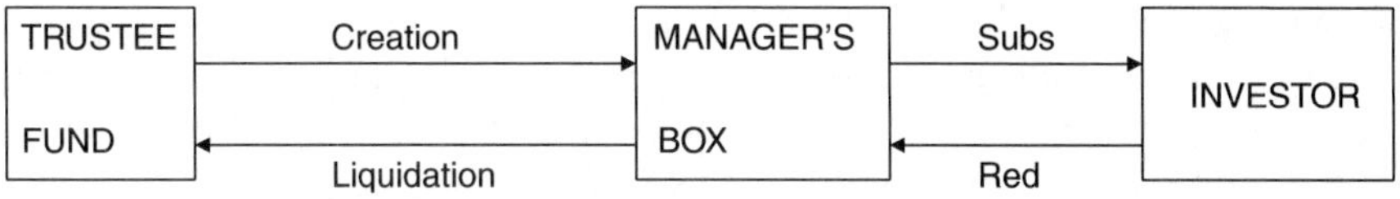

Figure 7.1 The Manager's box.

Many jurisdictions have issued regulations as to how managers and trustees/custodians of regulated funds should communicate regarding the creation/cancellation of units/shares. These are generally such that the manager is precluded from benefiting from hindsight, and therefore must take a calculated risk in holding shares/units for his own account.

Offshore regulations are not generally as stringent, and in some jurisdictions the manager will be permitted to enjoy the benefit of hindsight *as long as the fund is valued on a historic basis*. At all times, though, the manager will generally be under a duty to ensure that the box is not run to the detriment of investors. The onus will be on the manager, periodically scrutinized by the auditors, to ensure that this does not happen.

The procedures will be such that the manager buys units/shares from the fund, by way of a creation of these unit/shares. The fund will issue the units/shares to the manager against payment, increasing the number of units/shares in issue.

The manager is now in possession of a 'stock' of units/shares, which it can sell to investors. The manager will therefore, now only need to ask the fund to create new units/shares when the manager has no more units/shares in its box to sell to investors. At this point only will the number of units in the fund increase.

Managers can also sell units/shares back (and cancel them) to the fund by way of a liquidation/redemption. The fund will cancel units and pay the manager the proceeds of them, and the number of the units in the fund will at that point reduce.

Since a manager operating a box generally sells units from his own stock to investors, it is he who contracts with the investor to sell him units/shares in return for payment. The manager is empowered to collect and bank the investor's payment for his holding, and the fund is thus not itself involved in the transaction at this stage. The number of units/shares in issue stays the same, but the number of units/shares in the box reduces.

The reverse happens when the investor sells.

The regulatory controls in place over how a manager's box must be operated are generally as follows:

- The manager will not generally be allowed to deal in the box for its own gain to the detriment of unit/shareholders.
- It may not have a negative box (i.e. the manager cannot short-sell units/shares).
- It may not back-value creations/liquidations in the fund.
- It should generally only create/redeem shares to satisfy deals placed by investors (and not to generate a trading profit/loss for itself).

7.6 Pricing errors

We saw in Chapter 5, Section 5.14 that pricing errors can be damaging not so much for the fund itself (although its sponsors may suffer some reputational risk) but rather for the party whose error has caused the loss. To recap on these principles, we should put ourselves in the dealer's position. Remember, a pricing error could arise because the valuations team has miscalculated, *or* because the dealing team picks up the wrong price for a given dealing day:

- if the fund's price has erroneously been set too high, it is unlikely that the dealer will be able to recover any excess proceeds of sales (redemptions) already paid out to investors;
- similarly, if the price had been set too low, the manager may prefer not to suffer the embarrassment of telephoning a client to tell him that his units/shares are going to cost him more than the dealer had told him they would.

As an example of where the manager must pay compensation because of a valuations/dealing room error, and where the loss may be recovered from the fund, consider the following. The dealing room has mis-read the price per unit of a fund and has picked up too high a price.

- Investors who have sold shares will have been paid too much in proceeds. It is unlikely that the manager will be keen to contact them and ask for some money back (and they might well refuse!). However, it is also unreasonable for the fund to suffer as a consequence of the manager's error, so the manager would have to compensate the fund from his own pocket.
- Investors who have bought shares will have paid too much per share, and must be compensated – either with additional shares or with some money back. In this case, the manager can compensate them out of the assets of the fund (and will have to confess to his error!). However, the compensation can come from the fund, since this only puts it back into the financial situation it ought properly to have been in anyway – it is paying out cash/issuing shares which it ought to have done in the first place.

7.7 Large deals and their impact

The issue of large investor subscriptions/redemptions is of most importance in the context of open-ended schemes, mostly because of the corresponding impact they may have on the underlying portfolio. New money must be absorbed into the portfolio and invested so as to maintain an appropriate asset mix; money being withdrawn has to be sourced by liquidating underlying investments.

We saw in Chapter 2 that the inflow of new money to, and outflow from, open-ended funds should not in theory affect the NAV per share/unit. This is true in the broad terms; however, when large net subscriptions or redemptions are experienced the fund manager cannot net off the sales and repurchases through the manager's box.

This means that a significant amount of dealing must be undertaken in the underlying investment portfolio. For large net new inflows, this will take the form of investment purchases, to place the new money in such a way as to maintain the portfolio's asset allocation:

- firstly, a regulated fund will not be permitted to exceed prescribed liquidity levels for more than a short period;

- secondly, an overweighting of cash would in rising markets act as a drag on performance.

However, investing new money brings with it certain costs – stockbrokers' commissions, settlement charges, and in some markets (e.g. the United Kingdom) stamp duty.

For net outflows, again the fund will bear significant costs in liquidating sufficient underlying assets to raise the necessary cash.

The impact of these dealing costs could, if some remedial action was not taken, adversely affect investors remaining in the fund. Thus, in theory an investor taking no action could end up subsidizing the costs of accommodating another who has decided to invest or disinvest. This is clearly unfair, and so various mechanisms have arisen to ensure that 'static investors' are not disadvantaged because of the activities of active ones.

We looked at some of the mechanisms for these in Chapter 5, when we considered the means by which unit/share valuations might be adjusted in given circumstances. These included:

- pricing on a bid or offer basis (dual priced funds);
- dealing and dilution charges.

Many jurisdictions impose detailed prescriptions on how the valuations and unit/share pricing of a regulated fund must be calculated. In the United Kingdom the regulations laid down by the Financial Services Authority in connection with dual priced funds take into account the initial fee, the market bid and offer prices of the underlying securities, and the dealing costs of those securities – including stamp duty. The quoted buy and sell (offer and bid) prices may be positioned anywhere between the highest possible buying price (i.e. the creation price plus the initial charge) and the cancellation price.

As we saw, most of the time, the bid price – the price at which units are bought back from investors by the manager – will be greater than the cancellation price, unless the manager is experiencing a prolonged period when more unitholders are selling than buying. On large deals, that is, those over £15 000 (or whatever is specified in the Scheme Particulars as being 'large'), the manager may however choose to deal at the 'full offer price' on purchases or the cancellation price on repurchases, that is, at different prices from the normally calculated bid or offer price, during a given dealing period.

Managers need to accommodate such provisions, to ensure the dealing room is given a price which positions the fund appropriately in light of the net demand/supply of units from investors. So, for example, where the valuations team has produced its system-generated valuation, and is told by the dealing team that there appears to be significant net *demand* for units/shares, the valuation should be adjusted to accommodate this. The price per unit would be adjusted to an *offer* basis.

Conversely, if the valuations team is told by the dealing room that there is a net *redemption* of units/shares then it should move the pricing to a *bid* basis. That is, the team would simply value the fund's underlying assets on a *bid* basis, adjust for applicable accruals (e.g. income, charges), and apply the roundings.

The dealing room team therefore needs to take the following actions in connection with large deals:

- notify the investment manager/adviser (so they can consider what investment actions should be taken to accommodate the inflow/outflow of cash); and
- where applicable regulations are in force, consider any 'large deals' rules which allow for changes in the basis of dealing.

In addition, restrictions may be placed on the acceptance of large deals, so as to allow the impact of accommodating them to be spread or avoided altogether. For example, many schemes' offering documents provide that the directors may, at their discretion, decline subscriptions and/or (more commonly) redemptions of over a certain size. This size is sometimes set by reference to an absolute value (e.g. £150 000) but more commonly would be expressed as a percentage of the NAV of the fund as a whole (e.g. 5 per cent).

The issues we have looked at above do not normally affect closed-ended vehicles such as investment trusts. This is because investor purchases and sales are – excepting at the launch or windup of the fund – usually conducted between investors, via a broker.

7.8 Equalization and performance fees

We have come across the term 'equalization' already, in the context of income tax on income accrued in the purchase price of fund holdings. However, the term is also used in the context of performance-related investment management fees, a feature mainly encountered in the hedge fund industry.

To a degree, equalization calculations are becoming somewhat 'old hat', since administrators with appropriate systems now deal with the matter of performance fees by issuing different classes of share (the 'series approach'), which become merged with the main share class once the current calculation period has expired. However, a large number of administrators still use the equalization basis, and so we will spend a moment dealing with the administrative implications of this process.

Performance fees are typically paid to investment managers in such a way as to reward 'net new highs' in performance. That is, a manager should not expect to be rewarded for performance which has merely brought a fund's NAV per share back to $1, when the investor originally bought at $1 and has since seen the NAV fall to $0.50.

Share price 1 January 2003	$1
Share price 1 July 2003	$0.50
Share price 1 January 2004	$1

He would expect to see performance fees being levied only when his share price moves to (say) $1.25, or some other benchmark target.

However newer investors, who bought shares their shares at a price of $0.50, might be very happy to see performance fees being paid on a performance which has taken the value to $1: for them, this is a 'net new high'.

This introduces a complexity for the manager/administrator whose job it is to calculate and apply performance fees: all investors shares have the same NAV, yet some are liable for performance fees and some, perhaps, are not.

Let us consider the situation for Fund A, which has a built-in performance fee of 20 per cent:

RATIONALE FOR EQUALISATION IN FUNDS SUBJECT TO PERFORMANCE FEES

1. Traditional approach – no equalisation

Fund ABC has a volatile share performance, as follows:

	1 Jan	31 Mar	30 Jun	30 Sep	31 Dec
NAV before perf. fee accrual	100	140	160	120	130

The manager is entitled to a performance fee set at 20%; no equalisation calculations are carried out.

Shareholder Smith bought shares at the start of the incentive fee period:

- price = £100

Shareholder Jones bought shares on 31 March:

- price before performance fee accruals = £140
- price after performance fee accruals = £132, calculated as follows:
  - (£140 – £100) = £40
  - £40 X 20% = £8
  - £140 - £8 = £132

The accounting entries for Shareholder Jones' subscription should be:

Dr Cash	£132
Cr Share Capital	(£1)
Cr Share Premium	(£131)

The 30 September performance fee accruals and NAV per share will be calculated as follows:

Total NAV before performance fee accrual

£120 per share X 2 shareholders, being Smith and Jones)		£240
Less cost of subscriptions:	Jan £100.00	
	(£232.00)	£8.00
Total growth in portfolio	Mar £132.00	
Total performance fee accrual (20%)		(£1.60)
Total NAV, after performance fee accrual (£240 – £1.60)		£238.40
Shares in issue = 2		
NAV per share, after performance fee accrual		£119.20

Figure 7.2

The accounting entries to record the performance fee accrual at 30 Sept are as follows:

Dr Perf fee expense account £1.60
Cr Perf fee accrual account £1.60

2. Using equalisation

If Smith and Jones were assessed independently for the performance of their respective shareholdings, the performance fee accrual would be as follows:

Shareholder	Smith	Jones	Total
30 Sep NAV before performance fee accrual	£120.00	£120.00	£240.00
Less cost of subscriptions	£100.00	£132.00	£232.00
Growth in portfolio	£20.00	(£12.00)	£8.00
Total performance fee accrual @ 20%	(£4.00)	£0.00	(£4.00)

Using the approach set out at 1 above, the manager would retain £1.60 in performance fees.

Using the individually-assessed basis at 2 above, the manager would have retained £4.00 – an improvement of £2.40 through implementation of an equalisation policy.

Figure 7.1 Continued

Various methods of performing equalization calculations are in existence, some 'fairer' than others, and some having the benefit of ease of administration and in terms of explanations to investors. They include:

- Avoidance of the issue altogether (performance fees, without equalization); generally speaking this results in inequities to investors, but is simple conceptually and so has a marketing advantage.
- The series method; this suffers from the drawback in that over the course of a year, a monthly-dealing fund will end up with 12 different share series (and investors may hold several series if they are regular investors). However, for less frequently dealing (e.g. quarterly-dealing) funds this problem is not so severe, and in any event series will merge at the start of a new incentive fee period. At the start of each year, therefore, there will again be only one series.
- The equalization factor method; this suffers from a drawback in that it requires the retention of investor moneys in the fund for a period when otherwise the investor could have had access to that money. There is therefore an opportunity cost to the investor. There are also some administrative difficulties, especially where subscription levels are high.

- The share equalization method. This suffers from complexities in that investors' shareholdings change on an ongoing basis: however, all shares have the same NAV, and the approach does result in a 'fair' outcome.

The key for sponsors will be to ensure they understand the accounting and financial implications of each approach, and that they select an administrator with the systems capabilities to administer their chosen method.

8 Income distributions

8.1 Nature and source of income

Few funds earn no income at all on their underlying assets: even those which invest entirely in non-income producing assets will have a small amount of liquidity on hand which is likely to be earning some interest.

Typical sources include:

- interest on bank accounts;
- rental on properties (residential, commercial, ground rents);
- interest on debt instruments;
- dividends on equities; and
- distributions from unit trusts and other vehicles.

In most cases income will be easily recognizable as such (however you will recall that we encountered some potential complexities in Chapter 1 – refer back to Section 1.11 if you need to). Sponsors may find that a return, which they might have expected to be treated as capital in nature, is in fact regarded as income for certain purposes.

There are a number of ongoing developments in this area affecting particular markets, for example, in connection with:

- the provisions relating to UK distributor status (see below), which at the time of writing are under review; and
- the provisions arising out of the EU Savings Directive, especially those in connection with funds with in excess of a certain level of their assets in debt instruments (either directly or, for funds-of-funds, via investee funds) and where it is difficult to ascertain an investee fund's exposure to debt instruments at a given point. Again at the time of writing, the precise details, as they will be implemented at national level, have yet to be finalized – and indeed it is far from certain that the EU Savings Directive will in fact be implemented on its now-due date of 1 July 2005. However sponsors planning to target EU resident investors should be taking account of these issues so as to be prepared in the event.

Whilst for some funds the issues will be clear cut, in other cases sponsors will wish to take legal advice as to relevant tax authorities' attitude to:

- the characterization of returns on the type of underlying assets intended to be held within the fund; and

- the likely treatment both of distributions, and of realizations of holdings, in the hands of investors in the intended market.

8.2 Income distribution mechanics

We call the income distribution from an open-ended investment company (OEIC) a 'dividend', since dividends are what companies pay out on their shares. Where the fund is set up as a unit trust, we usually use the term 'distribution' instead. However, for simplicity the term distribution will be used for both types of payment here.

Distributions are paid to holders of units/shares who hold the appropriate class of unit/share (i.e. distribution units or income shares) at the record date on which that distribution is declared. Investors holding 'accumulation units' or rollup shares do not receive a payment: the income stays in the fund's portfolio, and as it is still in the bank (or is invested by the manager in other assets) continues to be reflected in the price of the units/shares. These unit/shares will therefore rise compared to the value of income units (whose net asset value (NAV) has been reduced by the cash payment away).

On the ex-dividend (XD) date, the fund will declare its distribution. This date will be the day after the last day of the distribution period to which it relates. The XD period runs from the XD date to the 'pay date'. On the XD date, the price of shares will reduce to reflect the 'stripping out' of the distributable income from the value of the fund. This is because the fund now has a liability to pay that dividend: and liabilities reduce the NAV of the fund.

Prices quoted during this period will have the suffix 'XD'. Investors who buy shares during this period are not entitled to the imminent distribution payment.

On the "pay date" (or distribution date), the fund will pay the distribution to holders. In many jurisdictions, the regulations prescribe the maximum XD period – that is, the rules may be such that the pay date may be no than 2 months after the XD date.

8.3 Price of shares/units

When a distribution is declared, we should expect the price of the units/shares to fall, to reflect the loss in value to the fund. The reason is that when a fund pays out its dividend, cash will leave its bank account to fund this payment. We know from Chapter 5 that cash is one of the assets of the fund; therefore the assets – and so the NAV – of the fund have fallen.

In fact this fall in value happens somewhat before the distribution is actually made: at the point at which the distribution is declared, it becomes a liability of the fund (an amount which is due to the relevant investors). This liability will be reflected in the books, thereby reducing the fund's NAV as of the *declaration date* (as opposed to the pay date).

8.4 Dividend/distribution re-investment

Some funds offer an automatic re-investment facility, whereby the distributions, on payment, are immediately used to buy more units/shares in the fund. Investors frequently confuse this re-investment facility with the holding of accumulation units, but the two are quite different and can have very different tax consequences.

Where distribution re-investment is offered, the number of units/shares held by the investor will increase. Cash has been paid out by way of the dividend, but it has then been used to buy more, newly issued, shares or units. The re-investment of the dividends will usually be carried out at the full offer price.

The tax authorities' perspective on re-investment is generally, understandably, that the investor has received an income payment on which tax is payable at the applicable rate. It is incidental, from a tax perspective, that the investor has chosen to use this cash to buy more shares, notwithstanding the fact that the re-investment facility has short-circuited this process in such a way that cash has never passed through the investor's hands (or bank account).

8.5 How often are distributions made?

Depending on the way the fund is established, the income it earns may (if it is to be distributed at all) be paid out annually, semi-annually, or – less commonly – quarterly or even monthly. The decision will be largely driven by:

- marketing consideration (i.e. the needs of the target investor market); and
- economic considerations (the individual distributions should not be so small that it is not economic to make them).

In certain jurisdictions, regulated funds will have little choice; for example, funds may be required to have a minimum of two income accounting periods, with provisions enabling them to include additional interim accounting periods if they wish.

8.6 Responsibility for the calculation and payment of distributions

A fund's manager is responsible for calculating the amount of income received by the fund during an accounting period. The trustee (of a unit trust) or the manager (of a corporate vehicle), in conjunction with the registrar, is responsible for distributing the income to the appropriate holders, in proportion to their holding in the fund.

In practice, of course and as we have already seen, the manager may also act as registrar itself; in this case if the fund is constituted as a unit trust, it will be the trustee who arranges for the distribution to be paid out, in accordance with the calculations generated by the manager.

Distributions may be paid by way of cheque or warrant (to which a tax voucher will usually be attached). Alternatively, payment can be made by bank-to-bank transfer, using the investor's banking details as collected on his application form. The advantage to the investor of the latter method is that there is no risk of the payment going astray in the post, and he does not have the administrative burden of paying the cheque or warrant in. In addition, bank charges may be reduced. For the Registrar, the paper handling and account reconciliation work is also reduced; there is a reduced incidence of cheques issued but not yet cleared against the fund's account by investors who have, for example, forgotten to pay their cheques in.

8.7 Calculation of distributions

The basic formula for calculating the income available for distribution in a given period is:

Add	Gross income (received and receivable during the accounting period); Income carried forward from the previous accounting period; In certain jurisdictions, a sum in connection with income tax equalization on units created during the period;
Deduct	Expenses and charges; Taxation, if any is applicable; A sum in connection with income tax equalization on units cancelled during the period; In some cases, charges levied on the assets of the fund; Income carried forward.

We will look at some of these components in more detail:

- *Gross income* (received and receivable during the accounting period) includes:
  - dividends on equities;
  - interest payments from interest bearing securities (e.g. bonds, gilts); and
  - interest on cash balances at the bank.

  The calculation can be complicated where derivative instruments including some element of income are included (e.g. swaps on debt instruments).

  The gross income may include:
  - *Income on which local tax has already been paid:* For a UK fund, for example, this would be referred to as 'franked income' and it would include dividends from UK companies which have been paid out after deduction of UK corporation tax at source, and on which no further corporation tax is therefore due to be paid in the hands of any UK fund vehicle.
  - *Income on which overseas tax has been paid:* depending on the nature of the fund, its location and any withholding tax treaties in place, the tax which has already been paid may be off-settable against any liability in the fund's home country.
  - *Income on which no tax has been paid – for example,* income from overseas shares debt instruments and bank deposits on which no tax has been paid. If the fund is located in a jurisdiction which exempts it from the need to pay local taxes, there may be no further tax to pay on this income in the hands of the fund.
  - *Equalization* is a time-apportioned distribution calculation, which is calculated in order to make the levying of income tax fair for all investors. It is levied in the

United Kingdom, and also in varying forms in certain other jurisdictions. It is levied in recognition of the fact that as time passes between one distribution point and the next, the income element which is reflected in the price of units/shares will increase as a proportion of their NAV.

Equalization need not be calculated for all funds, even in those jurisdictions in which it is provided for. It is only relevant for income funds. The calculation requires that shareholders are split into two categories – those who have purchased their holdings during the current distribution period (Group 2 shares) and those who were invested before the current distribution period (Group 1 shares). Group 2 shares will be allocated an equalization rate at the distribution date, so that their that tax paid on income is correctly calculated. Otherwise they would pay for an amount of accrued income in their unit/share price, and then receive it back – but be forced to pay tax on it – at the next distribution point.

- *Expenses* include managers' fees, other fees, bank and safe custody charges, etc. paid/payable during the period. Whether or not these are charged to income will depend on how the fund has been established, what regulatory or tax provision apply, and what has been provided for in the scheme particulars. In some cases charges are to be levied against income to keep the income to minimal levels, whilst in others they may be levied against capital so as to keep the distributable income as high as is possible.
- *Taxation* may include withholding taxes, income or corporation taxes depending on how the fund is constituted and what the tax regime is in the jurisdiction(s) in which it operates.
- *Income carried forward* will be any amount that the trustee/custodian and manager agree will be carried forward to the next accounting period. In many jurisdictions, regulatory provisions will preclude certain types of fund from carrying forward of more than a very minimal amount. This is intended to ensure that the fund distributes substantially all of the income it earns.

Part 3

Markets and Developments

9 Domestic funds regimes

9.1 The UK market

At first sight the UK market may, as a traditional 'domestic' funds environment, not seem a particularly appealing one from the perspective of international funds; however, it has a number of features which can make it an attractive base for an international fund offering. Funds may presently be established as Undertakings for Collective Investments in Transferable Securities (UCITS) or authorized, non-UCITS schemes, depending on the target market. They may of course also be set up as entirely unregulated schemes. For more information on UCITS, see Section 9.3 below.

For both UCITS, and authorized but non-UCITS funds, the United Kingdom offers some taxation advantages over its European competitors. In particular, the United Kingdom has a wider range of double taxation treaties than many of its competitors, which can enable the manager to reduce the impact of foreign withholding taxes on interest and dividend payments on the underlying portfolio.

The price to be paid for this slight tax advantage is that the United Kingdom suffers from a somewhat more rigid regulatory regime. Authorized non-UCITS schemes in the United Kingdom have to comply with the full range of investment and other restrictions applicable to their particular classification (a summary appears below), whilst in Luxembourg and Dublin a much lighter framework applies to their local equivalents; and indeed the authorities in Luxembourg and Dublin have been known to waive certain of the regulations that *do* generally apply, if the manager can present a good case for doing so.

9.1.1 UK authorization and regulation of collective investment schemes

The power to authorize schemes rests with the Treasury, which has appointed the Financial Services Authority (FSA) to take over this role. Thus, the FSA authorizes authorized unit trusts (UTs) and open-ended investment companies (OEICs) based in the United Kingdom, provided they meet the requisite standards.

Collective investment schemes operated in the United Kingdom (i.e. excluding Jersey, Guernsey and the Isle of Man (IoM), none of which are a part of the United Kingdom) can be either:

- regulated schemes, constituted as authorized UTs, or OEICs; or
- unregulated schemes, constituted as UTs or partnerships, but not as OEICs. This is because UK company law does not provide for the establishment of an open-ended company excepting where it is to be a fund authorized by the FSA.

OEICs are, in the United Kingdom, also known as Investment Companies with Variable Capital (ICVC) in the UK regulations.

For a UK open-ended fund to be marketable to the public, it must be authorized by the FSA – whether it is a UT or an OEIC. Authorization will be granted if the scheme complies with certain requirements and if the regulator is happy that the people operating that scheme are 'fit and proper'; that is, they are competent, solvent and have integrity. In terms of the investment restrictions which apply to authorized schemes, these are largely as for those set out in Chapter 3.

In terms of documentation requirements, those for the fund's scheme particulars are broadly as set out in Chapter 6. However a UK ICVC, instead of being governed by a memorandum and articles (M&As), is governed by its instrument of incorporation. UK ICVCs usually use as a template the model document put forward by the Institute of Fund Managers (the 'IFM'), formerly known as the Association of Unit Trusts and Fund Managers. However, even where the model is used, it is important to ensure that professional advice is taken so that the individual provisions reflect the needs of the specific ICVC – for example:

- the method of calculating the vehicle's net asset value (NAV);
- its investment objectives and parameters/restrictions; and
- the various share classes, and rights attaching to them.

The UK regulator, the FSA, is well acquainted with the IFM model and so new applicants need only highlight the variations from the model on their submission.

Again in connection with UK ICVCs, the offering document, as with any form of company, takes the form of a prospectus. The ICVC's prospectus must be made available to the investor before he invests, as would be the case for the Scheme Particulars of a UT.

9.1.2 *Promotion of funds in the United Kingdom*

The FSA exercises its powers in connection with open-ended schemes, and their operators, under the Financial Services and Markets Act 2000 ('FSMA') of the United Kingdom, and associated regulations and orders. FSMA does not only cover how schemes are operated in the United Kingdom but also how they may be promoted. Section 238 of the FSMA is the section which covers the marketing of domestic collective investment schemes in the United Kingdom. It states that to be promoted direct to the public, a scheme must be either Authorized or Recognized. Otherwise, UK unregulated funds must be sold in accordance with the provisions of the Financial Promotion of Collective Investment Schemes Order (the 'CIS order').

The CIS order gives certain exemptions to the prohibition on promoting unregulated schemes; mainly, that authorized persons will be able to promote unregulated schemes to private individuals who fall into the categories of 'high net worth individuals' and 'sophisticated investors'.

9.1.3 *UK ICVCs: the impact of European legislation*

As we saw earlier, one of the main drivers for the United Kingdom's introduction of OEICs – (ICVCs) was the perceived marketability of such funds in the European arena.

That is, corporate, single-priced funds were seen as being more attractive to European investors than dual priced unit trusts – which were at that time the sole option in terms of open-ended schemes.

In addition to improving UK fund managers' access to European markets, the expectation is that the ICVC legislation will:

- encourage other international fund managers – for example, those based in the United States – to establish funds in the United Kingdom under the ICVC legislation so as to target European markets (thereby boosting the UK funds industry as a whole); and
- encourage European fund managers to market their funds into the United Kingdom, improving investor choice and the diversity of available products.

There has been slow progress in this area, not least because at the outset the range of fund types which could be established as an ICVC was considerably narrower than that available as (say) unit trusts. However, this was remedied by way of changes brought in to the FSA's 'Collective Investment Schemes Sourcebook' in 2003, which *inter alia* will facilitate the development of products such as limited issue funds, and of guaranteed and protected funds.

Table 9.1 sets out some of the key comparisons and contrasts between UK unit trusts and ICVCs.

Other issues to bear in mind when considering whether to establish a UK fund as an ICVC or a unit trust are:

- For an umbrella ICVC, there is a single annual accounting date for all the sub-funds in the umbrella. (There is, however, scope for flexibility in the interim dates.)
- Although assets and liabilities are allocated to each sub-fund, there is a technical cross-liability between the sub-funds should one go into a deficit.

ICVCs may offer some useful flexibility in terms of the ability to set up multiple share classes. For example, a manager may do so, so as to offer:

- differential charging structures for retail and institutional investors;
- different currency classes; and
- different share classes for different classes of investor on grounds of eligibility, etc.

However, such flexibility brings with it administrative complications, and a sponsor wishing to establish multishare classes of this nature would be well advised to ensure that his administrator's systems and staff are capable of dealing with the complexities.

9.1.4 Single pricing

Single pricing is mandatory for ICVCs, and (at the time of writing) optional also for unit trusts. There are those who believe that the concept of single pricing is more easily understood by the investor – though the truly confusing aspect for UK

	ICVC	Unit trust
Constitution	**Company**	**Trust**
Constitutional documents	Instrument of incorporation	Trust deed
Offering documents	Prospectus	Scheme particulars (although these are often also referred to as the prospectus)
Key features document	Yes	Yes
Parties	Authorized corporate director	Manager
	May have independent directors	No scope for equivalent of independent 'directors'
	May have investment adviser	May have investment adviser
Investors' rights	Shareholders	Beneficiaries under a trust
AGMs	Required	Not applicable
Material contracts	• ACD and fund • Depository and fund • Investment manager/ adviser and fund manager • Administrator/registrar and fund	• Trustee and Fund Manager • Investment manager/adviser and fund manager • Fund manager and administrator • Fund manager or administrator (if any) and registrar
Regulatory regime	OEICs (Companies with Variable Capital) Regulations 2001 and the FSA 'Collective Investment Schemes Sourcebook'	The FSA 'Collective Investment Schemes Sourcebook'
Classes of capital	Multiple share classes available	Income or accumulation units available only
Pricing	Single pricing only. Option of swinging single price or midmarket single price with possible dilution levy on redemptions	Single or dual pricing. Unit trusts were formerly dual priced only, but for several years now have been able to adopt a single pricing basis
Charges	Restricted to • Initial charges • ACD remuneration • Redemption charges • Expenses as per the • Instrument of Inc (which may include establishment charges) Performance fees not permitted	Restricted to • Initial charges (Manager) • Periodic charges (Manager) • Exit charges (Manager) • Trustee fees • Certain other expenses as specified in the FSA • Unit Trust Regulations

Table 9.1 Key differences between UK unit trusts and ICVC

	ICVC	Unit trust
Fund categorizations	UCITS and non-UCITS Part 5A: • Securities funds • Warrant funds • Money market funds • Funds-of-funds • Umbrella funds • Futures and options funds • Geared futures and options funds • Property funds • Feeder funds not permitted	UCITS and non-UCITS Part 5A: • Securities funds • Warrant funds • Money market funds • Funds-of-funds • Umbrella funds • Futures and options funds • Geared futures and options funds • Property funds • Feeder funds for relevant pension schemes
Regulatory investment restrictions	As for the equivalent category of unit trust: see part 5 (UCITS) and 5A of the FSA's 'Collective Investment Schemes Sourcebook'	See part 5 ('UCITS scheme category') and 5A (other schemes) of the FSA's 'Collective Investment Schemes Sourcebook'
Capital gains tax	CGT exempt	CGT exempt
Income tax	Overall flow-through is usually reasonably efficient	Overall flow-through is usually reasonably efficient
Other		Specific provisions deal with the application of Stamp Duty Reserve Tax on the redemption of units
Listing	Possible	Possible
Time to establish	May be slightly longer than for a unit trust, due to need to ensure that the proposed authorized corporate director also has necessary FSA authorizations - and because an ICVC, in providing more flexibility, is necessarily often somewhat more complex	May be slightly quicker than an ICVC for an established UT manager

Table 9.1 Continued

investors is likely to be the existence of both dual and single pricing within a single funds regime.

ICVCs may choose to operate their single pricing mechanisms in one of two ways:

- mid-market with a possible dilution levy (see Chapter 5); or
- the adoption of a 'swinging single price'.

9.1.5 *Charging structures*

Broadly charging structures are as set out in Table 9.1. However, sponsors may need to take advice as to how the ACD is remunerated, especially if the investment management function is to be delegated. In particular, there may be value added tax (VAT) implications as to whether the ACD pays the investment manager itself, out of the fees it earns for its own role, or whether the investment manager is paid direct by the fund.

9.1.6 *UK authorization requirements for fund administrators*

As we noted in Chapter 3, it is not only funds themselves which may require authorization; in addition, certain functionaries will also require authorization. This authorization is also granted by the FSA, under the Financial Services and Markets Act 2000 (FSMA). We will consider here the implications for UK-based fund administrators and registrars.

The provisions as to what service providers will require authorization are set out in the Regulated Activities Order (RAO) 2002, an order made under FSMA. The RAO does this by designating certain activities as being regulated (and therefore requiring that a body is appropriately authorized before it carries on those activities). The activities most relevant to those administering funds are as follows:

- *Regulation 25(1) – arranging certain specific transactions*: For example, making arrangements for someone else to buy, sell, underwrite or subscribe for a particular investment (as opposed to investments in general). A fund administrator's role will generally involve its receiving subscription applications, dealing with the applications and if all is in order, placing the deal, notifying the registrar and issuing a certificate (if the fund is certificated). Similarly the administrator will deal with redemption requests processed under the trustees or directors' authority. Depending on how these deals are effected it is likely that certain of an administrator's activities will fall under this activity. (If, however, all subscriptions were made independently of the administrator – for example, by way of a previous agreement between manager and investor – then the administrator might arguably be settling the deal only and would not be involved in the making of the relevant arrangements.) There are some potential exemptions which might conceivably apply, and remove the requirement for the administrator to apply for authorization, but these will not generally be applicable and in any event specialist legal advice should be taken.
- *Regulation 25(2) – making arrangements with a view to transactions in investments*: This is wider than 25(1) above but it would be fair to say that if 25(1) is applicable to the administrator's activities, then 25(2) will also apply at the point at which the administrator contracts with the trustees (of a unit trust) or directors (of an investment trust).
- *Regulation 40 – Safeguarding and administering investments*: Many administrators' activities will fall squarely within this bracket. However, it is worth noting that for an administrator to be caught under this activity, it would need to be providing both the named services: that is, both safeguarding, and administering, investments. The definition of safeguarding includes arranging for someone else to

do that safeguarding, and it may be questionable as to whether the administrator had any hand in selecting a fund's trustee/custodian. In many cases administrators/registrars will be caught under this definition, although again some exemptions apply.

- *Regulation 45 – Sending dematerialized instructions*: This includes sending instructions via the UK settlement agent, CREST. Thus, administrators and/or registrars sending instructions via CREST in connection with fund holdings on behalf of an investor would most likely be caught. Again, there are certain exemptions, but their application will not be possible in the majority of circumstances and specialist advice should be taken.
- *Regulation 64 – agreeing to do any of the above*: Clearly, holding out as providing any of the above activities could, if the activity itself is regulated, also be regulated. However, a point to bear in mind in the context of international schemes is that even if the regulated activities themselves are to be carried on overseas – and would therefore not require authorization – the act of promoting a firm's ability to do them (overseas), that promotion being done from a sales office in the United Kingdom, could be a regulated activity and require authorization.

9.2 The US market

The main legislation affecting US mutual funds and providing for investor protection was introduced in the 1930s and 40s. It is:

- *The Securities Act of 1933 and the Securities Exchange Act 1934*, which collectively aimed to restore investor confidence after the events of October 1929, by providing for a more robust framework for regulatory oversight. These focused mainly on:
  - the standards of business to be observed by market practitioners in terms of fairness, honesty and integrity; and
  - disclosure issues relating to securities offerings.
- *The Investment Company Act 1940*, which required that every fund price its assets based on applicable market values; and, among other things:
  - prohibits certain transactions between a fund and its managers;
  - imposes leveraging limits;
  - imposes the requirement for independent directors;
  - imposes a regulatory burden not only on the fund itself, but also on its investment advisers, principal underwriters, directors, officers and employees;
  - mandates that mutual funds redeem their shares anytime upon shareholder request;
  - requires them to pay redeeming shareholders a price based on the next calculated NAV within 7 days of receiving a redemption request.

  The act makes provision for the regulatory regime in respect of (*inter alia*) mutual funds offered to the public, and focuses on disclosure of material information, including financial standing and investment policies.
- *The Investment Advisers Act 1940*. This act:
  - requires that all advisers to mutual funds must be registered (excepting for banks);

- imposes a general fiduciary duty on investment advisers;
- contains several broad anti-fraud provisions; and
- requires that advisers meet record-keeping, reporting, disclosure and other requirements.

In most cases, only advisers with more than $25 million of assets under management, and those advising registered investment companies (including mutual funds) need to register.

These pieces of legislation have been subject to numerous amendments over the years, but their key provisions continue to apply; they are therefore, despite their evolution, among the more mature pieces of legislation affecting the funds industry today.

Section 5 of the Investment Company Act 1940 also defines a mutual fund, as follows:

> a. Open-end and closed-end companies. For the purposes of this title, management companies are divided into open- and closed-end companies, defined as follows:
>
> 1. 'Open-end company' means a management company which is offering for sale or has outstanding any redeemable security of which it is the issuer.
> 2. 'Closed-end company' means any management company other than an open-end company.
>
> b. Diversified and non-diversified companies. Management companies are further divided into diversified companies and non-diversified companies, defined as follows:
>
> 1. 'Diversified company' means a management company which meets the following requirements: At least 75 per centum of the value of its total assets is represented by cash and cash items (including receivables), Government securities, securities of other investment companies, and other securities for the purposes of this calculation limited in respect of any one issuer to an amount not greater in value than 5 per centum of the value of the total assets of such management company and to not more than 10 per centum of the outstanding voting securities of such issuer.
> 2. 'Non-diversified company' means any management company other than a diversified company.
>
> c. Loss of status as diversified company. A registered diversified company which at the time of its qualification as such meets the requirements of paragraph (1) of subsection (b) shall not lose its status as a diversified company because of any subsequent discrepancy between the value of its various investments and the requirements of said paragraph, so long as any such discrepancy existing immediately after its acquisition of any security or other property is neither wholly nor partly the result of such acquisition.

The Sarbannes-Oxley Act of 2002 brought in a number of new provisions, *inter alia* amending the Investment Company Act of 1940, and affecting the operation of registered investment companies. These included:

- New rule 30a-2 under the Investment Company Act 1940, introduced by Sarbannes-Oxley, which requires that the principal executive and financial officers of registered investment companies which have to file periodic reports under the Securities Exchange Act 1934, must each certify the information so filed. Since many types of investment fund, including unitized investment trusts, will not have their own financial officers, the requisite forms are likely to be completed by the fund's sponsor, trustee/custodian.
- These new certification requirements also involve obligations relating to the investment company's internal controls and procedures.
- There is an obligation for such companies to establish a 'disclosure committee' which will report to the company's senior management on disclosure controls and procedures.
- There are new rules relating to the adoption by registered investment companies of 'codes of ethics' for their senior financial management. (Again, since unitized investment trusts do not typically have officers, the disclosures will relate to the adoption of codes of ethics by the vehicle's sponsor, trustee/custodian etc.)
- Sarbannes-Oxley also extends the requirements in connection with the audit committees of 'public companies', a definition which is likely to apply to registered investment companies. (The requirements apply to the audit committees of 'issuers', which will include a registered investment company.) It also set new conditions in connection with external audit, including the ancillary services which an external auditor may no longer provide to audit clients.

A further overhaul to the mutual funds regime in the United States took place by way of the Mutual Funds Integrity and Fee Transparency Act 2003, introduced as a result of concerns over abusive practices. The act places a duty on the Securities and Exchange Commission to establish further disclosure rules for the benefit of investors, mainly relating to the costs of investment. The act also enhances Sarbannes-Oxley-style corporate governance provisions and audit provisions to mutual funds. This includes a requirement for an independent audit committee, and the adoption by each mutual fund of a code of ethics and a chief compliance officer. There are likely to be some derogations from the more burdensome requirements for smaller funds.

Supervision of funds in the United States is carried out by the Division of Investment Management of the Securities and Exchange Commission. Disclosure requirements are largely dealt with under the Securities Act 1933, sometimes poetically referred to as the United States' 'truth in securities' legislation. This sets out registration requirements for securities (including fund offerings, whether established in the United States or overseas). The registration process incorporates requirements to file details of:

- the issuer's property and business activities;
- the security to be offered;

- the issuer's management; and
- certified financial statements.

There are filing exemptions in certain circumstances, the most relevant for our purposes being those for 'private offerings' (made only to a limited number of persons or institutions); and those for offerings of limited size.

Funds in the United States can be set up as mutual fund companies, trusts and limited partnerships. As with many other jurisdictions, they may be open-ended or closed ended (in which case the term 'investment trusts' is again often used). Closed-ended vehicles are, as in other jurisdictions, popular vehicles where the underlying investment portfolio is illiquid, and where the manager does not want the distraction of accommodating regular in- and out-flows of investor liquidity (see Chapters 1 and 2 to revisit the rationale for this). Real Estate Investment Trusts (REITs) are a good example of this.

The choice of structure will often be guided by taxation considerations, not only in terms of how returns are treated in the investor's hands, but also at fund and portfolio level. There are a number of specific investor types which have particular requirements, which will not be covered in depth in this text. These include, for example (but there are many others):

- *Tax exempt US investors*. Certain types of US investor are exempt from the requirement to pay US taxes, excepting in the case of 'unrelated business taxable income' (UBTI) returns. Investors who pay UBTI will have specific needs when investing in a fund vehicle. This is because capital gains, dividend income and interest income earned by the fund on its investment portfolio will not be included in the investor's UBTI assessment. However, any investments which the fund makes which are financed in part or in full by borrowings may be included. Care needs to be taken in connection with investments made by charitable remainder trusts since the receipt by the trust of income of this type can cause the entirety of the trust's income to become taxable.
- *ERISA requirements*. The Employee Retirement Income Security Act (ERISA) 1974 places complex requirements on funds in which more than a stated percentage of the fund's value is held for this type of benefit plan. For this reason fund sponsors often aim to structure their offerings so that they will be exempt from such requirements, usually by taking advantage of certain exemptions. *Inter alia* these include exemptions for operating companies (either Venture Capital Operating Companies or Real Estate Operating Companies) and for funds which do not have significant participation (i.e. 25 per cent by value of the fund) by way of benefit plan investors.

For this reason sponsors considering establishing a fund in the United States, or with a significant constituent investor base should take specialist legal advice.

Where the target client base is to be made up of US investors, the preference may be to establish the fund as a limited partnership or some other entity capable of being treated as a US partnership for US tax purposes. This is because partnerships are not taxable entities for US tax purposes; rather, there is a 'look-through' to each partner, both in terms of the quantum of income and (generally) to the characterization of that income. This is helpful for US investors since generally speaking the investments in a fund vehicle will be held for more than one year: and therefore US investors (partners in the partnership) will be taxed on the gain on the fund's investment activities at long-term capital gains tax rates.

Generally speaking a US fund vehicle will be required to register under the Investment Company Act 1940 (ICA); there are, however, certain exemptions. In particular, a fund will be exempted where the number of investors is not greater than 100; funds may also be exempted if their investor base is limited to 'qualified purchasers', who must meet an asset-based test in order to qualify.

A US sponsor may consider establishing the fund vehicle in a non-US jurisdiction for other reasons, predominantly – but not solely – regulatory (e.g. the avoidance of having to register the entity under the ICA). This is because:

- where the fund is established as a US-based entity, and the sponsor is hoping to rely on the 100-person cap as a means of avoiding registration under the ICA, non-US investors will count towards that 100-person maximum;
- however, if a fund is established outside the United States, its non-US investors will not count towards that 100-person maximum.
- similarly, if the sponsor hopes to rely on the 'qualified purchaser' exemption, where a fund is US-based then all the investors must meet the criteria for qualification.
- however if it is established in a non-US jurisdiction, then only US investors will need to meet the criteria.

In addition, another persuasive reason for establishing a fund set up as a partnership in a non-US jurisdiction may arise if there is a danger of its falling within US provisions in connection with publicly traded partnerships. This can bring about unwanted tax consequences; if this seems to be a possibility, perhaps because of the manner in which investors will be permitted to transfer or redeem interests in the vehicle, then the sponsor may again wish to consider establishing the vehicle outside the US.

The decision will also be coloured by the fund's intended investment activities. Where the underlying investments are themselves to be solely US-based there may be no issue. However, if the intention is to invest in non-US assets, and the investments may constitute a significant percentage of the investee entities' voting capital, then carrying out such activities through a US-based vehicle could work to the disadvantage of the US investors. This is as a consequence of the US provisions in connection with controlled foreign corporations; under these provisions, a US partnership is regarded as a single shareholder in the investee entity, whilst where the partnership is established elsewhere, it will not be regarded as a single investor; instead the ownership of the investee entity will be treated as if each of the individual investors owned an interest in it in proportion to their interest in the partnership. This is the case even if all the partners in the non-US partnership are themselves US persons.

9.3 The European market

Within the European Union (EU), the dominant legislative influence on various national markets has been driven in the main by European Directive *85/611/EEC on the coordination of laws, regulations and administrative provisions relating to*

Undertakings in Collective Investments in Transferable Securities (UCITS) – otherwise known as the UCITS I Directive. This legislation was aimed at providing investor protection in connection with publicly promoted collective investment schemes, under a set of standards which would be recognized and provide equivalent levels of protection throughout the union.

The UCITS I Directive introduced the so-called 'European Passport' for Undertakings in Collective Investments (UCIs) which met various criteria, including that they were invested only in transferable securities. This permits a collective investment scheme constituted and operated in one EU state to be registered in other EU Member States upon completion of a relatively brief and simple notification process; for an example of what is required see Section 10.2 of Chapter 10, in relation to the registration of overseas schemes in the United Kingdom.

Two new directives have since been introduced modifying UCITS I: collectively, they are known as UCITS III. They are Directives 2001/107/EC (known variously as 'the Management Directive' or 'the Profession Directive') and 2001/108/EC ('the Products Directive'). Member States were required to implement UCITS III in their national laws before 13 August 2003 and then had another 6 months (i.e. up until 13 February 2004) to bring them into effect.

Under UCITS III the concept of the European passport is maintained, but the range of investments in which a fund may invest whilst qualifying as a UCITS is extended beyond those defined as 'transferable securities'. It now permits investment in cash deposits, money market instruments, securities issued by other UCITS and by non-UCITS UCIs, and in a range of derivatives. We will look at the two directives more closely here.

The *Products Directive* came into force on 13 February 2002 and substantially extends the instruments a UCITS can invest into. Under UCITS I, funds were restricted to investing primarily in listed securities (i.e. mostly listed shares and bonds); the Products Directive extends this to include:

- Liquid transferable securities
- Cash
- Money market instruments
- Other funds (both UCITS and non-UCITS)
- Derivatives.

It also facilitates 'tracker' or 'index' funds.

As well as expanding the range of assets in which UCITS can invest, the Products Directive also extends the restrictions on concentration of investment, which apply to transferable securities, to money market instruments as well. It introduces an 'issuer restriction' such that a UCITS may invest up to a maximum of 10 per cent of its NAV in the securities of any one issuer (there are some exceptions for transferable securities or money market instruments which are issued or guaranteed by a government or local authority). On top of this it also introduces the concept of the 'group'. The impact of this is that a UCITS will not only have to comply with the various restrictions set out below: it will also have to ensure that the aggregate of its exposures to transferable securities, deposits, money market instruments issued by members of any one corporate grouping, and of OTC derivatives where a member of that corporate grouping is a counterparty, must not exceed 20 per cent of the fund's NAV.

Some other notable amendments relating to specific types of fund are:

UCITS funds-of-funds: under UCITS I, only 5 per cent of a UCITS could be invested in other funds: under UCITS III this limit has been lifted to 100 per cent, enabling funds-of-funds to be established. However, the funds in which the UCITS invests must themselves be UCITS, or if non-UCITS, must be 'subject to supervision considered by the UCITS' competent authorities to be equivalent to that laid down in Community law. ...' The precise definition of 'equivalent supervision' had, at the time of writing this text, yet to be clarified.

In addition:

- A UCITS fund-of-funds may not invest in another fund which itself is permitted to invest more than 10 per cent of its assets in funds; this is intended to prevent unhealthy levels of layering, which can carry the risk of multiple charges and in some cases of self-re-investment (see Chapter 3, Sections 3.11–3.18 on the general principle of, and rationale behind, investment restrictions).
- A UCITS fund-of-funds may not invest more than 10 per cent of its assets in any one fund (although individual Member States may choose to lift this limit to 20 per cent).
- Nor may it invest more than 30 per cent of its assets in non-UCITS funds.

A UCITS funds-of-funds must disclose the maximum management fees of the funds in which it invests in its annual report; it is also precluded from charging initial or exit charges for investments in any funds which are under common control or management with the investing UCITS.

At the time of writing, there is still some uncertainty over the application of the investment restrictions where the investee fund is an umbrella fund. The drafting of the directive does not appear to have contemplated umbrella funds, and the matter for debate is whether the investment restrictions on target funds should apply at umbrella, or sub-fund level.

UCITS Tracker Funds: the Products Directive makes tracker funds much more of a reality than they were under UCITS I. Under UCITS I, there were difficulties where one of the shares which it was necessary to buy accounted for a sizeable proportion of the index: the directive restricted investments in the securities of any one issuer to 10 per cent, but there have been several occasions on which a share's weighting has accounted for more than 10 per cent of an index of which it is a constituent. Under the Product Directive, this limit is raised to 20 per cent of the securities of any one issuer for a tracker UCITS (and in some cases 35 per cent) provided the fund's objective is replication of the index and the index is one which is recognized and published.

UCITS investing in derivatives: under UCITS III, funds may now have investment in derivatives as a stated investment policy (as opposed to being limited to 'Efficient Portfolio Management' (EPM) techniques and exchange rate risk management – see Chapter 3 on general principles of investment restrictions, for a description of EPM principles). A UCITS fund investing in derivatives must abide by the following restrictions:

- It must limit its exposure to over the counter (OTC) contracts to 10 per cent where its counterparty is a credit institution, and 5 per cent in all other cases;

- The counterparties must in all cases be institutions which are subject to some prudential supervision, and must meet other criteria.
- The underlying instruments to which the derivative relates must be instruments specified in the Products Directive, financial indices, interest rates, foreign exchange rates or currency instruments.
- Any OTC derivatives must be such that prices can be reliably obtained and verified on a daily basis. The UCITS must also be able to close them out, liquidate them or sell them at any time at a fair value price.
- The fund must employ risk management techniques and processes which allow it to monitor the risk profile of its positions, and of the fund itself.
- The total exposure of the fund to derivative instruments must not exceed the NAV of the fund itself.
- Where the fund invests in any security which incorporates an embedded derivative, that derivative must be included when calculating the fund's overall position for purposes of complying with the above investment restrictions.

As yet not all the issues relating to UCITS' investments in derivatives are clear: in particular, some areas of uncertainty exist in connection with the calculation of 'risk profiles' and risk exposures, both in general and particularly in connection with OTC transactions. These are expected to be ironed out as information supplied by Member States on such issues as current values, counterparty risk, market movements and the time available to liquidate positions is sent on to the European Commission, considered and absorbed. As yet, in light of the lack of clarity, there is some uncertainty over the way in which capital protected funds – which often employ the use of OTC transactions – may be treated.

Money Market UCITS: UCITS funds can now invest in money market instruments. Money market instruments are defined as 'instruments normally dealt in on the money markets which are liquid, and have a value which can be accurately determined at any time; ... .' The following provisions apply:

- where the money market instrument is not traded on a regulated market, it must be issued by a body which is itself regulated; and
- it must be issued or guaranteed by *either* a central, regional or local authority of a Member State; or if not of a Member State, by such a body which is itself subject to prudential supervision.

UCITS investing in cash deposits: Under UCITS III a fund may now invest directly in cash deposits (prior to UCITS III, cash could only be held for 'ancillary purposes' – e.g. the maintenance of 5 per cent or so of NAV to meet redemptions). Deposits are defined as placements of cash which are 'repayable on demand or have the right to be withdrawn, and maturing in no more than 12 months'. The following restrictions apply:

- The UCITS may invest no more than 20 per cent of its NAV in the deposits of any one institution, or with institutions which are members of the same group.
- Deposits may only be placed with credit institutions whose registered office is in a Member State, or (if in a non-Member State) the institution must be subject to prudential supervision equivalent to that operated under EU law.

At present, there seem to be differing interpretations, from one Member State to another, as to whether the funds which a UCITS retains as 'ancillary cash' are viewed as contributing to the 20 per cent maximum; or whether only deposits held for investment purposes are to be counted.

Prospectus issues: Under the Product Directive, there are new disclosure obligations, including the requirement that the category into which the UCITS falls must be disclosed. In addition, prominent disclosure must be made if the fund's investment policy allows it to invest in other funds, or in deposits or derivatives.

Use of subsidiaries: Under the Products Directive, UCITS established after 13 February 2002 may not establish subsidiary entities in non-EU Member States as investment vehicles (in the past some UCITS have established subsidiary vehicles in 'offshore' jurisdictions such as Cyprus and Malta).

Changes under the *Management Directive* must also be taken into account: this element of UCITS III deals with and imposes rules on Member States in connection with the management companies of UCITS III funds. UCITS will be permitted to appoint a management company if they wish, or remain self-managing.

Both management companies and self-managed investment companies are explicitly permitted to delegate certain of their activities under the Directive. However, there are restrictions upon this: in particular the core function of investment management may not be delegated to the 'depository' (custodian), nor to any other entity whose interests may conflict with those of the management company or the fund's investors. The Directive is not explicit about whose interests may be regarded as conflicting, and so it appears it will be a matter for individual Member States to set their own rules on this.

Where a management company is appointed, the Directive imposes new capitalisation, internal administration and accounting requirements on it (the 'substance requirements').

In general, such management companies now have greater powers: they will be allowed to passport their activities and to carry on a wider range of activities. In particular:

- The management company of a UCITS authorised in one Member State may provide services in another Member State by establishing a branch there. This will be subject to approval by the regulatory authority in the host Member State; but the host state authority will not be permitted to make such approval subject to any additional local authorisation or capital adequacy requirements, above and beyond those in the Directive. The effect should be to enable management companies to passport their services into Member States other than their home state.
- Management companies are required to maintain minimum capital of €125 000 or (where assets under management exceed €250 million), 0.02 per cent of assets under management with a maximum capital requirement of €25 million.
- Those UCITS companies which do not have separate management companies must have an initial capital of €300 000.
- UCITS with no management company must also comply with a formal code of conduct, and with requirements relating to the delegation of investment activities.

- The Management Directive also introduces the concept of the 'simplified prospectus', as an additional source of information for investors. UCITS must now produce both a full prospectus, and a simplified version containing key information. This is analogous to the 'Key Features' document which we looked at in Chapter 6. The final details of what will be contained in the simplified prospectus is not yet clear in all jurisdictions, but a key point is that in theory, it will be able to be used across all Member States for marketing purposes without the need for any amendments (excepting for translation).

The 'substance requirements' are proving to have very different implications from one Member State to another: in some jurisdictions, laws and regulations already exist which are substantially the same as those under the Directive. In others, the requirements are entirely new and in addition to the intended results are bringing with them a host of ancillary complications relating to tax, VAT and so forth.

Timing and transitional issues: From 13 February 2004 Member States were required to apply the provisions of UCITS III. At present many member states are in a transitional period, and the provisions can be complex; in particular:

- The 'grandfathering provisions' are such that any UCITS established before 13 February 2002 will have 5 years (i.e. until 13 February 2007) to comply with the new rules. For funds established post-13 February 2002, compliance with the new rules had to be achieved by 13 February 2004.
- The new prospectus regime applies to all UCITS, whenever established, from 13 February 2004.
- It is not at this stage entirely clear whether one EU Member State is obliged to recognise a UCITS established in another Member State (the 'host' state) where that host has not yet itself implemented the Product Directive.
- Whilst newly-established funds can now invest in derivatives, a strategy which was largely unavailable to them before, they are also now required to employ risk management processes and calculate exposures – on a basis of which the details are not yet finalized.
- Management companies established prior to 13 August 2004 are also 'grandfathered', in that they may continue their existing operations until 13 February 2007 – by which time they must comply with the new Management Directive in full.
- The fact that the Directive does not take account of umbrella funds also means that it is as yet unclear what will happen when an existing (pre-2002) umbrella UCITS, which falls within the grandfathering provisions described above, wishes to establish a new sub-fund.

10 Distribution regimes: selling foreign schemes into regulated jurisdictions

10.1 The regulatory environment: recognition of foreign schemes

Few jurisdictions nowadays allow overseas funds promoters unfettered access to their investors. Most will wish to regulate access to their market, for some or all of a number of reasons:

- the protection of investors resident in their jurisdiction;
- protection of their local market place from overseas operators who may be able to offer financial products on more competitive terms; and
- in order to limit the opportunities for residents to place their assets overseas and avoid paying local taxes, either through legitimate planning or by non-legitimate means (such as non-disclosure).

In order to manage access to the local market, most financial services regulators therefore operate a system of approval whereby overseas providers can apply for their products to be 'recognized' (the terminology varies from country to country).

This process normally involves some form of assessment of the overseas product, and its provider, against similar criteria to those which the regulator would apply if it were to be assessing a new local provider. However, in view of the fact that the local regulator will have little in the way of regulatory sanctions over the foreign provider, the regime usually places some weight on the level of regulation in the provider's home country. Preference will be given to providers based in a country with whose financial services regulator the prospective host country's regulator has a Memorandum of Understanding (MoU) or some other mutual assistance agreements in place, since this will support any regulatory action which needs to be taken as a result of abuses by the foreign provider in the host country.

In order to gain an understanding of the typical processes involved, we will look at the regime in one particular country (the United Kingdom) for recognition of foreign schemes. We will consider the approach taken firstly from a purely regulatory perspective, and secondly from a tax perspective.

10.2 Overseas schemes: regulatory distribution issues in the United Kingdom

The legislation in connection with the promotion of financial products, including funds, in the United Kingdom is dealt with under the Financial Services and Markets Act 2000 (FSMA), and the associated regulations and orders made under it.

Offshore funds which are not recognized are not, generally speaking, permitted to be marketed in the United Kingdom direct to the public (e.g. 'off the page' or by direct contact with the investor). They can only be sold through appropriately authorized intermediaries/agents in accordance with specific regulations, as we have noted earlier (the CIS Order). There are some exclusions from the regulations, for example, in connection with:

- promotion to high-net worth individuals;
- promotion to sophisticated investors.

There are three routes available for offshore funds to be freely marketable in the United Kingdom alongside authorized unit trusts/open-ended investment companies (and subject to UK marketing rules). The following sections of the FSMA are the sections which are of most interest to us here, covering as they do the *'recognition'* by the United Kingdom of non-UK collective investment schemes in order that they can be marketed to the general public:

- Section 264 (European Economic Area schemes, that is, Undertakings in Collective Investments in Transferable Securities (UCITS)). This section implements the European passporting regime we looked at in Chapter 9;
- Section 270 (designated territory schemes). These are countries which the UK Treasury has determined operates an investor protection regime which offers equivalent measure of investor protection to that which is afforded under the UK domestic regime; and
- Section 272 (individually recognized schemes). These are schemes which are neither UCITS, nor operated under the appropriate regime of a designated territory. Such schemes must go through a more lengthy process than schemes applying under sections 264 and 270, since with a s272 scheme the FSA cannot rely on the fact that the scheme is operated under an overseas regulatory regime which it has already assessed as providing equivalent protections to its own.

Notifications and applications: where a s264 or s270 scheme operator wishes to market that scheme in the United Kingdom it makes a notification to the FSA. Where a s272 scheme is involved, its operator makes an application to the FSA.

Consider the difference between the two: in a **notification**, the scheme operator simply informs the FSA of what it intends to do. In the case of an **application**, on the other hand, the manager must ask the FSA for permission, before it proceeds. The rationale is that in the case of UCITS and schemes operated under the appropriate regime in a designated territory, the FSA should not need to look closely at the scheme; it has already been authorized to standards deemed equivalent to UK authorization standards, by an overseas regulatory authority of appropriate standing. In the case of a s272 scheme, the FSA cannot rely on this and so must review the scheme in detail before giving permission for it to proceed.

The FSA lays down rules as to how notifications and applications to it must be framed: for each section there is a separate set of regulations. As an example, the requirements for s264 schemes are contained in the FSMA (Collective Investment Schemes Constituted in Other EEA States) Regulations 2001. We will look briefly at the requirements for each type of recognition.

Section 264 – schemes constituted in other EEA States. This covers UCITs schemes constituted in another European Economic Area (EEA) member state. As we saw in Chapter 9, the first UCITS directive was adopted in Europe in 1985, and is aimed at permitting cross-border selling of schemes between EU Member States; and broadly speaking, the requirements are that UCITS must invest in transferable securities, and operate risk spreading.

All collective investments which comply with the directive within the countries of the EU are enabled to apply to any other EU country for permission to be marketed. As the United Kingdom is a Member State of the European Union, it is obliged to admit the UCITS funds of other EU Member States. This section does not apply to Channel Islands or Isle of Man schemes, since these territories are not member states of the EU or, for these purposes, the EEA.

The rules for making a **notification** to the FSA for s264 schemes are contained in the FSMA (Collective Investment Schemes Constituted in Other EEA States) Regulations 2001. They require the following:

- The notification and all relevant documents must be in English, or accompanied by a translation.
- They must be certified by the scheme operator as being true copies of the originals.
- They must include:
  - name of the scheme;
  - legal form of the scheme;
  - name and address of operator;
  - address in the United Kingdom for service of notice and other documents;
  - name and address of any supervisory authority regulating the scheme in its home state;
  - whether the scheme is to be marketed in the United Kingdom in a way which constitutes a regulated activity in the United Kingdom;
  - name and address of the depository (custodian);
  - address in the United Kingdom where the scheme facilities will be maintained;
  - details of the arrangements for marketing units in the United Kingdom, for example,
    - proposed start date;
    - whether sales will be through any employed sales force (tied agents), authorized persons (intermediaries) or by way of unsolicited calls;
  - any order or certificate from the home EEA state authorities showing that the scheme complies with the UCITS Directive;
  - a copy of the instrument constituting the scheme.
  - a copy of the prospectus; and
  - a copy of the latest annual report and any subsequent half-yearly report.

Any changes to the information supplied to the FSA must also be advised to them.

Section 270 – schemes operated under the appropriate regime, from countries with Designated Territory Status. This covers schemes which have 'Authorised' (or the local equivalent) status in a country which itself has Designated Territory Status. At the time of writing these countries were:

- The Isle of Man
- Jersey
- Guernsey
- Bermuda.

A country with Designated Territory Status will offer substantially equivalent investor protection to that of the United Kingdom. The UK authorities satisfy themselves that this is the case by examining that country's legislation and regulations, and by periodic visits to inspect the overseas regulator. Usually, they will also visit the operators of several such schemes to gain a first-hand impression of the regime's implementation in practice. If the UK authorities are happy with what they have seen they will issue a 'Designation Order', which states that the country has designated territory status in respect of *certain* categories of scheme only. Note, the Order does not cover *all* schemes from that country; only those which are run in accordance with rules very similar to those of the FSA in the Uinted Kingdom.

Again the provisions for giving notice will be very similar to that required for s264 EEA applicants:

- The notification and all relevant documents must be in English, or accompanied by a translation.
- They must be certified by the scheme operator as being true copies of the originals.
- They must include:
  - name of the scheme;
  - legal form of the scheme;
  - name and address of operator;
  - address in the United Kingdom for service of notice and other documents;
  - whether the scheme is to be marketed in the United Kingdom in a way which constitutes a regulated activity in the United Kingdom;
  - name and address of any person to whom the schemes assets are entrusted for safekeeping; that is, the depository (custodian) or trustee;
  - address in the United Kingdom where the scheme facilities will be maintained;
  - details of the arrangements for marketing units in the United Kingdom, for example:
    - proposed start date;
    - whether sales will be through any employed sales force (tied agents, appointed representatives), authorized persons (intermediaries) or by way of unsolicited calls;
  - a copy of the instrument constituting the scheme; that is, the Trust Deed or Certificate of Incorporation;
  - a copy of the Prospectus or equivalent document (Scheme Particulars);
  - a copy of the latest annual report and any subsequent half-yearly report;

- a copy of any document affecting the rights of participants in the scheme (*note, this is different to the requirement for a s264 application)*;
- a copy of the authorization from the home (Designated Territory) regulator confirming that the scheme is of a class covered by the designation order.

Again the FSA will wish to be notified if there are any changes to the information which has been supplied.

The FSA has powers to refuse recognition of a s270 scheme under S271.

Section 272 – schemes individually recognized by the FSA. This covers schemes that require recognition in their own right – that is, because they are constituted outside the EEA or the countries having Designated Country Status. The procedure for recognition is more lengthy than under sections 264 or 270, because the FSA does not have the comfort of knowing that the scheme has already been reviewed by another regulator which it know to have similar investor protection standards to its own.

The section might also include a fund that *was* constituted in a Designated Territory or EEA Member State, but which was unable to achieve the right status in its home territory because some of its features were outside the scope of the local legislation. In this case, it might still be possible for the scheme to be acceptable under the UK provisions (and indeed this has on occasion happened).

Such schemes make an **application** (not a notification). Their application will contain almost exactly the same information as for s270 schemes. However:

- it ill not include a confirmation from the local regulator that the scheme falls into any category covered by a Designated Territory order (because, of course, it does not);
- the prospectus must include a statement that says 'Complaints about the operation of the scheme may be made to the FSA;'
- the prospectus must state whether or not investors would be covered by the United Kingdom's Compensation Scheme; if so how and who to contact. This is not necessary for s264 and s270 schemes since these should be covered by schemes in their own countries.

The FSA has powers to refuse recognition of a s272 application under s276.

10.3 Facilities to be maintained by foreign schemes recognized in the United Kingdom

Foreign schemes recognized for sale in the United Kingdom under sections 264, 270 or 272 of the FSMA are required to maintain certain facilities at an address in the United Kingdom, intended to make life easier for their UK investors. The address must be disclosed in the Prospectus and will most likely be the scheme operator's principle place of business in the United Kingdom.

The facilities must include somewhere where investors can, free of charge:

- inspect the constitutional documents of the scheme (and any documents amending them);

- obtain a copy of the most recent Prospectus, and the latest annual and half-yearly reports;
- get up-to-date sale and repurchase prices for units; and
- make complaints about the operation of the scheme, which will be passed back to the operator.

The facilities must also allow the investor to redeem units bought, and get payment, in the United Kingdom, unless the fund's units/shares can be sold on an exchange at a price which is not significantly different to the net asset value (NAV). However, the facilities must then instead advise investors how and where to do so.

The scheme operator must ensure that the prospectus and annual/half-yearly reports are offered to a prospective UK investor before the sale of units to him is completed.

In the unlikely event that the fund issues **bearer shares**, the facilities must also include arrangements for holders to receive, free of charge:

- payment of dividends due (free of charge);
- copies (in English) of the most recent annual and half-yearly report; and
- any notices which have been sent out to participants.

10.4 The UK distributor status regime

'Distributor status' is a term arising under the Income and Corporation Taxes Act 1988 of the United Kingdom, schedule 27 paragraph 15. It is a status which may be grated to an offshore fund by the UK Inland Revenue, provided that fund can satisfy certain conditions. Broadly, these are that the fund:

- distributes the bulk of its income (i.e. **more than 85 per cent** of the greater of its income as computed for UK tax purposes, and its accounting profits) annually in such a manner as to make that income taxable for UK resident investors; and
- observes certain investment restrictions.

It is quite possible for a fund to be distributing without having distributor status – for example, if its strategy is such that it will not adhere to the relevant investment restrictions, or indeed if its manager simply does not apply for distributor status because the UK market is not an important target market. A manager may also not bother to apply for distributor status for a fund, if it is intended that any UK investors should hold it by way of structures which will remove any tax problems arising from non-distributor status.

The most important implications for UK resident and domiciled taxpayers of holding non-distributor funds as against those with distributor status are the following:

- gains on the disposal of shares of a non-distributor status fund will be treated as income for tax purposes, and income tax will be payable on them;
- gains on a fund with distributor status fund will be treated as capital gains. The investor's capital gains tax (CGT) allowance may cover this gain, meaning that there is the potential for him to pay little or no tax on the realized gain.

On top of this there are some other benefits for a fund in of having distributor status:

- The income tax charged on a non-distributor fund is taxed under 'Schedule D Case VI'. In brief this means that there can be no set-off against trading losses incurred elsewhere.
- On the sale of shares in a distributor fund, any loss is treated as a capital loss and can be offset against other gains made elsewhere, for CGT purposes. This is not so for funds without distributor status.
- The 'gain' made on the cost price of a non-distributor fund is not indexed for inflation when calculating the amount liable to income tax. Gains on distributor funds, being charged to CGT, benefit from indexation.
- In the event of the death of the investor, a distributor status fund would be 'stepped up' to its then market value without any liability to UK CGT. Inheritance tax will then be levied on the market value. Where a non-distributor fund was held, income tax would be levied on the difference between the cost price and the market value at the date of the investor's death; inheritance tax would then be levied on the market value, less the amount already paid in income tax.

Clearly, this has implications for the marketing of funds in the United Kingdom. We have seen that a UK resident shareholder of a Distributor fund is able to treat gains on disposals of shares as capital gains, not income, and offset any losses against gains, whilst a UK resident shareholder of a non-Distributor fund must treat gains on disposals of shares as income. Therefore, for most UK resident retail investors it would be advantageous to invest in a fund with Distributor Status.

11 A comparison of some international funds centres

11.1 Bermuda

Bermuda has generally been regarded as operating a somewhat more rigorous regulatory regime for funds than many of its Caribbean competitor jurisdictions. Whilst this may have cost it something in terms of the volume of business based there, the Bermuda funds industry has nonetheless grown rapidly.

The Bermudan regulator in connection with funds business is the Bermuda Monetary Authority (see at www.bma.bm). One of the main pieces of applicable legislation is the Bermuda Monetary Authority Act 1969, which *inter alia* defines a collective investment scheme (CIS) as either a unit trust or a mutual fund. The Companies Act 1981 builds on this, defining a mutual fund as a company '... limited by shares and incorporated for the purpose of investing the moneys of its members for their mutual benefit and having the power to redeem or purchase for cancellation its shares without reducing its authorised share capital and stating in its memorandum that it is a mutual fund' (s156A of the act). In addition to this, any company incorporated by a private act which has the power to redeem or purchase its shares for cancellation at the option of, or on the request of, a member is deemed to be a mutual fund for the purpose of the Companies Act 1981.

As to the definition of a unit trust, section 1 of the Stamp Duties Act 1961 defines one as ' ... any arrangements made for the purpose of, or having the effect of, providing, for persons having funds available for investment, facilities for the participation by them as beneficiaries under a trust, in profits or income arising from the acquisition, holding, management or disposal of any property whatsoever.' Most open-ended funds are established as mutual fund companies; however sponsors targeting some specialist markets will generally prefer unit trust vehicles, usually established under a 'declaration of trust', so as to obviate certain potential complexities that can otherwise arise.

Schemes may also be established as limited partnerships, under any of:

- The Partnership Act 1902 as amended;
- The Limited Partnership Act 1883, as amended; or
- The Exempted Partnerships Act 1992.

Partnership vehicles may be attractive where fiscal transparency is a prerequisite for the fund's target audience. Vehicles established as Bermudan Limited Partnerships may have their partnership interests listed on a stock exchange (including overseas stock exchanges, subject to provisions allowing for a 'branch register' of limited partners' interests being maintained outside Bermuda).

As with many 'international' funds centres, Bermuda operates a number of different regulatory categories of fund. (This is in contrast with those jurisdictions, such as the United Kingdom, which only have a two-tier system - that is, a scheme is either regulated, or it is completely unregulated.) Unit trusts and mutual funds are categorized by reference to the Bermuda Monetary Authority (Collective Investment Scheme Classification) Regulations 1998. The regulator may exempt a scheme from the requirements of these regulations in certain circumstances - primarily those where it is clear that a fund is not to be offered to the public, and that it will be marketed to fewer than 20 persons; or where it is dormant for a reasonable length of time.

United Kingdom Class Schemes (shortly to be reclassified as 'Bermuda Recognized Schemes')

Bermuda is one of the four countries which has been granted Designated Territory Status under the Financial Services and Markets Act 2000 (FSMA) (we looked at this concept in Chapter 10). This means that a scheme complying with the requirements of the UK Class Scheme (Bye-Laws) Regulations Act of Bermuda may apply to the Bermuda Monetary Authority for certification as a UK Class Scheme. The benefit to the sponsor of taking this step is that it may then notify the UK regulator, the Financial Services Authority (FSA), that it is applying for 'recognition' – which should allow the scheme to be promoted direct to the public in the United Kingdom.

Such schemes are subject to a compensation fund, which provides protection to eligible investors in the event that the manager is unable to repay investors the sums they are due.

Broadly, the requirements for a UK class scheme are as follows:

- the custodian must be a Bermudian bank;
- the manager must be a Bermuda-incorporated company and must be separate and apart from the custodian bank, and, as such, the custodian and manager must fulfil their respective duties completely independently from one another; and
- the scheme must be operated in accordance with provisions which are broadly similar to those applicable to UK domestic authorized schemes. These are clearly fairly rigorous and allow little room for flexibility, when compared with the regime for institutional funds set out below.

At the time of writing, it was intended that Bermudan UK Class schemes should, subject to finalization of certain details, be re-designated as 'Bermuda Recognized Schemes'. However, at this point no date by which this must happen had been set.

Bermuda institutional schemes

These schemes are subject to a considerably lighter and more flexible regime, reflecting the reduced levels of investor protection accorded to the target investor base. They may only be offered to institutional or sophisticated investors. There are various requirements which must be satisfied before a scheme can qualify as an institutional scheme:

- The administrator must be a local, exempted or overseas ("permit") company or partnership, with a physical presence in Bermuda.
- Any change in the administrator must be advised in writing to investors.
- The administrator must be independent of the scheme and of any other service provider to it, excepting where the Bermuda Monetary Authority has given its prior approval for any variation to this principle.
- The following statement must be prominently included in the offering documentation: '[the scheme] has been classified as a Bermuda Institutional Scheme. As such, the scheme is exempted from the need to appoint a Bermuda custodian and may not be supervised to the same degree as other schemes which are regulated and supervised by the Authority. Therefore, the scheme should be viewed as an investment suitable only for investors who can fully evaluate and bear the risks involved.'

Bermuda Institutional Schemes are exempt from the need to appoint a Bermuda custodian, provided that:

- the fund has a minimum initial offering size of Bermudan Dollars 50 000 000 or foreign currency equivalent; and
- the minimum investment is Bermudan Dollars 100 000 per investor, or foreign currency equivalent.

Bermuda standard schemes

Schemes which are neither Institutional Schemes nor UK Class/Recognized Schemes will be classified as Standard Schemes. The Collective Investment Schemes Regulations set out the terms on which such schemes must be established and operated, and include financial reporting, prospectus and disclosure obligations. Such schemes are generally required to appoint the following parties, all subject to the regulator's approval:

- an investment manager or adviser;
- an administrator; a registrar;
- a custodian/trustee; and
- an auditor.

The functionaries may appoint delegees, but remain responsible for the performance of these delegees. The custodian of a Standard Scheme must generally be a Bermudan financial institution, or the subsidiary of such an institution; exceptions may be made where the proposed appointee is based in a jurisdiction, and subject to supervision, which the Bermudan authorities regard as appropriate, and subject to the scheme administrator itself meeting certain criteria.

The authorities may exempt a standard scheme from the need to appoint a custodian in certain circumstances, namely:

- where the scheme is a feeder fund (see Chapter 2) and the master fund has appointed a custodian or approved prime broker;

- where the scheme is a fund-of-funds, and its assets mainly comprise registered shares/units in the underlying funds and cash at bank; and
- where the scheme has, with the regulator's approval, appointed a prime broker based in an appropriate jurisdiction and subject to regulatory supervision.

11.2 The British Virgin Islands

The British Virgin Islands (BVI) have long enjoyed a reputation as one of the more flexible jurisdictions in which to establish fund vehicles. The downside of this flexibility has been, perhaps, that it has not been regarded as so well regulated as some of its peers. Nonetheless, many sponsors have found the BVI to be an excellent place in which to incorporate or constitute their schemes, in light of its flexible regime and tax-friendly status, then opting to have the scheme managed and/or administered from a jurisdiction which imposes the comfort of a more robust regulatory overlay – with the risk management and marketing benefits which this may bring.

The primary legislation in the BVI relating to open-ended schemes is the Mutual Funds Act 1996, as amended by the Mutual Funds (Amendment) Act 1997. As in most jurisdictions, closed-ended vehicles are not caught within the scope of this legislation. The three main forms used for the establishment of funds in the BVI are:

- limited companies; and in particular international business companies (IBCs) formed under the International Business Companies Act 1984;
- unit trusts; and
- international limited partnerships, established under the Partnership Act 1996. There is no requirement for the general partner of an international limited partnership established under BVI law to have a local general partner.

11.3 Cayman

The Cayman Islands has, as with several Caribbean jurisdictions, enjoyed a reputation for a highly flexible and cost-effective base from which to establish and operate funds. As with the BVI (see Section 11.2), this flexibility has on occasion brought with it the disadvantage of a reputation for less rigorous supervision than some other jurisdictions enjoy. However, this has not proved a hurdle to the growth of the funds industry in this jurisdiction, in part because:

- of the Islands' tendency to attract funds targeted at institutional, sophisticated or high-net worth investors (in which cases sponsors do not usually require the same level of investor protection as that required for retail funds); and
- because it is frequently attractive for a sponsor to establish a scheme under the flexible Caymanian regime, but then to have it managed/administered in a jurisdiction which provides for a more robust supervisory overlay.

A further attraction is the ability to list mutual funds on the Cayman Islands Stock Exchange (see Chapter 1 for an indication of the requirements and benefits of this).

The regulatory authority in connection with Cayman Islands funds is the Cayman Islands Monetary Authority. The applicable legislation is the Mutual Funds Law of 1993 (as amended by the Mutual Funds Law 2003 Revisions). This defines a mutual fund as 'any company, trust or partnership either incorporated or established in the Cayman Islands, or outside the Cayman islands, which issues equity interest redeemable or repurchasable at the option of the investor, the purpose of which is the pooling of investors' funds with the aim of spreading investment risk and enabling investors to receive profits or gains from investments.' As with many of the other jurisdictions we have looked at, closed-ended vehicles are outside the scope of the legislation. Further, funds with fewer than 15 investors, where those investors are capable of appointing or removing the scheme functionaries (i.e. a scheme's trustee/custodian, directors or general partner as the case may be), may also be exempted from the registration requirements.

Cayman funds may be established as companies (usually exempted companies), unit trusts and partnerships. In addition, there is provision for funds to be established as 'segregated portfolio companies', an increasingly popular vehicle for umbrella structures.

The regulatory provisions are extremely flexible:

- There is no requirement for a local trustee/custodian, a manager or local directors.
- Nor are there any specific requirements in respect of investment objectives or restrictions.

However, the fund's offering documents must describe the nature of investors' interests comprehensively and accurately, and provide sufficient information with regard to its objectives, risk factors, functionaries etc. for a prospective investor to make an informed decision.

Funds registered in Cayman may be:

- Licensed;
- Registered; or
- Administered.

11.4 Dublin

Until relatively recently the Central Bank of Ireland (CBI) was responsible for the regulation of fund administrators, in Ireland, and you will still see the CBI referred to in much documentation. However, responsibility of this has now passed to the Irish Financial Services Regulator (IFSRA), which was established on 1 May 2003.

Differing requirements are imposed on administrators of Irish-incorporated funds and non-Irish incorporations:

- For funds constituted in Ireland, at least the following activities must be done in the jurisdiction:
  - maintenance of financial books and records;
  - retention of documentation supporting the books and records;
  - NAV calculations;
  - calculations in respect of income and expense accruals;

  - calculations and payment of dividends/distributions, if applicable;
  - payment of fund expenses; and
  - supervision of the liquidation and dissolution of the fund, when the time comes.
- For funds constituted elsewhere, the requirements are less rigorous and state simply that the administrator must ensure:
  - submission of the administration agreement between itself and its client fund to IFSRA, together with any other documentation mentioning the administrator; and
  - that there is a statement to the effect that the fund is not regulated by IFSRA.

Otherwise, IFSRA imposes little else in the way of obligations on overseas funds to which services are provided by Irish administrators. Further, so long as the overseas fund's 'mind management and control' is carried on outside Ireland, the fund will not be subjected to Irish tax.

The Dublin IFSC

Dublin's fund industry has profited from the existence of the International Financial Services Centre. A number of fund sponsors who do not maintain a full physical presence in the territory have established Irish-registered Managed Managers there: a managed manager is a concept we have come across before in Chapter 3 – that is, dedicated management companies which are service and administered by IFSC Fund Administration Companies. In Ireland, you may also see them referred to as Agency Management Companies.

This is the case for unit trusts, which as we saw in Chapter 3 require a manager: however even for those fund vehicles which do not necessarily require a manager (e.g. an ICVC/OEIC, which may be self-managing), the sponsor may wish to establish a managed manager both as a fee vehicle, and as a central point for co-ordinating relationships between the various service providers and the fund (i.e. administrator, investment adviser, etc.). The managed manager will be appointed by the fund to undertake such activities on its behalf, and will receive a fee for doing so.

11.5 Guernsey

Guernsey is a self-governing dependency of the British Crown. It is a member of the OECD, and like Bermuda, the Isle of Man and Jersey, it has designated territory status under the UK FSMA. Despite its relationship with the United Kingdom, Guernsey, like the other UK Crown Dependencies, generally enjoys a large amount of autonomy in terms of its internal government – including the setting of taxes.

Guernsey law is derived in part from the customary laws of Normandy. This foundation is strongly overlaid – in particular, in company and commercial matters – by influences derived from English law. The Judicial Committee of the Privy Council of the United Kingdom is the ultimate court of appeal for Guernsey.

The statutory framework for funds in Guernsey is established by way of:

- The Protection of Investors (Bailiwick of Guernsey) Law 1987, which establishes the statutory and regulatory framework for the establishment and administration of open-ended investment funds in Guernsey; and

- The Control of Borrowing (Bailiwick of Guernsey) Ordinances 1959–2003 (COBO), which provide the considerably less restrictive regime for closed-ended schemes. In essence closed-ended schemes are subject to the COBO regime, and to Guernsey company law.

Open-ended schemes may be established as quasi-OEICs (see Chapter 2, Section 2.2), unit trusts or partnerships.

Closed-ended vehicles are essentially similar to the investment trusts we have looked at in the context of the United Kingdom and other similar jurisdictions. The Guernsey Financial Services Commission issued clarification on its policy in November of 2003, in connection with closed-ended schemes (essentially schemes which operate as Investment Trusts). It set out the minimum disclosure requirements it would expect to see fund sponsors providing, and it also provided further guidance on a sponsor's ongoing notification requirements and other obligations.

As we have seen in connection with several other 'international' fund centres – notably the Isle of Man and Bermuda – Guernsey's regulatory regime provides for several different levels of regulation, from the tightly prescribed to the more flexible. The categorizations are as follows:

- *The Class A Rules*, which were updated in 2002 to accommodate changes to the UK regime. Class A schemes are those which accord with Guernsey's 'designated territory' status, as accorded under the FSMA of the United Kingdom (see Chapter 10, Section 10.2). Class A schemes are thus required to meet detailed requirements in terms of their constitution and operation, and these are largely modelled on the UK authorised schemes regime. They may be seen as a parallel to the 'Authorized Scheme' regime of the Isle of Man (see Section 11.6 below) and to the 'UK Class Schemes' regime of Bermuda (see Section 11.1 above), although Guernsey has been somewhat quicker to update its regime for recent changes to the UK provisions than its peers in the other designated territories.
- *The Class B Rules* were issued in 1990, and cover a wide variety of other types of scheme, primarily those where the level of prescription afforded under the Class A rules is not felt to be necessary or appropriate to the target market. The regime is considerably more flexible than that of Class A schemes. For example, the investment restrictions deal with the requirement for adequate diversification, but do not otherwise prescribe in detail the nature of the assets in which such a scheme may invest, nor its borrowing or hedging powers. Rather, scheme sponsors may make their case to the Guernsey regulator, explaining why the intended strategy is appropriate to the intended investor base. A Class B scheme might therefore be appropriate to an institutional investor base, or indeed for a retail investor base in a jurisdiction where the recognition requirements are less stringent than, or at least significantly different from, those of the United Kingdom (to which the Class A rules are attuned).
- *The Class Q rules* were issued in 1998, and deal with funds established for 'qualifying professional investors': that is,
  - governments, local or public authorities;
  - the trustees of trusts which have net assets in excess of £2 million;
  - companies or limited partnerships where the investing entity, its parent or subsidiary has net assets in excess of £2 million; or

- individuals who, together with any spouse, have a minimum net worth excluding their main residence of £500 000.

  As with the Class B rules, the Class Q rules are not prescriptive as to investment strategy. They provide further flexibility in that whilst a Guernsey-domiciled custodian must be retained by the fund, its duties are limited to controlling the assets of the fund and overseeing the sufficiency of any sub-custodians to which they delegate duties.

Guernsey gained something of a competitive advantage over its Crown Dependency peers when it introduced legislation facilitating the establishment of protected cell companies under the Protected Cell Companies (PCCs) ordnance 1997 of Guernsey (see Chapter 2, Section 2.6 for a note on the operation of PCCs). Whilst this did not result in a deluge of business, a number of umbrella funds have since been set up using the PCC structure.

In November 2003, the Guernsey Financial Services Commission issued a consultation paper on the regulatory framework for hedge funds in that jurisdiction. This focused on the regime for open-ended hedge funds, and sought to address difficulties arising in connection with four main areas:

- client money segregation;
- asset segregation;
- NAV and share/unit price estimation; and
- the role of the custodian as it relates to the activities of any prime brokers.

Sponsors considering establishing a hedge fund in this jurisdiction should monitor changes arising out of the consultation, as it may be that the outcome will be to resolve a number of areas of potential ambiguity.

11.6 Isle of Man

The Isle of Man is generally seen as having a stricter regulatory regime than many of its international fund centre counterparts; this perception extends not only to the broad scope of the legislation in force, but also, generally speaking, to its detail and implementation. In the past this has been blamed for holding back the Island's growth in terms of funds business, though it has also been of some benefit in terms of its reputation for investor protection.

In 2003, various legislative and tax changes were introduced to the Island's funds regime which removed many regulatory and cost burdens which had previously acted as a hurdle to business: the Island now presents a much more flexible base from which to administer international funds, coupled with the benefits of a European time-zone and the comfort of well-regulated service providers.

The Island is not, however, a part of the European Union and so suffers from a lack of access to European retail markets. In addition, at the time of writing, there was some uncertainty as to the detail of how the EU Savings Directive, to which the Island is partially subject, will impact on certain types of fund. These disadvantages are shared by a number of other offshore centres, including Jersey, Guernsey and (in the context of the EU Savings Directive), Cayman, Luxembourg, Dublin and the BVI. In terms of access to European markets, Dublin and Luxembourg, being members of the Union and therefore able to offer Undertakings for Collective Investments in Transferable Securities (UCITS), have some advantages in terms of retail offerings.

Like Jersey, Guernsey and Bermuda, the Island has 'designated territory status' as provided for under the FSMA of the United Kingdom; indeed it was the first country ever to be accorded such a status. This means that subject to certain conditions, Isle of Man schemes may be promoted direct to the public in the United Kingdom.

The financial services regulator responsible for investment offerings and activities is the Isle of Man Financial Supervision Commission. The main relevant legislation in connection with funds is:

- The Financial Supervision Act 1998 (FSA88); and
- The Investment Business Act 1991–3

and the regulatory codes, orders and regulations made thereunder.

The FSA88 is the main piece of legislation regarding Collective Investment Schemes. *Inter alia* it:

- Defines what constitutes a fund for the purposes of the legislation, at s30 of this act, as follows: 'In this Act "a collective investment scheme" means ..., subject to the provisions of this section, any arrangements with respect to property of any description, including money, the purpose or effect of which is to enable persons taking part in the arrangements ... to participate in or receive profits or income arising from the acquisition, holding, management or disposal of the property or sums paid out of such profits or income'.
- Defines various categories of scheme:
  - Authorized – Section 3. This is the category of scheme to which the Island's 'designated territory' status relates.
  - International (formerly Restricted) – section 11. This category covers any Isle of Man scheme which is not an authorized scheme.
  - Recognized – section 12 (Designated Territory schemes) and 13 (other schemes). These are foreign schemes which the Financial Supervision Commission has agreed may be promoted to the public in the Island, following a recognition regime not dissimilar to that which we looked at in Chapter 10 for the United Kingdom.

The Financial Supervision Act also requires that Manager and Trustee of an Authorized Scheme both be 'authorized persons': in practice this means that:

- the Manager will have an Investment Business Licence issued under the Investment Business Act 1991–3; and
- the Trustee will be a locally authorized bank.

The Investment Business Act 1991–3 (the IBA) is the main piece of legislation regulating investment business, and it establishes the requirement for those carrying on 'investment business' to hold a licence issued under section 3 of it, unless they fall within a range of exemptions. The Investment Business Order 1991, made under the IBA, defines:

- what is an investment; and
- what is investment business.

Operation of Schemes

The Financial Supervision (Authorized Collective Investment Schemes) Regulations 1988 (the Authorized Scheme Regulations) cover the constitution and operation of these schemes in detail. Supporting Guidance Notes assist managers and trustees in understanding how to apply the Regulations.

The Financial Supervision (International Schemes) Regulations 1990 cover International Schemes. They are much less detailed and are also supported by Guidance Notes, which address interpretation in connection with International Collective Investment Schemes *excepting* for two sub-categories of international scheme: the Professional Investor Fund, and the Experienced Investor Fund (see below).

Advertising and literature

The Financial Supervision (Scheme Particulars) Regulations 1988 cover what needs to be in an Authorized fund's Scheme Particulars or Prospectus.

The Financial Supervision (Restricted Schemes) (Advertising and Scheme Particulars) Regulations 1995 ('Advertising and Scheme Particulars Regulations') cover promotion of International Schemes. Among other things they require that any adverts comply with the Advertising Regulatory Code above. They are supported by Guidance Notes for Operators of Restricted Collective Investment Schemes on the Interpretation of the Financial Supervision (Restricted Schemes) (Advertising and Scheme Particulars) Regulations 1995.

The statutory Compensation Scheme

In order to demonstrate equivalence with the United Kingdom for the purposes of 'designated territory status', the Island - like the other designated territories – has a compensation scheme, which will make payments to eligible investors in the event that a manager cannot pay investors what they are due. The Authorized Collective Investment Schemes (Compensation) Regulations 1988 cover the Isle of Man compensation scheme, which extends to Authorized Schemes only. The scheme provides for payments to a maximum of:

- 100 per cent of the first £30 000 of an investor's holding; and
- 90 per cent of next £20 000, with
- a maximum total of £48 000 per eligible investor.

Categories of scheme

The categories of scheme provided for in the Island under the FSA88 are as follows:

- *Authorized schemes*, as provided for under section 3 of the FSA88. Authorized schemes are required to meet detailed requirements in terms of their constitution and operation, and these are largely modelled on the UK authorized schemes regime.
- *International schemes*, as provided for at section 11 of the FSA88. These are all Isle of Man schemes other than Authorized schemes.

- The following sub-categories of International scheme are also provided for (any international scheme which does not fall under one of the following sub-headings is simply an ordinary international scheme):
  - Exempt International schemes;
  - Professional Investor Funds;
  - Experienced Investor funds; and
  - Overseas funds.

In terms of the promotion of foreign schemes to the public in the Isle of Man, recognition may be applied for under sections 12 and 13 of the FSA88. Section 12 covers those schemes based in a territory designated as having equivalent investor protection standards to those provided for in the Isle of Man; section 13 covers those schemes operated in any other jurisdiction, or indeed a scheme from a designated territory which does not meet the applicable requirements for authorization in that territory.

11.7 Luxembourg

The financial services regulator in Luxembourg has, since 1 January 1999, been the *Commission de Surveillance du Secteur Financier*, or 'CSSF'. Prior to this financial services regulation was undertaken by the Luxembourg Central Bank (1 June–31 December 1998) and the Luxembourg Monetary Institute (the period up until 31 May 1998). Consequently, you may see references to regulatory notices introduced by all three of these bodies.

Luxembourg is currently in a transitional period (lasting from 1 January 2003–13 February 2007) in connection with public Undertakings for Collective Investments (UCIs); these are:

- **The law of 30 March 1988 on UCI** ('the Law of 1988'), which implemented *European Directive 85/611/EEC on the coordination of laws, regulations and administrative provisions relating to Undertakings in Collective Investments in Transferable Securities* (UCITS) – otherwise known as the UCITS I Directive; and
- **The law of 20 December 2002 on Undertakings for Collective Investment** ('the Law of 2002'), which implements the changes arising to UCITS I which arise from Directives 2001/107/EC (the Profession Directive) and 2001/108/EC ('the Product Directive'). Collectively, the Profession and Products Directives are known as the 'UCITS III Directive'.

The Law of 2002 follows much the same format as its predecessor, in that it perpetuates the distinction between Part I Funds (those which are subject to UCITS III and which are therefore passportable throughout the European Union) and Part II Funds, which cannot be passported. The new law also introduces a few changes not arising from UCITS III, generally bringing the regime up-to-date.

We have looked in Chapter 9, Section 9.3, at the main changes introduced by UCITS III; in particular, the fact that the transitional period between UCITS I and UCITS III carries some intepretative difficulties. In Luxembourg, this has been handled by way of the period of parallel operation of the Laws of 1988 and of 2002 above. On

13 February 2007, the Law of 1988 will effectively fall away; meanwhile, since 13 February 2004, elements of the Law of 2002 are being introduced progressively.

The CSSF communicates the regulations which it introduces to underpin the Law by way of Circulars. ***Luxembourg Monetary Institute (LMI) Circular*** **91/75**, which was issued on 21 January 1991, clarified the scope and purpose of the Law of 1988 and replaced a number of earlier circulars applicable to Luxembourg UCIs. At the time of writing, the CSSF is reviewing this circular in the context of the Law of 2002, and is likely to amend or replace it.

The Law of 19 July 1991 governs UCIs which are not for public offering (i.e. specifically, those aimed only at institutional investors).

CSSF Circular 2002/77, which was issued on 27 November 2002, improved investor protection for Luxembourg-domiciled UCIs. *Inter alia*, it established a robust investor compensation regime covering losses from incorrect NAV calculations and breaches of a UCI's investment mandate. It replaced an earlier circular, CSSF 2000/8.

In December 2002, the CSSF issued Circular 2002/80, establishing and clarifying the regulatory regime for hedge funds.

Open-ended funds may be established in Luxembourg either as "Founds Communs de Placements" (FCPs) or as "Societés d' Investessement ā Capital Variable" (SICAVs); the SICAV is essentially the same as an OEIC (i.e. it is a company and has separate legal personality). The FCP is a purely contractual vehicle, and has no legal personality.

12 Miscellaneous

12.1 Insurance issues: when things go wrong

When a prospective fund sponsor sets about establishing his first fund, one of the furthest things from his mind may be things going so badly awry that litigation ensues. However, in an increasingly litigious environment, and one in which corporate governance and the focus on the role of directors (both on the board of the fund company itself, and on its service providers) is growing, it is essential that adequate thought is given to maintaining appropriate indemnities and insurance cover.

The types of events we are discussing here include:

- Breach of fiduciary duty. The fund's board of directors is appointed to make decisions on behalf of the fund, and they have a personal liability in this regard (Figure 12.1). Yet in many cases, the fund's actions manifest themselves through the activity of a third party – the manager or administrator – over whom the directors have a limited amount of oversight. If push comes to shove, will the directors of the fund be able to show that they exercised adequate oversight over the actions of the administrators they have appointed?
- This leads us onto the possible vicarious liability of the directors of the investment trust or open-ended investment company (OEIC), via the fund itself, in appointing appropriate service providers and overseeing their activities.
- A disgruntled investor may take complaints to an ombudsman or (more rarely, since they tend not to get involved in individual disputes) a regulator. Failing this they will resort to the courts and may choose to take action against the fund itself – of which in their eyes they are as much a customer as a shareholder – and via the fund, against its directors/advisers.

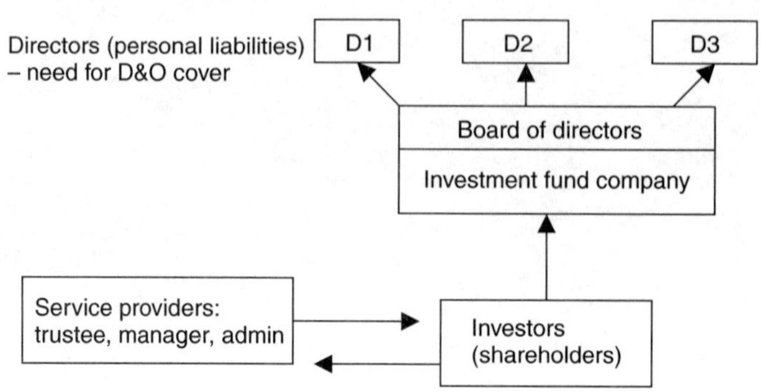

Figure 12.1 Liability Flows.

- Potential claimants include:
  - Shareholders, alleging:
    - poor performance of the fund;
    - deviations from the mandate as set out in the prospectus;
    - breach of contract or fiduciary duty;
    - although it is as yet rare to see shareholder class actions in the United Kingdom, some quasi-class actions may be in view in connection with split capital investment trusts.
  - The fund itself:
    - the fund company could conceivably take action against the directors, alleging breach of contract. However, many directors do not have a contract *per se*, preferring to consider that their duties and powers are as set out in the company's Memorandum and Articles (M&As) and in the applicable company law; and/or breach of fiduciary duty;
    - following change in a company's board, this could conceivably include action against former directors who have now lost control.
  - Creditors, for example, in the case of default on a loan provision;
  - Regulators, for breach of statutory or regulatory duties;
  - Official receiver/liquidator after investigation into the conduct of the company and/or its directors.

Directors of a fund company are potentially vicariously responsible to their shareholders for the services which the fund itself contracts out to third parties; that is, management companies, distributors, administrators and the like. In most cases, the directors will have a fiduciary duty to satisfy themselves that such services are being adequately provided.

In certain cases the directors of the fund company may be indemnified by the company itself. However, this may not be the case (or the indemnity may be worthless) where:

- the fund company becomes insolvent or has insufficient assets to meet any claim;
- the company itself is the claimant against its board, for breach of fiduciary duty;
- the indemnity is withdrawn for any reason, or does not extend to the particular circumstances; and
- the director has resigned and the indemnity no longer extends to him.

Many of the potential risks and liabilities discussed above will be insurable: and the prospective directors of a new fund company (and indeed of any managed manager) should consider carefully whether such insurance should be taken out, and the precise terms of such cover. The most appropriate form of insurance is generally Directors' and Officers' (D&O) cover, and in many cases, fund management groups which already have a group Professional Indemnity policy with a D&O extension simply add any new in-house funds to the schedule of assureds, subject to agreement from their underwriters.

D&O cover protects directors and officers of a company against such matters as:

- legal costs where they are defending claims or allegations of wrongful acts, including:
  - Neglect, errors and omissions
  - Mis-statements

  - Errors and omissions
  - Breaches of duty, warranty or trust;
- the cost of any compensatory or damages awards made; and
- awards of plaintiff's legal costs.

For sponsors setting up schemes where the management company (if any) and the fund itself is to be serviced by a third-party administrator, it is well worth discussing whether that administrator has arrangements in place with an established underwriter who understands the nature of the risks applicable to funds. However, in these circumstances prospective directors should consider carefully:

- Who is taking responsibility for the arrangement of the insurance, including the completion of any proposal forms?
- What protection will the directors have if it is the manager who arranges cover, and the manager makes an incorrect statement or warranty on the proposal form?
- Does the manager itself have appropriate professional indemnity insurance cover to provide protection, in the event that a loss arises from its inept handling of the D&O application process?
- Will there be any conflict of interest if it is the manager who eventually sues the fund and/or its directors?

As ever, if in doubt professional legal advice should be taken.

12.2 Some useful checklists

- Sample sponsor due diligence form;
- Sample fund takeon checklist;
- Sample pre-launch checklist

Sample Sponsor Due Diligence Form – where sponsor is a private company	
Proposed Scheme Name: .... Name of Sponsor: .... Registered Office: .... Correspondence Address, if different: .... Purpose of Fund: .... Services to be Provided: .... by administrator If you have been introduced by: .... a third party, please advise us of their identity and address Please attach the following items	
Details of the sponsor company's beneficial owners, which should include all parties' full names, addresses (with postcode), occupation/profession and percentage of ownership.	
For each beneficial owner controlling 5% or more of the voting rights in the sponsor company: ■ Satisfactory reference from each beneficial owner's main banker, or from an internationally recognised accounting or legal practice.	
■ Proof of identity. This may be by way of a certified copy of their passport, national identity card or equivalent document. This must incorporate a photograph, signature, nationality, date and place of birth of each beneficial owner.	
■ Verification of home address. This may take the form of an original or certified copy of a recent utility bill, bank statement, mortgage statement or similar provided this is addressed to the residential address and not a PO Box.	
Details of at least 1 Executive and one other Director of the sponsor company, and that of at least 2 authorised signatories if different – to include name, address (with postcode) and occupation/profession.	
For each of the Executives/Directors/Signatories identified above: ■ Proof of identity. This may be by way of a certified copy of their passport, national identity card or equivalent document. This must incorporate a photograph, signature, nationality, date and place of birth of each beneficial owner.	

■ Satisfactory reference confirming integrity, financial standing and length of relationship.	
Background details of shareholder's/and or director's career histories together with the latest audited financial statements and reports of funds with which the company has been, or still is, associated; or, if this is not available, other evidence of their investment advisory expertise.	
A complete list of shareholders with evidence of their identity.	
Reference on shareholders (5% or over holding) from their main banker, international accounting practice or international legal practice.	
For an established company, a reference from the company's main recognised bankers, international accounting practice or international legal practice.	
Latest audited financial statements, where available.	
Outline of proposed distribution channels.	
A copy of the sponsor's due diligence procedures with respect to potential investors into the fund.	
Agreement to annual compliance visits/checks.	
Certified copy of the company's certificate of incorporation, or similar document	
Certified copy of the company's Memorandum & Articles	

NEW FUND QUESTIONNAIRE – ADMINISTERED FUNDS

Name/proposed name of Fund:

Proposed jurisdiction of constitution:

Listing requirements:
Do you anticipate applying for a listing and if so on what exchange?

Structure:

Open-ended (Please specify Unit Trust/LP/OEIC/Other)

Closed Ended

Guaranteed

Umbrella

Multiple classes (please specify)________________________________

Subsidiary entities

Capital:

Ordinary shares

Participating redeemable prefs

Different share classes

Currency of denomination:

$ £ € other

Proposed investment objectives: Please also explain your investment philosophy

Proposed investment strategy:

Asset classes:

Money-market

Equities

Bonds

Commodities

Derivatives

Property

Other

Investment restrictions:

Please list any restrictions which will apply other than those applicable by way of regulatory status

On which markets is it anticipated that the fund will trade?

Recognised exchanges only (Please list if known):

Inter-bank and OTC:

Other:

Dealing (open-ended funds only):

Daily Weekly Monthly Other ____________

Please specify the notice period for redemptions ____________

Please specify the minimum subscription accepted ____________

Accepted in other currencies? Yes/No

Please specify minimum top-up subscription ____________

Will fractions of shares be issued? Yes/No

Pricing

Single or Dual?

Share certificates:

Will share certificates be issued? Yes/No/Optional

Distribution policy:

Is it anticipated that the fund will pay dividends/distributions? Yes/no

Frequency? Please explain your proposed dividend policy

Launch:

Proposed launch date Proposed initial offer period

Please specify the minimum initial subscription anticipated

Please state the size to which you anticipate the fund growing after 1 year (per your business plan)

Please state any maximum fund size you expect to impose

Proposed parties to the fund:

Please give full details. Alternatively if you require a recommendation please specify.

Sponsor
Address and contact

Manager (if separate from administration)
Address and contact

Custodian/Trustee
Address and contact

Bankers, if different to Custodian/Trustee
Address and contact

Registrar and Transfer Agent (if not to be provided by the Administrator)
Address and contact

Broker(s)
Address and contact

Legal adviser
Address and contact

Auditors
Address and contact

Investment manager/adviser (please specify which)
Address and contact

Tax advisers
Address and contact

Other parties

Company secretary: Name of company Name of individual Address and contact
Board: Please list the names, addresses and contact details for all. Additional details will be required.
Fees and charges: Please specify the quantum/% proposed Initial charges/Front End Loads? Exit or redemption charges? Commissions to intermediaries? Will any of these be negotiable? If so please specify on a separate sheet. If multiple share classes with different charging structures are anticipated, please specify on a separate sheet the structures proposed. **Management Fee** Please specify the % Has a flat minimum been quoted? Please specify how frequently this will be levied **Administrator's fee [a flat minimum may be quoted]** Please specify the % Please specify how frequently this will be levied

Investment Manager/Adviser Fee (please specify which)

Please specify the %

Please specify how frequently this will be levied

If a performance fee is proposed please describe the basis, including any provisions for high watermark:

Custodian/Trustee Fee

Please specify the %

Per transaction fees?

Has a flat minimum been quoted?

Please specify how frequently fees will be levied

Other fees

Please specify any other fees you have ascertained:

Brokerage

Audit

Legal

Other

Establishment costs

Do you propose to amortise the costs from the Fund?

Over how long?

Will the fund bear additional marketing expenses?

If so how much and what will these comprise?

Marketing:

Will you require that the fund's share price is published?

In which publications?

At the expense of the fund?

Will the fund pay brochureware and marketing expenses?

Will the fund's brochureware require translation? Please give details of all languages aside from English, and identify who will be responsible for costs.

If so what budget has been estimated?

Will the fund have a website?

Investor base:

What is the intended profile of the fund's investor base?

Retail

Institutional

Professional/experienced investor

Private placement

Other (please explain)

Please explain why the fund is aimed at these classes of investors.

Distribution

Where and by whom will the fund be sold?

Countries (please list all):

Distribution:

NEW FUND PRE-LAUNCH CHECKLIST

Name of fund
Sponsor 1
Sponsor 2
General Partner
Custodian
Investment Manager
Legal Adviser
Auditor
Proposed launch date
Offering period

		Date	Initial
Sponsor due diligence completed (see separate checklist)			
Local Head of Division's approval received			
Draft PPM/Scheme Particulars received			
Draft PPM/Scheme Particulars circulated to:	In-house legal		
	External (fund's) legal counsel		
	Custodian		
	Administrator		
Fund-specific compliance of Offering Document (*necessary only if the fund falls into a special category: e.g. IoM EIF/PIF, and where additional disclosures/investor screens are required*).			
Draft Offering Document agreed and finalised			
Draft Mem & Articles received			

		Date	Initial
Draft Mem & Articles circulated to:	In-house legal		
	External (fund) legal advisers		
	Custodian		
	Administrator		
Fund-specific regulatory Mem & Articles checklist completed and signed off			
Draft Mem & Artilcles agreed and finalised			
Form 1/resolution of initial subscriber appointing directors completed/received			
Directors' 1st meeting minutes completed and signed off			
Sponsor, administrator and legal adviser to sign off Offering Document to confirm agreement			
Directors' responsibility statements received			
Draft Admin/Custody/Management/Investment Adviser Agreements received			
Draft Agreements circulated to	In-house legal		
	External (fund) legal advisers		
	Custodian		
	Administrator		
	Manager		
	Investment Adviser		
All agreements agreed			
All agreements signed			
Instructions to Custodian/Banker to open bank accounts issued			
Mandates received from Custodian			
Mandates signed and returned to Custodian			

	Date	Initial
Auditors' letter of consent to be named in offering document received		
Auditors' letter of engagement received		
Letter sent to investment adviser requesting rationale for all investment recommendations (if required)		
Broker/trading account documentation received (if required)		
Broker/trading account documentation completed and returned (if required)		

Completed by:	Signed:
	Date:
Notes:	

Index